FAITH DISCIPLESHIP

Faith Reaching Out to World Religions

FACILITATOR GUIDE

Tal Davis, Bill Gordon, N. S. R. K. Ravi, Jimmy Furr, Cky Carrigan, Jim R. Sibley,
Randy Bernard, John Jackson, Paul C. Reed, Wayne C. Reynolds, Robert L. Zinn

⊕

LifeWay Press
Nashville, Tennessee

ISBN 0-6330-0892-3

Dewey Decimal Classification: 248.5

Subject Heading: WITNESSING \ CULTS \ EVANGELISTIC WORK WITH CULTS

Scripture quotations marked NASB are from the NEW AMERICAN STANDARD BIBLE,
© Copyright The Lockman Foundation, 1960, 1962, 1963, 1968, 1971, 1972, 1973, 1975, 1977, 1995.
Used by permission.

Scripture quotations marked NIV are from the Holy Bible,
New International Version © copyright 1973, 1978, 1984 by International Bible Society.

Scripture quotations marked NKJV are from the *New King James Version*,
© 1979, 1980, 1982, Thomas Nelson, Inc., Publishers. Used by permission.

Scripture quotations marked KJV are from the *King Ja*____ ___ ___*le.*

The FAITH Sunday School Evangelism Strate___ _____ _____ ____ _____istian Resources
of the Southern Baptist C_____ ___ ___ ___ ___ ___ Board.

FAITH church ____ ___
LifeWay ___ ___
127 Ninth Avenue, North; ___ ___
by faxing (615) 2___

For information about FAIT___

We believe that the Bible ha___ ___
without any mixture of error, for its ___ ___
The 2000 statement of *The Ba*___

*Printed in th*___ *.ca*

LifeWay Press
127 Ninth Avenue, North
Nashville, Tennessee 37234-0151

As God works through us, we will help people and churches know Jesus Christ and seek His kingdom
by providing biblical solutions that spiritually transform individuals and cultures.

Contents

The Writers

The content of *Faith Reaching Out to World Religions* was written by associates and missionaries on the Interfaith Evangelism Team at the North American Mission Board of the Southern Baptist Convention.

Tal Davis, B.A., Florida State University; M.Div., Southwestern Baptist Theological Seminary; D.Min., New Orleans Baptist Theological Seminary

Bill Gordon, B.S., Louisiana State University; M.Div., Criswell College; M.Div. and Th.D., New Orleans Baptist Theological Seminary

N. S. R. K. Ravi, B.A., Nizam College; B.D., Sarampore College; M.A., Columbia International University; M.Div. and Ph.D., Mid-America Baptist Theological Seminary

Jimmy Furr, B.S., Delta State University; M.Div., New Orleans Baptist Theological Seminary

Cky Carrigan, B.A., Criswell College; M.Div. and Ph.D., Southeastern Baptist Theological Seminary

Jim R. Sibley, B.A., Baylor University; M. Div., Southwestern Baptist Theological Seminary; S.T.M., Dallas Theological Seminary

Selected FAITH elements for this course—A Quick Review, Your Discipleship Journey, and For Further Growth—were written by a team of staff members at Immanuel Baptist Church in Highland, California.

Randy Bernard, minister to adults and discipleship, has taught several FAITH Discipleship courses, as well as sessions at FAITH Clinics and Institutes.

John Jackson, associate pastor, has a broad knowledge of world religions and sees this course as a valuable tool for witnessing to their followers.

Paul C. Reed, minister of missions, has facilitated FAITH Discipleship courses and has promoted FAITH in new church starts.

Wayne C. Reynolds, minister of education, has taught FAITH Advanced, as well as sessions at FAITH Clinics and Institutes.

Robert L. Zinn, pastor, is heavily involved in FAITH at Immanuel and participates in several FAITH Clinics and banquets every year.

Expression of Commitment

FAITH Discipleship: Faith Reaching Out to World Religions

I commit myself to **FAITH** Sunday School
evangelism training in my church. I recognize **FAITH** training
as a way to help my church, to grow as a Great Commission Christian,
and to obey God's command to be an active witness.

Signed _____

Address _____

City _____ State _____ ZIP _____

Phone number (home) _____ (business) _____

Email _____ Fax _____

I will faithfully attend and participate in this 16-week semester of FAITH
training as: ❑ a Team Leader ❑ an Assistant Team Leader ❑ a Team Learner
❑ a prayer partner ❑ other: _____

My Team members _____

My Sunday School department/class _____

Introduction

Congratulations for completing semesters of FAITH evangelism training and for making a commitment to further growth as a Great Commission Christian through FAITH Discipleship. In FAITH Basic and Advanced you concentrated a great deal on going to the lost, and you learned many skills and biblical teachings that are important for disciples to know and practice. In FAITH Discipleship courses you learn more about what it means to be a disciple of Jesus Christ and to make disciples of others.

Here are some specific ways FAITH Discipleship courses equip you further as a Great Commission witness.
- By teaching you important biblical truths you need to understand and exemplify as a growing disciple
- By equipping you to respond to difficult questions you may encounter in witnessing
- By helping you develop as a life witness for Christ, taking advantage of daily opportunities to share God's love
- By giving you opportunities to practice what you have learned in witnessing situations
- By helping you develop as a Team Leader
- By suggesting ways you can disciple others

This stop on your FAITH Discipleship journey is *Faith Reaching Out to World Religions*. The proliferation of world religions over the ages illustrates humanity's persistent longing to experience and worship God in a meaningful way. Tragically, many of these religions teach that God is self, nature, or another false god, and they deny God's Son, Jesus Christ.

Today America is a patchwork of world religions. Although our nation's largest religious faith is Christianity, increased immigration to the United States during the past 40 years has brought followers of many other religions to our neighborhoods and workplaces. Millions of Jewish people, Muslims, Hindus, and Buddhists live in this country, and other non-Christian philosophies like New Age and secular humanism have an impact on culture and government that is far greater than the number of their adherents might suggest.

The influence of these world faiths presents a clear challenge to Christians in America today. Although their followers practice their religions with sincerity and devotion, the truth is that God, who " 'made the world and everything in it, ... commands all people everywhere to repent. For he has set a day when he will judge the world with justice by the man he has appointed. He has given proof of this to all men by raising him from the dead' " (Acts 17:24-31, NIV). It has been said that the world's religions are humans' attempts to reach God through their own efforts, while biblical Christianity is God's reaching down to humans through Jesus Christ. All religions that do not profess Jesus Christ as Savior and Lord can offer only empty hope to their followers.

Christians have an obligation and opportunity to share the good news of salvation through Jesus Christ. *Faith Reaching Out to World Religions* was designed to equip you to be a competent witness to those who are lost in a sea of false religious teachings and practices. This course will guide you to examine the claims of several world religions and to formulate a biblical response to these claims. You will also learn witnessing strategies for each world religion, based on the truth of God's Word. Here are the specific purposes of *Faith Reaching Out to World Religions*.

1. *You will increase your understanding of historic biblical doctrines.* Bank tellers are trained to recognize counterfeit money by handling authentic money throughout their training. Similarly, during this study you will be immersed in the true doctrine of God's Word so that you can identify the biblical doctrines that world religions pervert. You will learn how to use historic biblical teachings to present the truth to followers of world religions. Here are some of the biblical doctrines you will use to refute world religions' claims.
   - The deity of Jesus Christ
   - The nature of God
   - A biblical understanding of the Trinity
   - The sole authority of the Bible
   - The nature of humanity
   - The reality and effects of sin
   - Salvation by grace through faith
   - The nature of the church
   - The afterlife
   - Characteristics of a true prophet of God

2. *You will gain confidence in confronting followers of world religions with the truth of the gospel.* Do you feel intimidated by followers of other religions? If so, maybe it is because you lack experience in countering their false teachings and their methods of seduction. Following is practical information you will learn to increase your confidence in confronting followers of world religions.
   - The history of individual world religions
   - Ways world religions violate biblical truth
   - Biblical responses to specific religions' beliefs
   - World religions' deceptive use of Christian terminology
   - World religions' use of tradition and intimidation to recruit and control followers
   - Why world religions believe that they are the only true faith
   - A witnessing strategy for encountering each world religion

3. *You will develop Christian compassion for followers of world religions.* Many followers of world religions honestly seek a relationship with God but have been deceived to believe teachings that violate God's revealed plan. Their eternal future hangs in the balance as they face death without Christ. Because most of these people have been taught that Christians are their enemy, they have never had anyone with a loving heart and an equipped mind to point out, in the power of the Holy Spirit, the fallacy of their beliefs. You will be such a person. You can have a life-changing impact on followers who discover that you genuinely care for their souls.

Faith Reaching Out to World Religions will help you, as a growing disciple, anchor your Christian life deeper in the eternal truths of God's Word. You will also grow as a Great Commission witness by learning how you can present Jesus Christ as a beacon of hope for those who are lost, tossed about by the waves of false teachings. Your investment of 16 weeks will make an eternity of difference in the kingdom of God.

FAITH Visit Outline

Preparation

INTRODUCTION

INTERESTS

INVOLVEMENT

Church Experience/Background
- Ask about the person's church background.
- Listen for clues about the person's spiritual involvement.

Sunday School Testimony
- Tell general benefits of Sunday School.
- Tell a current personal experience.

Evangelistic Testimony
- Tell a little of your preconversion experience.
- Say: "I had a life-changing experience."
- Tell recent benefits of your conversion.

INQUIRY

Key Question: In your personal opinion, what do you understand it takes for a person to go to heaven?

Possible Answers: Faith, works, unclear, no opinion

Transition Statement: I'd like to share with you how the Bible answers this question, if it is all right. There is a word that can be used to answer this question: FAITH (spell out on fingers).

Presentation

F is for FORGIVENESS

We cannot have eternal life and heaven without God's forgiveness.

"In Him [meaning Jesus] we have redemption through His blood, the forgiveness of sins"
  —Ephesians 1:7a, NKJV.

A is for AVAILABLE

Forgiveness is available. It is—

AVAILABLE FOR ALL

"For God so loved the world that He gave His only begotten Son, that whoever believes in Him should not perish but have everlasting life"—John 3:16, NKJV.

BUT NOT AUTOMATIC

"Not everyone who says to Me, 'Lord, Lord,' shall enter the kingdom of heaven"—Matthew 7:21a, NKJV.

I is for IMPOSSIBLE

It is impossible for God to allow sin into heaven.

GOD IS—
- LOVE
  John 3:16, NKJV.
- JUST
  "For judgment is without mercy"—James 2:13a, NKJV.

MAN IS SINFUL

"For all have sinned and fall short of the glory of God" —*Romans 3:23, NKJV.*

Question: But how can a sinful person enter heaven, where God allows no sin?

T is for TURN

Question: If you were driving down the road and someone asked you to turn, what would he or she be asking you to do? (change direction)

Turn means *repent.*

TURN from something—sin and self

"But unless you repent you will all likewise perish" —*Luke 13:3b, NKJV.*

TURN to Someone; trust Christ only

(The Bible tells us that) *"Christ died for our sins according to the Scriptures, and that He was buried, and that He rose again the third day according to the Scriptures"* — *1 Corinthians 15:3b-4, NKJV.*

"If you confess with your mouth the Lord Jesus and believe in your heart that God has raised Him from the dead, you will be saved" —*Romans 10:9, NKJV.*

H is for HEAVEN

Heaven is eternal life.

HERE

"I have come that they may have life, and that they may have it more abundantly" —*John 10:10b, NKJV.*

HEREAFTER

"And if I go and prepare a place for you, I will come again and receive you to Myself; that where I am, there you may be also" —*John 14:3, NKJV.*

HOW

How can a person have God's forgiveness, heaven and eternal life, and Jesus as personal Savior and Lord?

Explain based on leaflet picture, FAITH (Forsaking All, I Trust Him), Romans 10:9.

Invitation

INQUIRE

Understanding what we have shared, would you like to receive this forgiveness by trusting in Christ as your personal Savior and Lord?

INVITE

- Pray to accept Christ.
- Pray for commitment/recommitment.
- Invite to join Sunday School.

INSURE

- Use *A Step of Faith* to insure decision.
- Personal Acceptance
- Sunday School Enrollment
- Public Confession

FAITH Participation Card

Name _____ Semester dates _____

Address _____ Phone _____

Sunday School department _____ Teacher _____

Other Team members _____

Check one: ❏ FAITH Team Leader ❏ FAITH Assistant Team Leader ❏ FAITH Team Learner

	1	2	3	4	5	6	7	8	9	10	11	12	13	14	15	16	Totals
Class Participation *Place a check to indicate completion for the appropriate session.*																	
Present																	
Home study done																	
Outline recited																	
Visitation *Indicate a number for the following areas.*																	
Number of tries																	
Number of visits																	
Number of people talked with																	
Type of Visit (Assignments)																	
Evangelistic																	
Ministry																	
Baptism																	
Follow-up																	
Opinion Poll																	
Gospel Presented																	
Profession																	
Assurance																	
No decision																	
For practice																	
Gospel Not Presented																	
Already Christian																	
No admission																	
Sunday School Enrollment																	
Attempted																	
Enrolled																	
Baptism Explained																	
Committed																	
No decision																	
Life Witness																	
Profession																	
Assurance																	
No decision																	

Faith Reaching Out to World Religions: An Orientation

In this session you will—

HEAR IT by learning the purpose of this course and the topics to be covered;

SAY IT by practicing the *Preparation* portion of the FAITH Visit Outline;

STUDY IT by overviewing Home Study Assignments.

IN ADVANCE

- Preview the content of all sessions.
- Read the teaching suggestions and content for session 1. Pay special attention to the distinctives of FAITH Discipleship and to the description of this course (see pp. 13–16). Decide whether to use the session 1 computer presentation or the overhead cels.
- Prepare the room for teaching.
- Review your Sunday School testimony and evangelistic testimony. Update them to reflect your recent experiences.
- Pray for participants.
- Distribute Journals as participants arrive. When you are ready to begin the orientation, direct participants to open their Journals to page 12.

TEACHING TIME

HEAR IT

Step 1 (5 mins.)

Welcome participants to *Faith Reaching Out to World Religions*. Ask participants to recall things God has done in their lives and the skills they have learned through their previous semesters of FAITH. Pray, thanking God for the lives that have been changed forever and that you have another opportunity to grow as Great Commission Christians.

Step 2 (5 mins.)

Ask participants to turn to page 13 in their Journals and to fill in the blanks as you present the benefits of FAITH Discipleship courses. Use the computer presentation or the overhead cels.

Goals of
FAITH
Discipleship

Where Your Journey in FAITH Has Led

Congratulations for completing semesters of FAITH evangelism training and for making a commitment to further growth as a Great Commission Christian through FAITH Discipleship. Perhaps your journey thus far has taken you to places you had never been before—into the lives of lost persons who need to know our Lord Jesus Christ. Although your way may have been difficult at times, we hope that your journey has also taken you to new heights in your relationship with God as you learned to rely on Him for power and boldness in sharing His love for people.

In *A Journey in FAITH* you learned to use the FAITH Visit Outline to present the gospel to lost persons. You also learned to use your Sunday School testimony in witnessing visits. You learned the value of making Sunday School ministry visits. You gained valuable experience in making witnessing visits, as well as in sharing FAITH in everyday situations.

In *Building Bridges Through FAITH* you learned the importance of following up with new Christians to lead them to their next steps of growth and commitment. You learned and practiced additional skills for connecting people with Christ, the church, and Sunday School. You saw how these vital connections occur in daily life, in intentional visits, in ministry actions, and in other ways.

The next phase of your journey is FAITH Discipleship.

Goals of FAITH Discipleship

FAITH Discipleship grows from solid biblical principles like Jesus' Great Commission: " 'Go and make disciples of all nations, baptizing them in the name of the Father and of the Son and of the Holy Spirit, and teaching them to obey everything I have commanded you. And surely I am with you always, to the very end of the age' " (Matt. 28:19-20, NIV). Notice Jesus' dual emphasis on going and making disciples. In FAITH Basic and Advanced you concentrated a great deal on going to the lost, and you learned many skills and biblical teachings that are important for disciples to know and practice. In FAITH Discipleship courses you learn more about what it means to be a disciple of Jesus Christ and to make disciples of others.

Discipleship has been defined as "a personal, lifelong, obedient relationship with Jesus Christ in which He transforms your character into Christlikeness; changes your values into Kingdom values; and involves you in His mission in the home, the church, and the world."[1]

Do you see the way FAITH Discipleship complements FAITH evangelism training? From your growing relationship with Jesus come motivation, skills, and knowledge for witnessing and ministering to others. Here are some specific ways FAITH Discipleship courses equip you further as a Great Commission witness.

- By teaching you important ___**biblical**___ ___**truths**___ you need to ___**understand**___ and ___**exemplify**___ as a growing disciple
- By equipping you to ___**respond**___ to difficult ___**questions**___ you may encounter in witnessing
- By helping you develop as a ___**life**___ ___**witness**___ for Christ, taking advantage of daily opportunities to share God's love
- By giving you opportunities to ___**practice**___ what you have learned in ___**witnessing**___ ___**situations**___
- By helping you develop as a ___**Team**___ ___**Leader**___
- By suggesting ways you can ___**disciple**___ others

Perhaps you have already studied the first FAITH Discipleship course, *Sharing a Living Faith*. If so, you formed a biblical belief system that serves as a foundation for your further growth as a disciple. You also learned ways to respond to difficult questions and to share your beliefs with others who are willing to listen.

If you studied the FAITH Discipleship course *Faith at Work in Your Relationships*, you learned a variety of skills for developing witnessing relationships with lost persons who are not initially open to the gospel. You also learned ways to take advantage of opportunities to witness to lost persons you encounter in the everyday patterns of life.

Perhaps you have also studied *FAITH Discipleship: Faith Reaching Out to Cults*. That experience strengthened your understanding of historic biblical doctrines as you gained confidence in confronting cult members with the truth of the gospel and developed Christian compassion for cult members.

This stop on your FAITH Discipleship journey is *Faith Reaching Out to World Religions*.

Purposes of Faith Reaching Out to World Religions

Religion is humanity's explanation (beliefs) and expression (practice) of its relationship to its ultimate concern (its god).[2] God created people to be religious beings, and we give our primary devotion to that which we value most. The proliferation of world religions over the ages illustrates humanity's persistent longing to experience and worship God in a mean-

Step 3 (15 mins.)

Direct participants to turn to page 14 in their Journals and to fill in the blanks as you present the three purposes of *Faith Reaching Out to World Religions*. Participants will—

- increase their understanding of historic biblical doctrines;
- gain confidence in confronting followers of world religions with the truth of the gospel;
- develop Christian compassion for followers of world religions.

Use the computer presentation or the overhead cel to explain each purpose.

Purposes of
*Faith Reaching
Out to World
Religions*

ingful way. Tragically, many of these religions teach that God is self, nature, or another false god, and they deny God's Son, Jesus Christ.

Today America is a patchwork of world religions. Although our nation's largest religious faith is Christianity, increased immigration to the United States during the past 40 years has brought followers of many other religions to our neighborhoods and workplaces. Millions of Jewish people, Muslims, Hindus, and Buddhists live in this country, and other non-Christian philosophies like New Age and secular humanism have an impact on culture and government that is far greater than the number of their adherents might suggest.

The influence of these world faiths presents a clear challenge to Christians in America today. Although their followers practice their religions with sincerity and devotion, the truth is that God, who " 'made the world and everything in it, … commands all people everywhere to repent. For he has set a day when he will judge the world with justice by the man he has appointed. He has given proof of this to all men by raising him from the dead' " (Acts 17:24-31, NIV). It has been said that the world's religions are humans' attempts to reach God through their own efforts, while biblical Christianity is God's reaching down to humans through Jesus Christ. All religions that do not profess Jesus Christ as Savior and Lord can offer only empty hope to their followers.

Christians have an obligation and opportunity to share the good news of salvation through Jesus Christ. *Faith Reaching Out to World Religions* was designed to equip you to be a competent witness to those who are lost in a sea of false religious teachings and practices. This course will guide you to examine the claims of several world religions and to formulate a biblical response to these claims. You will also learn witnessing strategies for each world religion, based on the truth of God's Word.

Let's overview the specific purposes of *Faith Reaching Out to World Religions*.

1. You will increase your understanding of historic <u>biblical</u> <u>doctrines</u>.

Bank tellers are trained to recognize counterfeit money by handling authentic money throughout their training. Similarly, during this study you will be immersed in the true doctrine of God's Word so that you can identify the biblical doctrines that world religions pervert. You will learn how to use historic biblical teachings to present the truth to followers of world religions. Here are some of the biblical doctrines you will use to refute world religions' claims.
- The deity of Jesus Christ
- The nature of God
- A biblical understanding of the Trinity
- The sole authority of the Bible
- The nature of humanity

- The reality and effects of sin
- Salvation by grace through faith
- The nature of the church
- The afterlife
- Characteristics of a true prophet of God

2. You will gain _____confidence_____ in confronting followers of world religions with the truth of the gospel.

Do you feel intimidated by followers of other religions? If so, maybe it is because you lack experience in countering their false teachings and their methods of seduction. Following is practical information you will learn to increase your confidence in confronting followers of world religions.

- The history of individual world religions
- Ways world religions violate biblical truth
- Biblical responses to specific religions' beliefs
- World religions' deceptive use of Christian terminology
- World religions' use of tradition and intimidation to recruit and control followers
- Why world religions believe that they are the only true faith
- A witnessing strategy for encountering each world religion

3. You will develop Christian _____compassion_____ for followers of world religions.

Many followers of world religions honestly seek a relationship with God but have been deceived to believe teachings that violate God's revealed plan. Their eternal future hangs in the balance as they face death without Christ. Because most of these people have been taught that Christians are their enemy, they have never had anyone with a loving heart and an equipped mind to point out, in the power of the Holy Spirit, the fallacy of their beliefs. You will be such a person. You can have a life-changing impact on followers who discover that you genuinely care for their souls.

Name world religions with whose members you have had contact.

_____

How did you respond? _____

Write ways you would like the Lord to change and equip you to reach followers of world religions with the truth of the gospel.

_____

_____

Give participants a moment to respond to the questions. Then ask:
- Do you personally know any followers of world religions?
- Do you react to casual contacts with defensiveness, evasiveness, hostility, fear, or compassion?
- Are you knowledgeable or ignorant of their beliefs and an appropriate Christian response?

State that this semester participants will be challenged to engage other religions' beliefs in a way that is informed by biblical truth and is motivated by Christlike compassion.

Step 4 (10 mins.)

Review the Team Leader's roles as participants fill in the blanks on pages 16–17 in their Journals. Use the computer presentation or the overhead cel.

The Roles of a Team Leader

Point out that participants can refer to What Learners Need, which also appears in the margin on page 16 of their Journals, during the semester.

WHAT LEARNERS NEED

Learners need a Team Leader who will—

• hear them recite the FAITH Visit Outline every week during Team Time;

• contact and pray for them during the week;

• gently persuade them to share what they have learned in actual visits;

• motivate and encourage them;

• check off memory work every week;

• model the outline in visits;

• use the Opinion Poll correctly in visits;

• know how to adjust the pace of training to meet Learner needs/abilities;

• be with them and encourage them to attend Celebration Time.

Faith Reaching Out to World Religions will help you, as a growing disciple, anchor your Christian life deeper in the eternal truths of God's Word. You will also grow as a Great Commission witness by learning how you can present Jesus Christ as a beacon of hope for those who are lost, tossed about by the waves of false teachings. Your investment of 16 weeks will make an eternity of difference in the kingdom of God.

The Roles of a Team Leader

While you are meeting for this *Faith Reaching Out to World Religions* orientation, Team Learners are overviewing many important ingredients of FAITH. They will learn to depend on you to interpret and reinforce many of the things they are discovering for the first time. *Faith Reaching Out to World Religions* was intentionally designed for someone who has already learned the FAITH Visit Outline. Everything is planned to help you encourage and train individuals who are learning the outline for the first time. Although every participant in this course may not be a Team Leader, the importance of this role will be evident in this course.

If you are participating in this training as a Team Leader, you will learn specific ways to lead your Team through training. If you are participating in another way, you will still focus on actions you can take to enhance your skills in leading persons to faith in Christ. God may be preparing you for the time when you will lead a Team of Learners through FAITH.

If you are a Team Leader, you will fill several important roles.

1. You are a ___role___ ___model___.
You will serve as a role model in FAITH training by—
• demonstrating how to make a FAITH visit;
• being on time for Team Time;
• learning and demonstrating what you have learned and are learning in FAITH training;
• keeping up with all Home Study Assignments;
• making sure the Team has positive Visitation Time experiences;
• participating in Celebration Time.
You will also serve as a role model in Sunday School by—
• taking leadership roles;
• participating in weekly Sunday School leadership meetings;
• assimilating people, especially new members, into the class or department;
• looking for ways to disciple new believers through Sunday School.

2. You are an _____**encourager**_____ **and**
a _____**motivator**_____ **.**

As a Team Leader, you are responsible for—

- recognizing Learner needs;
- helping class and department members know about and want to be a part of the FAITH strategy;
- letting Learners know that you are praying for them;
- getting to know Learners and helping them feel comfortable with you during training sessions and throughout the week;
- assisting Learners as they memorize various parts of the FAITH Visit Outline during the week;
- encouraging Team members in things they are doing well before, during, and after visits;
- helping Learners during Team Time recite memory work and share experiences from home study;
- being sensitive to pressure points for Learners during the training;
- recognizing dropout signals;
- celebrating what Learners have memorized and completed by signing off on their assignments during Team Time;
- gently persuading Learners, when they are ready, to take the lead in specific parts of the visit.

3. You are a _____**growing**_____ _____**disciple**_____ **.**

Everything you do as a Team Leader assumes that you are growing in your faith. It will be obvious if you are not doing this. Everything done in FAITH Discipleship—witnessing, ministry, mentoring, Bible study, prayer—requires you to grow. Making yourself available to be used by God in these ways is essential.

The Process

Faith Reaching Out to World Religions follows the format of FAITH Basic and Advanced courses.

1. Team Time (15 mins.)
   - CHECK IT—Leading Team Time
2. Teaching Time (45 mins.)
   - KNOW IT—review of the previous week's material
   - HEAR IT—presentation of the current week's material
   - SEE IT—video segment supporting the week's material (selected sessions)
   - SAY IT—practice of the FAITH Visit Outline (selected sessions)
   - STUDY IT—preview of Home Study Assignments

State: You will grow in faith as you put into practice 2 Timothy 2:1-2. You have accepted the privilege of mentoring two new Learners. They will be uncertain, concerned, excited—just as you once were. Keep in touch during the week. Explain why you handled a visit a particular way. Pray for Learners and seek to help them.

Step 5 (25 mins.)

Recall the FAITH training schedule. Quickly review the parts of the process participants are familiar with. Spend more time on the new features of this course.

Review the dynamics of Team Time, using the computer presentation or the overhead cel.
• FAITH Visit Outline
• Other Home Study Assignments
• Debriefing of Previous Session
• Help for Strengthening a Visit

Team Time
Agenda

Pages 8–9 contain the FAITH Visit Outline in its entirety for participants to refer to throughout *Faith Reaching Out to World Religions* as needed. No new memory work is required for *Faith Reaching Out to World Religions*. The same FAITH Visit Outline is used in visits. Team Leaders will grow in their relationship with God and will learn ways to relate more effectively to lost persons, Team Learners, and Sunday School members and visitors. New Learners become familiar with the presentation for the first time as they attend separate training sessions for FAITH Basic (*A Journey in FAITH*). During Team Time, as each Learner recites appropriate points of the FAITH Visit Outline each week, the Team Leader should check off these points in the Learner's *A Journey in FAITH Journal*.

3. Visitation Time (110 or more minutes, depending on your church's schedule)
   • DO IT
4. Celebration Time (30 mins.)
   • SHARE IT

What Happens During Team Time

Team Time is a very important part of the schedule for FAITH Learners. During these 15 minutes Learners debrief, practice, and recite the portion of the FAITH Visit Outline they have been assigned to learn up to that point. Since learning the entire FAITH Visit Outline is such a significant part of FAITH training, Team Time becomes a time of accountability.

If You Are a Team Leader

Your job is to help Learners rehearse the outline so that they feel more comfortable and natural in making a visit. Although Team Time is only 15 minutes during most sessions, Learners will increasingly see it as a much appreciated checkup and practice time.

Each session of this resource provides help to prepare for and lead Team Time. Although Team Leaders are responsible for conducting Team Time each week, everyone who has completed FAITH Basic will have an important role.

Team Time begins in session 2. Because good use of time is extremely important throughout this training, it is vital that you begin and conclude on time each week. (Session 12 is an extended Team Time, in which Learners spend the entire session practicing material they have learned.)

Each week ask Learners to recite the assigned portion of the FAITH Visit Outline as designated in the Team Time portion of *A Journey in FAITH Journal*. Hold the Learner's FAITH Journal and follow the outline as each person recites it.

Notice that these same assignments are capsuled in your resource in the section Leading Team Time, which begins each session. This feature will make you aware of what Learners are expected to know. Your copy of the FAITH Visit Outline is on pages 8–9 in this resource.

During the first few sessions you will likely have adequate time for both Team members to recite. Be aware that the longer the recitation, the greater the likelihood that only one person will be able to complete the outline during the 15 minutes before Teaching Time. Some of this work can continue in the car as the Team travels to and from visits.

In early sessions ask the person who feels most comfortable reciting to share first. Try not to put a Team member on the spot.

As a general rule and especially in later sessions, try to call on the person who most needs practice to share first. Do so with sensitivity and gentleness.

As a Team member correctly recites each line or phrase of the outline, place a check mark in the box beside the phrase. If the Learner has difficulty, does not recite it appropriately, or overlooks any portions, write notes in his copy of the FAITH Journal for his review. Be prepared to answer any questions the Learner might have about the outline and suggest ways to strengthen sharing the outline. When a Team member has successfully recited the assigned portion of the outline, sign off by writing your name or initials in the space provided in the member's Journal.

Overview the Learner's Home Study Assignments from the previous week. Feel free to raise questions and to discuss any aspect of the assignments. Doing so can help reinforce many important concepts taught through these assignments—concepts that may have been only introduced during the session. Again, sign off in the Learner's Journal any assignments that have been completed and that call for your approval.

As you debrief assignments or answer questions about the previous session, highlight ones that will appear on the final written review (ses. 16). Weekly, help reduce Learners' concerns about the final review.

Although you will not read the Learner's Your Journey in Faith pages, it will be significant to check to see that the Learner is keeping a written journal of his experiences throughout FAITH. It is easy to overlook this important aspect of home study.

However, journaling brings an enriching dimension to FAITH training. Suggest that Team members record their experiences and reflections on the Bible study. Encourage Learners to review previous journaling pages, particularly during times of discouragement. At the end of this semester both you and your Learners will be asked to write testimonies of what FAITH has meant personally, so your Journal is a wonderful record.

If You Are Not a Team Leader
Even if you are not a Team Leader, you will still need to participate in Team Time by being prepared to recite the FAITH Visit Outline, review the Home Study Assignments, and discuss ways to strengthen a visit. You may be asked to assist the Team Leader by working with a Team member who needs help and encouragement in learning and reciting the FAITH Visit Outline.

As Team members ride together to and from the visits, Learners can continue to practice sharing the outline and to discuss ways to strengthen a visit.

What Happens During Teaching Time
During Teaching Time you and Team Learners will go in separate directions for a focused time to learn new information. While Teaching Time for Team Learners presents the concepts in FAITH Basic, you will study the content in this course, *Faith Reaching Out to World Religions*. You will spend 45 minutes each week focusing on a different

Introduce the segments of Teaching Time, using the computer presentation or the overhead cel. Ask participants to fill in the blanks on page 20 in their Journals.

Teaching Time Agenda

world religion. You will overview the history of each religion, examine its beliefs system, and identify ways the group departs from biblical teachings. You will also receive practical, biblical suggestions for reaching out to followers of these religions with the good news of Jesus Christ.

The following format will be used for Teaching Time.

A Quick ____Review____

The first segment of Teaching Time, A Quick Review, is a five-minute period of accountability. Principles from the previous session will be reviewed. Some of the material in A Quick Review will appear on the final review (ses. 16).

Session ____Content____

The session content, which the Facilitator presents in about 35 minutes, identifies teachings of world religions, presents a biblical response, and suggests ways you can share the truth of Jesus Christ with followers. As the Facilitator presents the content, you will fill in the blanks in your Journal. Sometimes the session content is enhanced by a video segment.

What Happens During Visitation Time

This period of 110 or more minutes, depending on your church's schedule, is the vital time when you and your Team come back together to practice what you have learned through prayer and training.

FAITH Teams

Three persons are on every FAITH Team. In addition to the Team Leader, who has been trained in the FAITH strategy, two Team Learners have been enlisted to be trained and to visit together. Each Team represents a designated Sunday School division, department, or class.

Write the names of your Team members. If a Team member has already received training but is not participating as a Team Leader, write that member's name and role on the Team (for example, Assistant Team Leader).

_____

_____

_____

Team Leader

FAITH Participation Card

One of the first things Team members are doing is preparing their FAITH Participation Cards. You will remember that this card is used

---

Left margin notes:

Lead participants to write the names of other members of their FAITH Team on the lines provided on page 20 in their Journals.

Lead participants to complete the personal information on their cards for the semester. Emphasize the importance of every Team's completing a weekly report.

each week as a name placard and to record numbers and types of visits attempted and made by the Team. If you have not already completed the top portion of your Participation Card, do so now. Make sure your name is printed in large letters on the reverse side of your name placard.

Review the categories of the Participation Card. You will be responsible for helping your Team members understand the categories identified on the card. You will also be responsible for helping them complete their cards following visits that begin with session 2.

The Participation Card is the basis for information on the FAITH Report Board. Remember that reports from the visits are summarized here. Your job is to orient your Team members to this process so that they can eventually report during Celebration Time.

Types of Visits

In all visits you should be ready to share the message of the gospel, as well as to invite unsaved persons to saving faith in Christ. You will look for opportunities to represent Christ by ministering to individuals in need, by enrolling some people in Bible study, and by helping others grow in their journey of faith. Each Team will make four types of visits.

1. Teams will make visits to Sunday School prospects, some of whom have had contact with your church as visitors to Sunday School, worship, or a special event. Some have been referred by a member, and others were discovered through a People Search opportunity. Generally, prospects are those who are open to a contact from or a relationship with your church.
2. Teams will make ministry visits to Sunday School members.
3. Teams will make visits using the Opinion Poll.
4. Teams will make follow-up visits to persons who have made significant decisions: to trust Christ, join the church, or enroll in Sunday School.

Although you will discover many new experiences when you make visits, Learners will be interested in knowing about each of these types of visits when they receive their assignments. Your experience, as well as what is taught during Teaching Time, will be particularly helpful as Learners determine ways to participate in each type of visit.

Visitation Folder

Each Team will have a visitation folder that has been prepared for that week's visits. Be prepared to explain the significance and use of each item before, during, and after visits.

Contents of the visitation folder may include these and other items designated by the church.

Visitation assignment forms. Each week you should have several of these forms. Some assignments will be to a specific person or family indicated as a prospect. Other forms might be for visits to members.

Review the types of FAITH visits that can be made.

Some forms will indicate the assignment as a follow-up visit. Each form should indicate the general nature of the assigned visit.

If the card does not indicate that the person is a Sunday School member, assume that you are visiting to cultivate a relationship on behalf of the church and the Sunday School. Approach the visit assuming that you may have an opportunity to share the gospel.

Lead your Team to make as many visits as are feasible during the designated time. If you are unable to make assigned visits and/or have extra time, use the Opinion Poll to identify opportunities for evangelism and ministry.

Information about the church and Sunday School. A diagram, list, or information sheet should include a basic overview of Sunday School so that you can help family members identify with and know where Sunday School classes meet.

A Step of Faith. Use this leaflet when sharing the gospel with a person and issuing an **Invitation**. Also use it to enroll a person in Sunday School and to record decisions made during a visit.

My Next Step of Faith. In session 3 of FAITH Advanced you received detailed help in using this leaflet to help a new believer take a next step of obedience through believer's baptism.

Opinion Poll cards. Use these forms to ask and record responses when making Opinion Poll visits.

Bible-study material used by your class. During a visit give a copy of current material to new enrollees and to nonattending members.

Believe magazine. This devotional magazine helps new believers understand who they are in Christ and become grounded in their faith.[3]

Church promotional information about upcoming special events and opportunities.

Identify the items in your packet that are unique to your church. How can these items help you make better visits?

_____

_____

_____

You will be responsible for demonstrating how to use each item in the visitation folder. Until Learners overview how to use these items and complete the forms, you will be responsible for training them in how to use them. Remember that you are the Learners' model, and they will follow the example you set. Whatever you do correctly or incorrectly will be multiplied by them in the future.

Let's briefly review what is expected in completing the visitation forms. No matter what type of record form is used by the church, you need to take the following actions.

1. Fill in every applicable ____**blank**____ in which information is requested.

2. If an assigned person is not at home or is not willing to respond to selected questions for information, ____**initial**____ the card (or blanks left incomplete) and indicate the ____**date**____ of the attempted visit and the ____**reason**____ information was not recorded.

3. ____**Print**____ information ____**legibly**____.

4. Write information discovered from the visit that will help in making any _____**follow-up**_____ _____**contact**_____.

5. Record information about all other _____**prospects**_____ discovered in the home.

6. Turn in the detachable _____**Response**_____ ____**Card**____ portion of *A Step of Faith*.

Direct participants to fill in the blanks on page 23 in their Journals as you emphasize the six points of completing all records.

Prayer and Practice

If you have a sufficient number of Teams participating in FAITH visits, the work of several Teams will be coordinated by a FAITH Group Leader. For the purposes of Prayer and Practice, one group of Teams will remain in the Teaching Time room each week to pray while other Teams make visits. This process will begin no earlier than session 3. Assignments for Prayer and Practice are made on a rotating basis and are noted in your weekly newsletter or in the visitation folder.

As soon as visiting Teams depart to make visits, the assigned Group Leader assembles Teams for prayer. Teams pray throughout Visitation Time specifically for the Team members visiting and for the individuals to be visited. They pray for divine appointments. The Group Leader might call the names of persons visiting and being visited.

During Prayer and Practice the Group Leader can also lead Teams to practice reciting the FAITH Visit Outline with one another. Team members can also spend time writing notes to prospects and members. When Prayer and Practice is over, the Group Leader leads participants to complete their session Participation and Evaluation Cards.

Explain how prayer and practice will be done in your church, as well as how this information will be communicated.

What Happens During Celebration Time

This is a 30-minute time to report Team and FAITH-strategy victories. Each week you will be responsible for leading your Team to report about visits attempted and visits made. This can become a very meaningful and motivational time. In addition to helping Team members update and submit their Participation Cards, Evaluation Cards, and visitation-assignment cards, help them know how to complete the Report Board.

Particularly during the first few weeks of training, Team members will look to you to share verbal reports during the report time. Even if

Highlight guidelines for giving reports during Celebration Time.

Using the computer presentation or the overhead cel, review the dates this course will begin and end, as well as the times Team Time, Teaching Time, Visitation Time, and Celebration Time will begin each week.

Our
Schedule

Step 6 (10 mins.)

Emphasize the importance of current Sunday School and evangelistic testimonies. Give participants an opportunity to briefly identify ways their testimonies need to be updated. Encourage them to update or rewrite their testimonies, if necessary, before session 2.

Remind participants that they will assist Team Learners in developing their testimonies as well. Encourage participants to share their updated testimonies with other Team members.

Break (10 mins.)

a Team seemingly has not had a productive visit, Team members share in the ministry's victories during this period.

Keep these guidelines in mind as you lead and help your Team members verbally report.

1. *Be brief.* The amount of time needed will be determined by the number of Teams reporting.
2. *Be precise.* Do not give unnecessary details.
3. *Be positive.* Discuss problems or negatives in another setting, such as with your Group Leader.
4. *Be enthusiastic.* You and your Team have been attempting the greatest opportunity in the world!
5. *Be accurate.* Do not embellish what really happened.
6. *Be careful.* Do not report anything confidential that was shared with your Team. Use only the first names of the persons you visited.
7. *Be thankful.* Even if no decision was made or no one allowed you to share, be grateful for the opportunity to talk.
8. *Be affirming.* If Joe shared a Sunday School testimony for the first time in a visit and did a great job, tell the entire group. You not only encourage Joe but also motivate other Teams.

Your Testimony

By now you have been involved in FAITH training for at least two years, maybe longer. Many things can take place in that length of time.

Because Sunday School is an essential part of the FAITH process, it is important to keep your Sunday School testimony current. What changes do you need to make in your Sunday School testimony you developed for your first semester of FAITH to better describe what is happening in your class today?

_____

_____

You may also need to update your evangelistic testimony. What has God been teaching you in the past 18 months? How has your spiritual life changed? What adjustments do you need to make in your evangelistic testimony to make it current?

_____

_____

Growing as a Life Witness

While overviewing the Participation Card, you may have noticed the Life Witness line. One goal of FAITH training is to develop believers committed to sharing the gospel in today's world. This means sharing Christ more than the scheduled two hours a week. Sharing Jesus must become a part of your lifestyle if you are to be a true Great Commission Christian. You will be encouraged to grow as a life witness during *Faith Reaching Out to World Religions* through the following expectations.

1. The _____**Growing**_____ as a __**Life**__ _____**Witness**_____ portion of your Home Study Assignments will remind you of your responsibility to witness and minister to others during the week, besides during FAITH visits.

2. In addition to your prayer partners in your Sunday School class or department, you will have an _____**accountability**_____ _____**partner**_____ throughout the semester who will—

- __**ask**__ whether you have had witnessing and ministry opportunities during the past week, other than FAITH visits;
- __**pray**__ for specific persons you identify, for your participation in FAITH Discipleship training, for your effectiveness as a Team Leader, and for your use by God in divine appointments;
- _____**discuss**_____ problems or questions you may have in witnessing encounters or in completing Home Study Assignments and ways new concepts can be applied;
- periodically _____**practice**_____ the FAITH Visit Outline.

My accountability partner is _____

Phone number(s): _____

Your Resources

Faith Reaching Out to World Religions will enhance and reinforce your earlier FAITH training. Here are important resources you will use.

FAITH Visit Outline
There is no new memory work; you will continue to practice the FAITH Visit Outline.

Faith Reaching Out to World Religions Journal
As was true in FAITH Basic and Advanced, the Journal will be your main resource. After you have filled in the blanks during each session's

Step 7 (10 mins.)

Explain what it means to be a life witness and the importance of looking for opportunities to witness and minister in daily life. Ask participants to fill in the blanks on page 25 in their Journals as you point out ways this study will emphasize growing as a life witness.

Assist in selecting accountability partners and explain the responsibilities throughout the course. Facilitate the exchange of phone numbers. If you have an odd number of participants, you will need to serve as someone's accountability partner.

SAY IT

Step 8 (10 mins.)

Ask accountability partners to practice sharing the **Preparation** portion of the FAITH Visit Outline with each other.

HEAR IT

Step 9 (10 mins.)

Overview the resources available through participants' Journals and group sessions. The following items are provided in the Training Pack.

• *Facilitator Guide.* This guide contains the same sessions trainees have, plus answers and teaching suggestions.

• *Journal.* Each participant needs a copy of the Journal.

• *Videotape.* Video segments present fictional encounters with followers of world religions. Segments support selected training sessions. The video also provides a brief promotional segment. You have permission to duplicate the video for additional training groups.

• *Overhead cels.* This set of 70 overhead cels is used during Teaching Times to support session content.

• *CD-ROM.* You may prefer an Adobe Acrobat® presentation to overhead cels. Choose the medium of teaching support best suited for your church and training room. The CD-ROM provided is Macintosh®/Windows®-compatible and includes Acrobat Reader software.

• *Order form.* Copies of the *Journal, Facilitator Guide,* and *Training Pack* may be ordered, as well as items used in previous FAITH courses.

Draw attention to the comparison chart on page 272. Encourage participants to use it throughout the course to review the primary beliefs of the religions they are studying.

Teaching Time, it can be helpful during home study to reread that session to get the big picture. Besides the content studied during Teaching Time, the following sections are included in your Journal.

• *Leading Team Time.* The Leading Team Time suggestions each week will help you as a Team Leader debrief, practice, and review with your Team. Suggestions are based on Learners' *A Journey in FAITH Journal* Team Time agenda for each week.

• *Home Study Assignments.* Each week your Home Study Assignments reinforce the session by helping you apply what you have learned. Home Study Assignments consist of the following sections.

—*Your Discipleship Journey.* Assignments in this section focus on your development as a disciple.

—*Growing as a Life Witness.* This section reminds you of your responsibility to witness and minister to others during the week.

—*Your Weekly Sunday School Leadership Meeting.* This section allows you to make notes about the way your FAITH Team influences the work of your Sunday School class or department. As you and other leaders meet to plan for next Sunday's Bible-study time, identify actions that need to be taken through Sunday School as a result of prayer concerns, needs identified, visits made by the Team, and decisions made by the persons visited. You may also identify ways you can disciple others in your Sunday School class or department and in your church.

—*Discipling Your Team Members.* This section suggests ways you can disciple your Team members as you prepare to lead your FAITH Team's group time at the beginning of the next session and as you mentor and support members through the week. You will find reminders about the things the Learners have studied, as well as some tips to help you be a better Team Leader.

—*For Further Growth.* This section challenges you with optional long-term reading or discipleship activities. Because the person of Jesus Christ is the central issue in discussions with followers of world religions, For Further Growth activities this semester help you answer the question, Who is Jesus Christ? Each week's activities focus on one of Jesus' attributes to increase your understanding of who Jesus is and who you are in Him.

—*FAITH Tip.* Selected sessions include optional readings that explore biblical teachings about a variety of doctrinal issues.

—*FAITH at Work.* Selected sessions include testimonies about the difference FAITH has made in participants' lives.

• *Comparison chart.* The chart on page 272 compares the beliefs of most religions studied in this course.

In-Session Training Resources

Your Facilitator will use the following resources to help you learn.

- Videotape segments, in which you will see examples of FAITH participants who interact with followers of selected world religions
- Computer presentation or overhead cels to help you fill in the blanks and understand that session's teachings

Sunday School Ministry

Your Sunday School class or department is a primary resource. Sunday School is the unique dynamic of FAITH. Your class/department can be a place where names become people, needs become visible, and assimilation becomes more than a term. This link is created by attending the weekly Sunday School leadership meeting (and the Group Leader meeting, if appropriate).

Your Walk with God

Three components of your walk with God will provide essential spiritual direction as you participate in this course.

- *Your willingness to join God's work.* Evangelism is God's activity, and you must be willing to be on His agenda and timetable in this endeavor. Ask that His Holy Spirit will guide what you say and do; empower you for divine confidence, strength, and wisdom; and prepare each lost person's heart for the seeds you will sow. During the next 16 weeks, expect God to work in your life, in your Sunday School/church, in the lives of people you meet, and in your Team.
- *Bible study.* You will be exposed to a lot of biblical content during this course. Your Facilitator will not have time to cover in-depth each passage in your Journal. Spend time between sessions reading and reviewing the passages so that you will be better prepared "to give the reason for the hope that you have" (1 Pet. 3:15, NIV). Never underestimate the power of God's living and active Word to speak with an authority of its own (see 2 Tim. 3:15-17; Heb. 4:12).
- *Prayer.* Prayer is your most important and most powerful resource for FAITH training. The Lord has promised to hear us when we call on Him (see Matt. 18:19-20; 21:22; Luke 11:9-13). Call on Him throughout *Faith Reaching Out to World Religions.* In addition to personal prayer, you should enlist two faithful prayer partners in your Sunday School class to uphold you in prayer for the next 16 weeks. Your Sunday School class as a whole should also pray for your involvement in FAITH. Your class's prayer leader can make members aware of your prayer needs; lead the class to pray for divine appointments for your FAITH Team, for evangelism and ministry opportunities to be evident, for people to be saved, and for believers to grow as Great Commission Christians; give brief reports from FAITH Team visits; and report prayer concerns and results to Sunday School leaders.

Remind participants to enlist two prayer partners from their Sunday School classes to support them in prayer throughout the semester.

STUDY IT

Step 10 (5 mins.)

If you have not already done so, describe the nature of Home Study Assignments in FAITH Discipleship. Overview Home Study Assignments for session 1.

Remind the group that home visits will begin in session 2. Close by asking accountability partners to pray with each other, asking for God's strength and guidance as they seek to grow as His disciples and to enhance their witnessing skills.

Home Study Assignments

Home Study Assignments reinforce this session by helping you apply what you have learned.

Your Discipleship Journey

Journaling activities in Your Discipleship Journey are an important part of your development as a Great Commission Christian through FAITH training.

1. One purpose of FAITH Discipleship is to help you grow in your relationship with God. Each FAITH Discipleship course begins by asking you to assess your personal discipleship habits. Rate yourself in each area below, using the following scale.

   1 = never   2 = seldom   3 = sometimes   4 = usually   5 = always

I have a daily quiet time.	1 2 3 4 5
I make Christ number one in my life.	1 2 3 4 5
I stay close to the Lord throughout the day.	1 2 3 4 5
I read my Bible daily.	1 2 3 4 5
I study my Bible in depth.	1 2 3 4 5
I memorize a Scripture verse each week.	1 2 3 4 5
I keep a prayer list and pray for those concerns.	1 2 3 4 5
I recognize answers to my prayers.	1 2 3 4 5
I include praise, thanksgiving, confession, petition, and intercession in my prayers.	1 2 3 4 5
I live in harmony with my family and other believers.	1 2 3 4 5
I seek reconciliation when it is needed.	1 2 3 4 5
I attend worship services.	1 2 3 4 5
I attend Bible study.	1 2 3 4 5
I pray for lost persons by name.	1 2 3 4 5
I share my testimony with others.	1 2 3 4 5
I share the plan of salvation with others.	1 2 3 4 5
I witness each week.	1 2 3 4 5
I follow up on persons I have led to Christ.	1 2 3 4 5
I serve in my church.	1 2 3 4 5
I give at least a tithe through my church.	1 2 3 4 5
I minister to others.[4]	1 2 3 4 5

   Examine your responses to the inventory and determine where you need to improve. Write one action you will commit to take to grow in discipleship.

   _____

   _____

2. Record goals you have for this semester of FAITH Discipleship.

A goal for your personal discipleship: _____

_____

_____

_____

A goal for witnessing: _____

_____

_____

_____

A goal for discipling Team members and Sunday School members:

_____

_____

_____

Growing as a Life Witness

Growing as a Life Witness reminds you of your responsibility to witness and minister to others during the week.
1. Talk with your accountability partner and plan the way you will communicate each week during the semester.
2. Discuss any persons you are cultivating through ministry or witness.
3. Pray for each other's growth as disciples, as Team Leaders, and as witnesses.

Prayer Concerns	Answers to Prayer
_____	_____
_____	_____
_____	_____
_____	_____

Your Weekly Sunday School Leadership Meeting

A FAITH participant is an important member of Sunday School. Encourage Team members who are elected Sunday School leaders to attend this weekly meeting. Use this section to record ways your FAITH Team influences the work of your Sunday School class or department. Use the information to report during weekly Sunday School leadership meetings. Identify actions that need to be taken through Sunday School as a result of prayer concerns, needs identified, visits made by the Team, and decisions made by the persons visited. Also identify ways you can disciple others in your Sunday School class or department and in your church.

1. Think back to your first day of FAITH training and recall as much as you can about your Sunday School class then. Who else from your class was in FAITH training?

   _____

   _____

2. Think about your class now. How has it changed? How many of the people in your class are new believers or new members of your church? Who has joined you in FAITH training? What role has FAITH played in these changes?

   _____

   _____

   _____

3. A new semester of FAITH is under way. How does the Team's preparation for every Sunday through this weekly leadership meeting need to consider the needs of individuals or families visited through FAITH?

   _____

   _____

   _____

4. This time together each week also can facilitate your growth as a disciple. Does your continuing commitment to FAITH training include a commitment to attend this important weekly meeting?

Discipling Your Team Members

This weekly feature suggests actions the Team Leader can take to support Team members, prepare for Team Time, and consider ways to improve visits. This work becomes part of the Team Leader's Home Study Assignments. Add any actions suggested by your church's FAITH strategy.

Support Team Members

❑ Contact Team members during the week. Explain to them that you will pray for them during this semester of FAITH. Discuss their orientation to FAITH. Emphasize the importance of being on time for Team Time. Briefly remind them of their role during Team Time.

❑ As you talk with Learners this week—
   • find out whether they understood their Home Study Assignments, especially the writing of their Sunday School testimonies;
   • ask whether they have a prayer partner from their Sunday School class;
   • suggest that they preview the FAITH Tip for session 2, "Helpful Visitation Tips," in *A Journey in FAITH Journal*.

❑ Remind members to bring a small Bible with them to take on visits. Teams will make visits after session 2, then return for Celebration Time.

❑ Record specific needs and concerns shared by Team members.

_____

_____

_____

Prepare to Lead Team Time

❑ Review Team members' Home Study Assignments.
❑ Preview Leading Team Time for session 2.

Prepare to Lead Visits

❑ Review the FAITH Visit Outline.
❑ Be prepared to explain the contents of the visitation folder.
❑ Be ready to model a visit in which Team members are asked to share their Sunday School testimonies.

Link with Sunday School

❑ Prepare to share with other Sunday School leaders a brief summary of what you will study during this semester of FAITH Discipleship. Ask that they pray for you as you continue to learn and grow in your witnessing skills.

For Further Growth: The Eternality of Jesus Christ, Part 1

For Further Growth may include additional reading or activities that will enhance your growth as a disciple and a discipler of others. These assignments are intended to be long-term projects and do not have to be completed during this semester of study.

1. The most basic difference between Jesus and any other religious leader is that Jesus is the eternal Son of God. Read the following Scriptures and note how they verify the eternality of Jesus: John 1:1; 8:58; 17:5,24.

2. Read one or more of the following resources.
   • Millard J. Erickson, *Christian Theology*, part 7, "The Person of Christ," chapter 32, "The Deity of Christ" (Grand Rapids: Baker, 1985), 683–704.
   • R. C. Sproul, *Essential Truths of the Christian Faith*, part 4, "Jesus Christ" (Wheaton: Tyndale, 1992), 77–108.
   • Millard J. Erickson, *The Word Became Flesh*, part 3, "The Construction of a Contemporary Incarnational Christology," chapter 22, "The Logic of the Incarnation" (Grand Rapids: Baker, 1991), 551–76.

3. As you study world religions this semester, you might want to do further reading in one or more of the following resources.
   • David A. Brown, *A Guide to Religions* (London: SPCK, 1975)
   • Milton Steinberg, *Basic Judaism* (New York: Harcourt Brace, 1975)
   • Walter Martin, *The Kingdom of the Cults* (Minneapolis: Bethany, 1997)
   • John L. McKenzie, *The Roman Catholic Church* (Garden City: Image, 1971)
   • Sir Norman Anderson, *The World Religions* (Grand Rapids: Eerdmans, 1976)
   • Josh McDowell and Don Stewart, *Understanding Non-Christian Religions* (San Bernardino: Here's Life, 1982)

---

[1]Avery T. Willis Jr., *MasterLife 1: The Disciple's Cross* (Nashville: LifeWay, 1996), 5.
[2]Tom Wolfe, lecture at Golden Gate Baptist Theological Seminary; Brea, CA; spring 1995.
[3]*Believe* and *essential connection* magazines are available by writing to LifeWay Church Resources Customer Service, MSN 113; 127 Ninth Avenue, North; Nashville, TN 37234-0113; by calling toll free (800) 458-2772; by faxing (615) 251-5933; by ordering online at *www.lifewaystores.com*; or by emailing *customerservice@lifeway.com*.
[4]Willis, *MasterLife 1*, 29–30.

An Introduction to World Religions

N. S. R. K. RAVI

In this session you will—

CHECK IT by engaging in Team Time activities;

KNOW IT by reviewing distinctives of this course from session 1;

HEAR IT by discovering characteristics of world religions;

STUDY IT by overviewing Home Study Assignments;

DO IT by leading your Team in making visits;

SHARE IT by celebrating.

IN ADVANCE

- Overview content.
- Preview teaching suggestions. Prepare key points. Decide whether to use the session 2 computer presentation or the overhead cels.
- Prepare the room for teaching.
- Pray for participants and for Teams as they prepare for their first home visits.
- As Teaching Time begins, direct participants to open their Journals to page 36.

If the computer presentation is used, display the agenda frame for Team Time. Add other points as needed.

CHECK IT agenda:
- ✔ FAITH Visit Outline
- ✔ Sunday School Testimony
- ✔ Other Home Study Assignments
- ✔ Session 1 Debriefing
- ✔ Help for Strengthening a Visit

Leading Team Time

All Team members participate in Team Time. They are primarily responsible for reciting the assigned portion of the FAITH Visit Outline and for discussing other Home Study Assignments.

As you direct this important time of CHECK IT activities with your Team, keep in mind that Learners look to you as a role model, motivator, mentor, and friend. Team Time activities can continue in the car as the Team travels to and from visits.

Lead CHECK It Activities

Since this is the first time for Team Time activities, provide any additional explanation that is needed. Make good use of the 15 minutes that begin each session.

✔ FAITH Visit Outline

❑ Team members should be ready to recite all aspects of *Preparation* up to INQUIRY and the key words in *Presentation* (FORGIVENESS, AVAILABLE, IMPOSSIBLE, TURN, HEAVEN) and *Invitation* (INQUIRE, INVITE, INSURE).

❑ Indicate your approval by signing or initialing Journals. Encourage Learners.

✔ Sunday School Testimony

❑ Ask Team members for their written Sunday School testimonies, due this session. Help evaluate each testimony to make sure it includes one or two of the following aspects: friendship/support received, assistance received during a crisis, personal benefits of Bible study through the class, or ways they have grown as a Christian through experiences in or through the Sunday School class. Discuss how benefits can and do change, reflecting different experiences.

❑ If the written testimony is acceptable, make sure each Team member understands the importance of learning to share it naturally, in his or her own words. Ask for permission to print the testimony in any church materials that publicize FAITH and/or that encourage persons to share their testimonies.

✔ Other Home Study Assignments

❑ Are Learners on track with Home Study Assignments? Provide any feedback or help they may need.

✔ Session 1 Debriefing

❑ Make sure major concepts from session 1 are understood, since this session provides an orientation to the course.

✔ Help for Strengthening a Visit

❑ This is the first session in which Teams will make home visits. Encourage members and try to ease any concerns. Explain that the Team Leader will take the lead in the INTRODUCTION portion of the visit(s) following this session.

❑ Identify a Team member(s) who would be prepared to share a Sunday School testimony at the Team Leader's prompting during a visit. Be sensitive to persons who are ready to share.

Notes

_____

_____

_____

_____

_____

_____

Actions I Need to Take with Team Members This Week

_____

_____

_____

_____

_____

_____

_____

Transition to classrooms for instruction on the content of the session. (5 mins.)

KNOW IT

Step 1 (5 mins.)

Direct participants to locate A Quick Review on page 36 in their Journals and to check the correct goals of FAITH Discipleship. Then give the answers, using the computer presentation or the overhead cel.

A Quick Review

After participants have filled in the blanks, review the three purposes of *Faith Reaching Out to World Religions,* using the computer presentation or the overhead cel.

HEAR IT

Step 2 (5 mins.)

Direct participants to fill in the blanks as you present the key points in The World at Your Door. Use the computer presentation or the overhead cel.

The World at Your Door

A Quick Review

Faith Reaching Out to World Religions is a FAITH Discipleship course. Check the ways FAITH Discipleship courses equip you as a Great Commission witness.

☑ 1. By teaching you important biblical truths you need to understand and exemplify as a growing disciple
☐ 2. By exploring major themes of the Psalms
☐ 3. By helping you overcome the effects of codependent relationships
☑ 4. By equipping you to respond to difficult questions you may encounter in witnessing
☑ 5. By helping you develop as a life witness for Christ, taking advantage of daily opportunities to share God's love
☐ 6. By surveying government agencies that assist immigrants
☑ 7. By giving you opportunities to practice what you have learned in witnessing situations
☑ 8. By helping you develop as a Team Leader
☐ 9. By identifying ways to involve internationals in civic affairs
☑ 10. By suggesting ways you can disciple others

Identify the three purposes of *Faith Reaching Out to World Religions.*
1. To increase your understanding of historic _____**biblical**_____ _____**doctrines**_____
2. To give you _____**confidence**_____ in confronting followers of world religions with the truth of the gospel
3. To encourage Christian _____**compassion**_____ for followers of world religions

The World at Your Door

Religion played a fundamental role in the formation of the American nation. In an effort to gain religious freedom, European settlers, representing a diverse array of Christian groups like Puritans, Anglicans, Quakers, Presbyterians, and others, settled in different parts of the early colonies, making America basically a Christian nation. A study of historical documents produced by the founding fathers indicates that the early citizens of this new nation were primarily practicing various forms of Christianity. Though Native American religions existed before the settlers brought Christianity, it was _____**Christianity**_____ that gave America a unique culture and society.

However, during the building and expansion of America as a nation, immigrants from various parts of the world arrived with diverse religious backgrounds: "From colonial times onward, many groups that joined in the adventure of building the American nation brought with them their religious hopes and founded in this country a particularly American expression of religions from all parts of the world: Africa, Asia, Europe, and Latin America."[1] America is a unique country in that it is a land of **immigrants**. Except for Native Americans, all of its citizens are immigrants. Here we find people from all around the globe. From America's beginning, its religious freedom and its openness to immigrants paved the way for great religious diversity.

Today a vast majority of Americans say that they are religious. Some surveys indicate that 92.5 percent of Americans believe in God.[2] Most accept the idea that America is "one nation under God." **Religiosity** is a basic trait of American society. America is not only a **religious land** but also a land of most **religions**. America's religious freedom has reduced geographical and cultural distances between religions. Today the United States is the home to nearly every religion in the world. In some major cities we see Christian churches, Buddhist pagodas, Hindu temples, and Muslim mosques on the same street. When we look in a telephone directory or a local newspaper, we see various religious worship activities listed. In our highly mobile society we see people from various religious backgrounds in our own neighborhoods.

As America has become more diverse, Christians have begun to be more frequently and aggressively confronted by those who argue that all faiths lead to God and that therefore Christianity is too exclusive in its claim to be the one true faith. After all, many non-Christian people appear to be happy and satisfied with their religious practices. Many believe that they will go to heaven or become gods. Can't these devoted religious people follow their own way to God? Aren't all religions right? Isn't it snobbish to suggest that they will be denied God's heaven simply because they don't believe in Jesus Christ as their Savior? Why should the majority of the world's population go to hell for not accepting the gospel? Isn't it unfair and heartless for God to send people to hell?

To unbelievers, these are difficult and logical questions, and they have been a stumbling block to many. The questions and issues are serious. They need to be answered, and the answers are found in God's Word. The Bible makes clear that all roads do not lead to **heaven**. The idea that God will save a Hindu or a Muslim who is faithful to the teachings of Hinduism or Islam is completely foreign to the teachings of the Bible. As you have seen throughout FAITH training, **Jesus Christ** is the only way to salvation (see John 14:6). It is your responsibility and privilege as a Great Commission witness to recognize the lostness of followers of other faiths, to build bridges of relationship and understanding, and to introduce them to Jesus Christ as the only answer to their need for salvation. This course will equip you to fulfill these obligations and opportunities.

Step 3 (20 mins.)

Ask participants to turn to page 38 in their Journals and to fill in the blanks as you present the key points in Characteristics of World Religions. Use the computer presentation or the overhead cels.

Characteristics of World Religions

Characteristics of World Religions

Supernatural experiences have been reported since the beginning of the human race. Ever since God created humanity in His own image, people have been spiritually hungry. Throughout human history religion has played a significant role in shaping human culture, society, politics, and economics. Religion has been a cardinal and pervasive feature of human experience. To understand any part of human history and human life, we must understand a people's religious experiences.

A world religion is a belief system that encompasses a large portion of the world's population. All world religions have elements and practices that convey their unique religious identities. By examining these distinctives, you can learn how people have traditionally expressed their spiritual nature, and you can begin to see how other faiths' beliefs and practices compare with those of Christianity.

1. World religions possess ___sacred___ ___writings___.
Every world religion has its own sacred writings that are preserved from generation to generation. These scriptures, which believers regard as authoritative, create unity among the followers of a religion and become their teacher and guide. Sacred writings can be divided into two groups: scriptures that are revealed supernaturally and scriptures that are written by spiritual men to guide their followers. Supernaturally given scriptures are prophetic in nature, and revelations are understood as the Word of God. The primary example of scriptures that are supernaturally revealed is the Bible. Christians believe that God gave His eternal Word through various human authors over long periods of time (see 2 Pet. 1:20-21). Yet its message is unified and without contradictions. It is God's prophetic Word. Jews share this view of the Old Testament but do not accept the New Testament as sacred scripture.

Islam claims that the Qur'an was revealed to the prophet Muhammad through the angel Gabriel. The Qur'an refers to the Bible in several of its chapters; yet it contradicts the words of the Bible. Because God cannot contradict His own words, the validity of the Qur'an is questionable.

Examples of the other type of scripture, that which is written by spiritual men and passed down to followers, can be found in the Baha'i Faith, Buddhism, Hinduism, and many other religions. These writings present the words and insights of holy men, mythical stories, fables, and narrative, interweaving everyday moral teachings that explain and exemplify the religion's beliefs.

As you witness to followers of other religions, realize that their faith is based on their sacred writings. They regard their scriptures as holy and unique, and their cultural values and worldviews are based on these scriptures. Be careful not to criticize the scriptures of the other religions in spite of the contradictions and human messages in them. Some religions, such as Hinduism and Islam, respect the Bible. Build on this foundation by emphasizing the Bible's uniqueness as the revealed Word of God with a universal, life-changing message.

2. World religions gather in ___worship___ ___centers___.

Worship is the most basic element of a religion. Most major world religions emphasize corporate religious experiences; therefore, they encourage the community of believers to gather in public worship. Such gatherings take place in special structures like churches, mosques, pagodas, synagogues, and temples. These facilities provide common locations for spiritual nurture, fellowship, and ministry. Every religion gives unique spiritual significance to its worship sites, often expressed in the magnificence and uniqueness of the architecture. Many times a structure's architectural design identifies the religious faith it represents.

Some religions consider their worship centers as the centers of spiritual power, where worshipers encounter God or the gods. For example, Muslims worship at mosques, with the Grand Mosque in Mecca as the most important. Hindus have temples dedicated to their many gods. Jews regarded the Jerusalem temple as a divinely inhabited building.

Christians do not view their churches as places of spiritual power. The New Testament teaches that a Christian's body, not a physical structure, is the temple of God (see 1 Cor. 3:16; 6:19). A church is a place of fellowship, teaching, ministry, and corporate worship.

3. World religions profess ___structural___ ___beliefs___.

Structural beliefs form the foundation on which a religion bases its worldview, its answers to life's meaning, and its solution to the way life should be lived. All world religions focus on a transcendent entity or entities, whom followers may perceive as personal, impersonal, or immaterial beings or as supernatural forces. For example, Christianity believes in a personal God who involves Himself in the lives of people. In contrast, Buddhism and Hinduism see God as an impersonal being who does not involve Himself in human lives.

Followers of world religions accept the existence of these entities as a matter of faith and/or by experience (in some cases by false experience). Followers believe that these entities guide them in their spiritual path and provide an understanding (or an illusion of understanding) of why things happen. These foundational understandings form the basis of the religion's structural beliefs, which are often expressed in confessions or statements of principles. Roman Catholics and Muslims follow confessions, while Buddhists follow a statement of principles by vowing to Buddha to follow dharma (law). Structural beliefs satisfy emotional and spiritual needs in this life and provide comfort and assurance (or false assurance) of life after death.

Some Christian groups also express their beliefs in a structured manner. Anglicans and Lutherans follow formal creeds and confessions of faith. Baptists have adopted confessions of faith as a witness to the world and as doctrinal guidelines but not as statements to be imposed on individuals or churches. Baptists affirm the principles of soul competency and the priesthood of believers, "affirming together both our liberty in Christ and our accountability to each other under the Word of God."[3] Baptists insist that the sole authority for faith and practice is Scripture.

4. World religions engage in distinctive ___ceremonial___ ___practices___.

Ceremonial practices are repetitive rituals that express a religion's structural beliefs in a practical way. As followers learn and are involved in these rituals, they have opportunities to communicate with their deity and to gain a sense of control over the events of life. Rituals practiced by world religions may mark a particular stage of life, like child dedications, marriages, and funerals. Some ceremonial practices require religious specialists to lead and conduct the rituals.

Many ceremonial practices center on worship of the deity or express the values of the group's structural beliefs. For example, Muslims attend mosque during Ramadan to confess their faith and do good works by giving alms to the poor. Hindus may practice the spiritual discipline of yoga to achieve realization of inner divinity. Roman Catholics offer seven sacraments, believing that they impart saving grace to recipients.

Evangelical Christians' ceremonial practices are not observed in hopes of gaining favor with God but as expressions of a living relationship with Him. God desires wholehearted commitment to Him, not empty religious rituals (see Amos 5:21-24). Jesus' harshest criticism was leveled at the hypocritical religious practices of His day (see Matt. 15:3-9).

Evangelical Christians' ceremonial practices vary among religious, social, and ethnic groups. For example, instead of sacraments, Baptists observe the ordinances of baptism and the Lord's Supper, which are not observed as the means to salvation but as symbolic acts of obedience. Baptism represents the believer's faith in Christ as Savior, death to sin, the burial of the old life, and resurrection to new life in Christ. The Lord's Supper memorializes Christ's death and anticipates His second coming.

5. World religions adhere to codes of ___conduct___.

Most world religions prescribe codes of conduct, which include ethical and moral rights and wrongs. Examples are the Five Pillars of Islam, the Eightfold Path of Buddhism, and the Ten Commandments of the Old Testament. A religion's code of conduct accomplishes three purposes.
1. The code of conduct expresses the religion's structural ___beliefs___.

2. The code of conduct reinforces the religious group's **unity**.

3. The code of conduct maintains social **harmony** in general.

   Most codes of conduct are designed to earn a religious follower salvation, as in Islam; enlightenment, as in Buddhism; or a higher existence, as in Hinduism. Christianity, in contrast, bases its moral system on the New Testament, which teaches that a believer practices morality and good works in response to a personal relationship with Christ by grace through faith. These practices do not in themselves bring about salvation.

   Christians who witness to other religions can express appreciation for moral and ethical codes that benefit humankind. Use them as bridges to establish relationships and dialogue that lead to witnessing opportunities.

6. World religions celebrate **festivals**.

World religions observe festivals, which are days or periods of time set aside to celebrate specific religious events or seasons. They usually involve specific rites—religious rites, passage rites, death rites, seasonal rites, and sacrificial rites. Festivals generally originated in religious celebrations or ritual commemorations that included sacred community meals called feasts. Depending on the purpose of the festival, the celebration may be solemn, joyful, festive, or associated with fasting. Religious festivals promote solidarity, order, and tranquility in a religious group.

   An example of a religious festival is Ramadan, the ninth month of the Islamic calendar, which Muslims observe to remember Allah's provision of all of life's needs. Jews observe festivals and feasts to remember God's goodness. Passover reminds them of the exodus from Egypt, Pentecost commemorates the giving of the law to Moses at Sinai, and the Feast of Tabernacles is associated with the fruit harvest in early fall.

   By being aware of the meaning and purpose of religious festivals for your non-Christian friends and acquaintances, you can build relationships during these special days. And although Christians do not celebrate ritualistic festivals, we do observe spiritually significant events during the Christmas and Easter seasons. Use these opportunities to emphasize the historical uniqueness of Christmas and Easter and to point the way to salvation through the One who is the focus of these observances.

Sharing Christianity's Uniqueness

Have you ever wondered why so many religions exist? Because all religions seek God, can't they all be right? The Bible holds the answer to questions about the legitimacy of world religions. In fact, the origins of all religions can be found in Genesis 3.

Step 4 (10 mins.)

Ask participants to turn to page 42 in their Journals and to fill in the blanks as you present the key points in Sharing Christianity's Uniqueness. Use the computer presentation or the overhead cel.

Sharing Christianity's Uniqueness

- When Satan came to Eve in the form of a serpent, he asked her, " 'Indeed, has God said … ?' " (v. 1, NASB), implying that believable words exist other than God's words. This was the beginning of the deception of doubting God's word and the creation of other so-called sacred scriptures.
- In Genesis 3:4 the serpent said, " 'You surely will not die!' " (NASB). He implied that there is life after death, but he did not specify the kind of life he had in mind. Is it perpetual torment in hell or everlasting joy in the Creator's presence? This was the beginning of the deception of universalism, the belief that everyone will be saved.
- In Genesis 3:5 the serpent said, " 'Your eyes will be opened, and you will be like God' " (NASB). Here the implication seems to be that humans can achieve what only God can achieve and that they can become just like God. This was the deceptive beginning of humanity's thinking of itself as divine.
- In Genesis 3:6 Eve ate the forbidden fruit, choosing to satisfy her physical hunger rather than her spiritual hunger. This was the beginning of Satan's deceiving and blinding people from seeking the true God.

You have seen that Christianity shares certain observable characteristics with the other world religions. Yet Christianity claims to be unique among those religions. The reason is Jesus Himself. As the unique Son of God, who died for our sin and rose from the dead in power and victory, Jesus is the center of human history and the perfect revelation of God (see Col. 1:15-17). Only Jesus could make the claim " 'I am the way, and the truth, and the life; no one comes to the Father but through me' " (John 14:6, NASB). Only Jesus is uniquely qualified to save (see Acts 4:12) and to be our hope for heaven (see Rom. 5:1-2). Christianity is unique because Jesus is unique. All religious faiths that do not bow before Jesus as Savior and Lord are wrong.

The Christian message, then, is unique, and the people of the world need to hear it. We are living in a pluralistic society, where evangelicals encounter criticism in conveying the exclusive message of Jesus Christ. It is your holy mandate as a Great Commission witness to take the good news of Jesus Christ to those of other faiths (see Acts 1:8; Rom. 10: 13-15). As you study the beliefs of other religions this semester and begin to approach followers of other faiths with the gospel, keep in mind these general principles.

1. Seek power and direction through __**prayer**__.
Prayer is the key element in witnessing to persons of other faiths. Without God's power through prayer, any other preparation is futile. The Bible clearly states God's concern for the lost and our confidence in the power of prayer (see 2 Cor. 4:4-5; 2 Pet. 3:9; 1 John 4:4).

2. Be willing to __learn__.

Your participation in this course indicates that you care enough about followers of other religions to learn about their beliefs. When you meet persons of another faith, be willing to spend time learning about their faith and traditions, their lifestyle, what they eat, how they dress, their religious goals, their authority for beliefs and practices, and their beliefs about Jesus.

3. Respond with __love__ and __acceptance__.

Accept followers of other religions even though you do not accept their beliefs. Rather than ignore them or try to prevent the construction of their places of worship, love them as Christ loves them. When Jesus was on earth, He associated with all types of sinners (see Luke 5:27-32) and reached out to persons of other faiths (see John 4:7-30).

4. Develop __relationships__.

Through word and deed, build bridges of understanding and witness with the religion's followers. Relationships can be established through many areas of ministry, such as literacy missions and social activities. Take time to develop friendships through which you can show love and concern.

5. Ask __questions__.

Ask questions to clarify the meanings of words. Ask the right questions. To ask a Hindu, "Do you believe in Jesus?" may not be helpful. Rather, ask, "Who is Jesus to you?" or "Are you familiar with the Christian Bible?" Ask questions like "What do you expect your faith to do for you?" or "How do you deal with evil?" However, avoid asking embarrassing, intimidating, or hostile questions.

6. Build on __commonalities__.

Expressing admiration for another religion's emphasis on moral purity or spiritual discipline, for example, can build the relationship and can lead to a discussion of faith.

7. Define __terms__.

Define the words you use in a discussion of faith. The follower may not understand or may have different definitions. Terms like *salvation* may not mean anything in his faith. Beware of using exclusive church words.

8. Let the __Bible__ speak.

If the person is open, involve him in a Bible study. Through the work of the Holy Spirit, the Scriptures can convict and convince.

9. Emphasize __Jesus__.

Share the unique message of Jesus Christ and what He means to you.

STUDY IT

Step 5 (5 mins.)

Overview Home Study Assignments for session 2.

Transition to assemble with FAITH Teams to prepare for home visits. (5 mins.)

DO IT (110 MINS.)

SHARE IT (30 MINS.)

10. *Share the FAITH* ___gospel___ ___presentation___.
When the Holy Spirit leads, use the FAITH gospel presentation to explain the way to be saved. The FAITH approach is simple and flexible enough to be used with those of non-Christian backgrounds.

Visitation Time

Do It

1. The Team Leader guides preparation for all visits. Remind Team members to stay alert during Sunday School to prospect and ministry needs.
2. Alert Team members in advance if they need to be ready to give Sunday School or evangelistic testimonies.
3. Team members have been introduced to the Key Question. Discuss responses to the question and emphasize the importance of the **Preparation** phase of the visit.
4. Keep in mind the visitation tips Learners have been asked to review (p. 35, *A Journey in FAITH Journal*). Highlight any you feel are especially helpful or needed.
5. Most of all, encourage Team members as they make their first home visits. Be prepared to take the lead in all visits. Model a visit and debrief what happened so that Team members can learn.

Celebration Time

Share It

1. Explain the purpose and importance of Celebration Time and encourage members to stay for this time each week.
2. Encourage Team members to listen carefully as reports are shared, especially about decisions made in visits; the information can be helpful in follow-up.
3. Take the lead in sharing reports.
4. Complete the necessary forms:
   • Evaluation Cards
   • Participation Cards
   • Visitation forms updated with the results of visits

Home Study Assignments

Home Study Assignments reinforce this session by helping you apply what you have learned.

Your Discipleship Journey

Journaling activities in Your Discipleship Journey are an important part of your development as a Great Commission Christian through FAITH training.

1. Match each verse with the correct benefit of a personal relationship with God through Jesus Christ.

   ___ 1. John 15:11   a. Access to God
   ___ 2. Acts 10:43   b. Assurance of eternal life
   ___ 3. Romans 5:1   c. Forgiveness
   ___ 4. Romans 5:8   d. Hope
   ___ 5. Romans 8:1   e. Intercession
   ___ 6. Hebrews 4:15-16   f. Joy
   ___ 7. Hebrews 7:25   g. Love
   ___ 8. 1 Peter 3:15   h. No condemnation
   ___ 9. 1 John 5:11-13   i. Peace

2. Other religions look to their sacred writings as scripture. Christians believe that the Bible, as God's Word, is our sole authority. Match each group of Scriptures with the word or phrase that indicates what those verses teach about a Christian view of Scripture.

   1. 2 Timothy 3:16-17; 2 Peter 1:20-21   a. Totally sufficient for your needs
   2. Deuteronomy 4:1-2; Proverbs 30:5-6;   b. Accomplishes what it purposes
      Revelation 22:18-19   c. Authoritative
   3. Psalm 119:89   d. Complete
   4. 2 Timothy 3:16-17;   e. Inspired
      1 Thessalonians 2:13
   5. Isaiah 55:11

3. The primary difference between biblical Christianity and all other religions is the claim by other faiths that it is possible to work your way to God. Summarize what the following verses say about this belief.

   Habakkuk 2:4: _____

   _____

   Romans 1:17: _____

   _____

Romans 10:17: _____

_____

2 Timothy 1:9: _____

_____

Ephesians 2:8-9: _____

_____

Growing as a Life Witness

Growing as a Life Witness reminds you of your responsibility to witness and minister to others during the week.

1. Talk or meet with your accountability partner and share ways you have cultivated a lost person or have witnessed or ministered on occasions other than FAITH visits.
2. Discuss ways you can apply the session 2 content.
3. Pray for lost persons by name and for each other.

Prayer Concerns	Answers to Prayer
_____	_____
_____	_____
_____	_____
_____	_____
_____	_____

Your Weekly Sunday School Leadership Meeting

A FAITH participant is an important member of Sunday School. Encourage Team members who are elected Sunday School leaders to attend this weekly meeting. Use this section to record ways your FAITH Team influences the work of your Sunday School class or department. Use the information to report during weekly Sunday School leadership meetings. Identify actions that need to be taken through Sunday School as a result of prayer concerns, needs identified, visits made by the Team, and decisions made by the persons visited. Also identify ways you can disciple others in your Sunday School class or department and in your church.

1. FAITH Teams made or will make visits for the first time this week. If visits have been made, share reports and list any needs that affect your class or department.

_____

_____

_____

2. Indicate any individuals/families who are expected to attend on Sunday and whether a FAITH Team member will greet them. Make specific plans to involve other class members in making guests feel comfortable when they attend, such as sitting with guests in the worship service, introducing guests to other class members, and so forth.

_____

_____

3. Discuss ways Sunday's Bible-study lesson can involve members and guests in transformational Bible study and discipleship.

_____

_____

_____

4. Pray for FAITH Team members, teachers, and department directors.

Discipling Your Team Members

This weekly feature suggests actions the Team Leader can take to support Team members, prepare for Team Time, and improve visits. This work is part of the Team Leader's Home Study Assignments. Add any actions suggested by your church's FAITH strategy.

Support Team Members
❑ Call Team members and encourage them about their participation during the first home visits.

Prepare to Lead Team Time
❑ Preview Leading Team Time at the beginning of session 3.

Prepare to Lead Visits

❑ Review the FAITH Visit Outline to be able to model the entire process for Team members.

❑ Be prepared to explain the procedures in the car as you travel to and from the church, as well as the role of the Team Leader in making visits.

❑ Be prepared to model a visit in which Team member(s) are asked to lead in sharing a Sunday School testimony.

❑ Be prepared to model the use of the Opinion Poll in making visits.

❑ Be prepared to lead the Team to participate during Celebration Time.

Link with Sunday School

❑ Participate in your weekly Sunday School leadership meeting. Share pertinent information in this meeting, using Your Weekly Sunday School Leadership Meeting (pp. 46–47) and FAITH-visit results.

❑ Consider ways your Sunday School can ground members in the truths of the Word so that they recognize false teachings they encounter.

For Further Growth: The Eternality of Jesus Christ, Part 2

For Further Growth may include additional reading or activities that will enhance your growth as a disciple and a discipler of others. These assignments are intended to be long-term projects and do not have to be completed during this semester of study.

1. Read Hebrews 13:8. What does this Scripture say about Jesus?

2. Read Philippians 2:6-8. What does this Scripture say about the past, present, and future aspects of the person of Jesus Christ?

3. Read 1 Peter 1:20-21. When did the plan of salvation for humankind begin? What do we receive through Jesus?

4. Read one or more of the following resources.

   • Millard J. Erickson, *Christian Theology*, part 7, "The Person of Christ," chapter 32, "The Deity of Christ" (Grand Rapids: Baker, 1985), 683–704.

   • J. I. Packer et al., *Exploring the Christian Faith*, chapter 6, "Who Was Jesus?" (Nashville: Thomas Nelson, 1992), 40–56.

   • Herbert Lockyer, *All About God in Christ*, chapter 2, "His Incarnation" (Peabody, MA: Hendrickson, 1995), 19–62.

5. Read the FAITH Tip on page 49.

¹Jacob Nuesner, ed., *World Religions in America* (Louisville: Westminster/John Knox, 1994), 3.
²Ibid., 1.
³*The Baptist Faith and Message* (Nashville: LifeWay Christian Resources of the Southern Baptist Convention, 2000), 5.

Answers to matching activities on page 45:
Activity 1: 1. f, 2. c, 3. i, 4. g, 5. h, 6. a, 7. e, 8. d, 9. b
Activity 2: 1. e, 2. d, 3. c, 4. a, 5. b

FAITH TIP

Do All Roads Lead to Heaven?

- "I believe that eventually, everyone will be saved. I don't think a loving God would send anyone to an eternal hell."
- "I believe that all religions are good and lead to the same place. There are many roads to God."
- "I believe that if people are sincere, no matter what they believe, God will accept them."

Most Christians who have regularly shared their faith have probably heard one or more of these statements. They reflect two commonly held but unbiblical concepts that have crept into popular religious thinking over the past several decades: universalism and inclusivism.

Universalism is the belief that all people will eventually be saved and go to heaven and that no one will spend eternity in hell. Various advocates of universalism differ in their speculations on the way God will accomplish universal salvation. Some argue that God's unconditional love and grace completely override His judgment. Thus, everyone's sins are forgiven no matter how heinous they are and no matter whether the person accepts God's grace. Other universalists assert that God punishes sinners in a temporary state after death. Nonetheless, all people will repent and turn to God in that postmortem life, and eventually hell will be emptied.

The Bible, however, does not teach that all people will be saved. Only those who put their faith in Jesus Christ as Savior and Lord in this life will spend eternity in heaven (see John 1:12; Eph. 2:8-9; 1 John 5:13). The unsaved, sadly, will spend eternity separated from God in hell (see Matt. 18:8-9; 25:41-46; John 3:18,36). Scripture also does not teach that people can be saved after death. Salvation is received only in this mortal life, and then comes judgment (see Heb. 9:27).

Inclusivism is similar to universalism. However, those who hold this view are not necessarily universalists. They do not necessarily teach that everyone will be saved. Rather, their view is that all good people, even those who are not Christians, will be saved and go to heaven if they are sincere in their desire to serve God. Only wicked and unrepentant people will go to hell but only as a last resort if they refuse God's love after death.

Again, the Bible does not support any way of salvation apart from faith in Jesus (see John 14:6; Acts 4:12). Other religions and philosophies may teach moral principles, but salvation comes only by grace through faith in Christ.

FAITH AT WORK

Oh, no, not again. Why does this keep happening at the beginning of each FAITH semester? Last time it was my daughter. I was in the middle of a FAITH Clinic and got a call that my daughter had been hurt, having jumped off the top bunk and twisted her ankle. During the break between sessions we went to the hospital and, thankfully, found that the ankle wasn't broken. We returned for the evening service, hobbled down the aisle, and marveled at what God was doing in the lives of the people attending the Clinic.

The next semester of FAITH was about to begin. This time my son fell and broke his elbow. We returned from the emergency room just in time for the opening prayer. "OK, Lord, this is starting not to be funny."

The first two events might be seen by some as comical. And some might have used them as an excuse to drop out of any activity, especially an elective course on sharing your faith. But not me. No, I was a committed FAITH participant, and my children's injuries would not derail my training.

The third semester started uneventfully, but then a phone call came that my grandmother was ill. A week later she was gone. I didn't know what God had in store for us that semester or what the devil wanted to stop us from accomplishing. I just felt by this point that I was hurting and needed some time off. But I decided—I know now with the Lord's help—to continue. Weeks passed, and we didn't get an opportunity to lead anyone to Christ. But I knew that God was sovereign and that He must have a plan.

Soon we started to experience opportunity after opportunity to minister to member families. We went to the home of a young family that had completed an information card during church. On the first visit their 10-year-old son prayed to receive Christ. On our next visit we learned that this couple were new believers and were not yet married but living together. We shared God's plan for marriage and fidelity. They had heard enough sermons to know that we were speaking the truth. They became convinced that their lifestyle was ungodly, but they struggled with finding a way out. Our Sunday School class helped them with their wedding by providing flowers, a cake, and a gift. They became part of our Sunday School class and active FAITH participants.

The experience of making a difference in someone's life was repeated again and again. We would meet people, meet a need, and welcome them into our church family. Not everyone needed salvation, but in many cases fellowship with the Lord was restored. And while God was using me to bring comfort and healing to these new friends, He was comforting and healing me, too. In the midst of my serving Him, He met me there and used me for His purposes.

I accidentally caught my daughter's hand in the car window last night. Can you guess what begins at my church on Monday? I can't wait!

Anna Scott
Immanuel Baptist Church
Highland, California

SESSION 3

Judaism

JIM R. SIBLEY

In this session you will—

CHECK IT by engaging in Team Time activities;

KNOW IT by reviewing content from session 2;

HEAR IT by examining Jewish beliefs and by learning ways

to witness to Jewish people;

STUDY IT by overviewing Home Study Assignments;

DO IT by leading your Team in making visits;

SHARE IT by celebrating.

IN ADVANCE

• Overview content.
• Preview teaching suggestions. Prepare key points. Decide whether to use the session 3 computer presentation or the overhead cels.
• Prepare the room for teaching.
• Pray for participants and for Teams as they prepare to visit.
• As Teaching Time begins, direct participants to open their Journals to page 54.

If the computer presentation is used, display the agenda frame for Team Time. Add other points as needed.

CHECK IT agenda:
✔ FAITH Visit Outline
✔ Other Home Study Assignments
✔ Session 2 Debriefing
✔ Help for Strengthening a Visit

Leading Team Time

All Team members participate in Team Time. They are primarily responsible for reciting the assigned portion of the FAITH Visit Outline and for discussing other Home Study Assignments.

As you direct this important time of CHECK IT activities with your Team, keep in mind that Learners look to you as a role model, motivator, mentor, and friend. Team Time activities can continue in the car as the Team travels to and from visits.

Lead CHECK It Activities

✔ FAITH Visit Outline
❑ Be prepared to check off each Learner's memorization of all of **Preparation** (through Transition Statement) and the key words in **Presentation** and **Invitation**.
❑ Indicate your approval by signing or initialing each Learner's Journal. Encourage Learners as you do and indicate any notes you have jotted down that might be helpful.

✔ Other Home Study Assignments
❑ Give as much time as needed to helping Learners understand different responses people might make to the Key Question and ways to answer those responses in love. Indicate that such answers will become clearer throughout FAITH training/visits.
❑ Discuss how FAITH Tips and/or other readings can provide specific help or answer some questions from sessions.
❑ Indicate specific content areas that may appear again on the session 16 written review.

✔ Session 2 Debriefing
❑ Answer any questions that remain from session 2. Emphasize the importance of a good beginning in building trust that can ultimately result in the gospel's being shared. Highlight ways the Sunday School testimony helps build bridges to people.
❑ Review Learners' written Sunday School testimonies.
❑ Indicate specific content areas that may appear again on the session 16 written review.

✔ Help for Strengthening a Visit
❑ Answer any questions that emerged from home visits following session 2.
❑ Review ways to begin a visit.

❑ Identify actions Team members took during last week's visits that were particularly effective and others that might need to be changed.

❑ Suggest ways Team members can improve sharing their Sunday School testimonies.

❑ Call attention to the evangelistic testimony you shared during last week's visit(s). Mention that Team Learners will be introduced during this session to ways to share their testimonies during a visit.

Notes

_____

_____

_____

_____

_____

_____

Actions I Need to Take with Team Members This Week

_____

_____

_____

_____

_____

_____

Transition to classrooms for instruction on the content of the session. (5 mins.)

Direct participants to locate A Quick Review on page 54 in their Journals and to complete the activities. Then give the answers, using the computer presentation or the overhead cel.

A Quick Review

HEAR IT

Step 2 (5 mins.)

Direct participants to fill in the blanks as you present the key points in Reaching the Remnant. Use the computer presentation or the overhead cels.

Reaching the Remnant

A Quick Review

In session 2 you overviewed characteristics of world religions. Beside each statement, write *P* for *pluralism* if the statement can apply to most world religions and *C* if it applies only to evangelical Christianity.

P 1. Participate in festivals and ceremonies to increase a sense of community

P 2. Profess a body of structural beliefs

C 3. Emphasize a personal relationship with God through Jesus Christ

P 4. Seek to know God through their own efforts

P 5. Look to sacred writings for guidance

C 6. Believe that the Bible is God's Word and the standard for life and practice

P 7. Attend regular worship experiences

C 8. Believe that salvation is received by grace through faith

C 9. Teach that baptism and the Lord's Supper are ordinances of the church, not to be confused with sacraments

Fill in the blanks to identify general principles for witnessing to followers of other faiths.

1. Seek power and direction through ____**prayer**____.
2. Be willing to ____**learn**____.
3. Respond with ____**love**____ and ____**acceptance**____.
4. Develop ____**relationships**____.
5. Ask ____**questions**____.
6. Build on ____**commonalities**____.
7. Define ____**terms**____.
8. Let the ____**Bible**____ speak.
9. Emphasize ____**Jesus**____.
10. Share the FAITH ____**gospel**____ ____**presentation**____.

Reaching the Remnant

Judaism is the oldest of the world's three great monotheistic religions and is the parent of both Christianity and Islam. The Jewish people can be defined as an ethnic group composed of the physical descendants of Abraham, Isaac, and Jacob and the descendants of those who have joined the Jewish people throughout history. The Jewish people are unique among the peoples of the world in that God especially chose them for His purposes in history. About ___**2000**___ B.C. God appeared to Abraham (then Abram) and promised to bless him and to found a great nation (see Gen. 12:1-3).

The Old Testament recounts the subsequent history of the Jewish people: slavery in Egypt, the occupation of Canaan, the monarchy, and divided kingdoms. The northern kingdom fell to Assyria in **722** B.C., and the southern kingdom went into Babylonian captivity in **586** B.C., bringing the end of the Jewish people as an independent nation. Although the people later returned to Jerusalem, Jewish history primarily consisted of subjection to Babylonian, Persian, Greek, or Roman rule. An uprising in A.D. **70** brought the destruction of Jerusalem and the final dispersion of the Jewish people. Thereafter the Jewish people suffered intense persecution and longed for a return to their own land. This hope resulted in the Zionist movement and ultimately led to the creation of the modern state of Israel in **1948**.

The first Jewish immigrants to the United States arrived in 1654 from Brazil. They had been among a number of Jewish people who had fled religious persecution in Spain and Portugal. Thousands of Jewish people fled similar persecution in central Europe and arrived in the United States between 1840 and 1880. The Jewish community in the United States was the largest in the world by 1919. The Jewish population of the United States today is about **6,061,000**. The number of Jewish people in the world is about **13,092,800**.

Jewish Beliefs

A study of traditional Judaism may not shed much light on the beliefs of most Jewish Americans. Only a small minority of the North American Jewish population actively practices traditional Judaism. That's why it is important to deal with real people, not stereotypes, when relating to Jewish people.

In North America rabbinic Judaism is usually expressed in one of three different denominations: Orthodox, Conservative, or Reform. Within each of these exists a wide variety of doctrine and practice. In general, Orthodox Judaism strictly maintains traditional Judaism, Reform Judaism takes a fairly liberal attitude toward the Hebrew Scriptures and Jewish traditions, and Conservative Judaism tries to find a middle way. The overwhelming majority of Jews, however, are only marginally involved in the synagogue. In addition, many of North America's Jewish population are involved in Eastern and New Age spirituality. Most have embraced liberalism, humanism, and in many cases secularism. These ideologies are destroying the Jewish community and are leading to alarming rates of assimilation, which means that Jewish people are forsaking their Jewishness. Some in the rabbinic community, recognizing this trend, are trying to influence their people to adopt a more biblical value system.

Step 3 (20 mins.)

Ask participants to turn to page 56 in their Journals and to fill in the blanks as you present the main points in Jewish Beliefs. Use the computer presentation or the overhead cel.

Jewish Beliefs

Because of these divergent paths in Judaism, it is difficult to generalize about Jewish beliefs. Most Jewish people, however, hold in common some basic perspectives from traditional, rabbinic Judaism.

1. There is only one ___God___.

The defining verse of Scripture for traditional Judaism is Deuteronomy 6:4, commonly referred to as the Shema, a Hebrew word meaning *hear:* " 'Hear, O Israel: The Lord our God, the Lord is one' " (NIV). This God, the Creator of heaven and earth, has revealed Himself to the prophets of the Hebrew or holy Scriptures. God is personal, holy, and just.

The key word in this verse proclaiming the oneness of God is the Hebrew word *echad,* which refers to a composite unity. The same word is used in Genesis to refer to a man and a wife as "one flesh" (Gen. 2:24, NASB) and to the morning and the evening as "one day" (Gen. 1:5, NASB). However, Rabbi Maimonides, a 12th-century theologian and philosopher, used the word *yachid* to describe God. *Yachid* means *absolute and unqualified oneness.* This word does not allow for a trinitarian view of God, carrying rabbinic teaching away from biblical teaching.

Christians take seriously the triune nature of God as revealed in Scripture (see Gen. 1:26; Isa. 48:12-16). God has revealed Himself as Father, Son, and Holy Spirit; yet He is one God.

2. Scripture is inferior to ___tradition___.

The basis of Judaism is the Hebrew Bible, the Old Testament in the Christian Bible. The Hebrew Bible is divided into three sections: the Torah (the Law), Prophets, and Writings. The Torah, the first five books of the Bible, is the most important section. Later, rabbis gave oral interpretations of the Torah to adapt it to daily life. These oral interpretations and written commentaries on the Torah form the Jewish Talmud.

Rabbinic Judaism is based on human traditions, which are constantly shifting, changing, and evolving. The validity, indeed the authority, of this evolving, progressing theology is not to be challenged. Judaism teaches that even if a voice from heaven contradicts tradition, that voice is to be rejected.[1] So although rabbinic Judaism teaches that the Hebrew Scriptures are the Word of God, they do not carry the authority of traditional rabbinic sources.

Christianity is founded on God's Word. Our traditions, experiences, and scholarship stand under the authority of the Bible. Paul wrote, "All Scripture is inspired by God and profitable for teaching, for reproof, for correction, for training in righteousness" (2 Tim. 3:16, NASB). Our faith is built on the solid rock of biblical truth, epitomized in the person of Jesus.

3. Humanity is basically ___good___.

Are people to be understood in terms of their essential goodness and sufficiency or their basic sinfulness and insufficiency? Rabbinic Judaism holds that humanity is basically good, bearing God's image. The rabbinic position does not recognize the need for humanity's restoration, especially with respect to the Jewish people. In other words, Jews see no need for the good news because they do not believe the bad news of sin and separation from God.

Christians affirm humanity's creation in God's image, but we give full biblical weight to humanity's fall and its need for salvation (see Gen. 3). The Hebrew Scriptures emphasize the fact of our sinful condition and the need for atonement (see Gen. 6:5; Eccl. 9:3; Isa. 53:6).

4. Salvation must be ___earned___.

In rabbinic Judaism good and evil are always possibilities, but humans' dignity and basic goodness mean that they are inclined to choose good. Jewish people commonly think of sin in terms of almost criminal behavior. Usually, they would not consider themselves to be sinners.

Traditional Judaism is a religion of self-salvation with no room for a Savior or Redeemer who would die for the sins of the world. Salvation is to be earned through repentance, prayer, and good deeds. Orthodox Jews believe in a life after death, although they primarily emphasize life in the present. Most Jewish people in North America, however, either deny or express uncertainty about life after death.

Christians do not believe that salvation can be earned. Salvation is freely given as a gift from God to anyone who repents of sin and turns to God through faith in Jesus Christ (see Luke 13:3b; Rom. 10:9). Those who accept Christ's salvation spend eternity with Him in heaven (see John 14:2-3). The New Testament also teaches the need for holiness (see Matt. 5:20); however, a Christian's motivation for good works is not to earn salvation but to serve God and others in Christ's love.

5. Observing the ___law___, the ___Sabbath___, ___festivals___, and ___feasts___ is essential.

What Jewish people do is more important than what they believe. Observance of the Torah, which consists of the written law of Jewish Scripture, other rabbinical writings, and oral tradition, occupies a central role in the good deeds required to earn salvation. Dietary (*kosher*) laws, marriage ceremonies, festivals, mourning rites, *bar* or *bat mitzvah*, and other customs and ceremonies affect all aspects of life. A Jewish boy becomes a *bar mitzvah*, or a son of the commandments, at age 13 and is considered an adult. A Jewish girl becomes a *bat mitzvah* at the same age.

Jewish people observe the Sabbath, the seventh day of the week, as the day God rested from the work of creation (see Gen. 2:2-3). The Sabbath begins at sundown on Friday and ends at sundown on Saturday. Synagogue and temple services are held on Friday evening. Sabbath school may be held on Saturday morning.

Jewish people observe holy days besides the Sabbath. The Jewish

New Year is *Rosh Hashanah*. The Day of Atonement (*Yom Kippur*), or the Day of Coverings, is the holiest day of the year. In ancient Israel it included the sacrifice of an animal to cover or atone for the sins of the people (see Lev. 16:1-34). *Purim* celebrates the deliverance of the Jews in Persia, as described in the Book of Esther. *Hanukkah*, celebrated in December, commemorates the victory of Judas Maccabees over the Syrians and the rededication of the temple in 164 B.C.

Festivals and feasts call Jewish people to remember God's goodness. Passover (*Pesach*), recalling the exodus from Egypt, is the most important Jewish feast (see Lev. 23:4-14; Deut. 16:1-8). Pentecost (*Shavout*), or the Feast of Weeks, commemorates the giving of the law to Moses at Sinai. It is also associated with the wheat harvest (see Lev. 23:15-21; Deut. 16:9-12). The Feast of Tabernacles (*Succot*), or Booths, is associated with the fruit harvest in early fall (see Lev. 23:33-43; Deut. 16:13-17).

Christians do not observe Old Testament law, feasts, and festivals, because the law was fulfilled in Jesus Christ (see Matt. 5:17). Paul wrote to the Colossians, "No one is to act as your judge in regard to food or drink or in respect to a festival or a new moon or a Sabbath day—things which are a mere shadow of what is to come; but the substance belongs to Christ" (Col. 2:16-17, NASB). The Christian faith is a matter of the heart and not of religious ritual. However, we can enrich our faith by discovering its roots in the Old Testament, because the ritual observances recognized God's work in the lives of His people and foreshadowed the coming of Christ. An understanding of Jewish practices also gives us common ground for discussions of faith with Jewish people.

6. *Jesus' messiahship is* ___**denied**___.

Michael Medved, a noted film critic and social commentator who is also an adherent of Orthodox Judaism, has said: "The chief distinguishing characteristic of most American Jews is not what they do believe, but what they do not believe. They do not believe in Jesus as the messiah. Period. End of sentence, end of story. … Acceptance of Jesus is the one theological permutation that Jews of all persuasions find unacceptable, the only issue on which Jewish Americans from the militantly secular to the militantly Hasidic are ready to draw a common line."[2]

Rabbinic Judaism would like to avoid any consideration of Jesus, the gospel, or Christianity, but it is forced to deal with these topics because of the historic relationship between Judaism and Christianity and because of the strength of Western Christian culture. The dilemma for Jewish people is that Jesus is the most famous Jew to have ever lived, with overwhelming evidence for His historicity. Yet most Jewish people reject Him. Jesus must be denied His messiahship and divested of His deity to be acceptable to the Jewish community.

Jewish opinions about Jesus are varied and contradictory. Sometimes He is viewed as a future, though merely human deliverer; sometimes as a symbol for a future golden age; and sometimes in purely political terms, that is, as the modern state of Israel.

In contrast, for Christians, Jesus is the very center of our faith, thought, and life. We do not believe that a man became God but that God became a man in the person of the Messiah of Israel. He lived a sinless life, died on the cross, and rose again—all according to the Hebrew Scriptures—so that He might provide ultimate and final atonement for all who place their trust in Him.

Witnessing to Jewish People

1. Anticipate <u>defensive</u> <u>tactics</u>.
When witnessing to Jewish people, you may encounter defensive tactics.

- *Pluralism.* Because many modern Jewish people take refuge in pluralism, you may hear them say, "There are many roads to God" or "God has many names." It is strange that devout monotheists would grant legitimacy to polytheists, idolaters, and worshipers of false gods in order to avoid having to deal with Jesus. Pluralism cannot be maintained without deforming and perverting the other world religions or surrendering the concept of absolute truth.

- *Offense.* Jesus is the central issue dividing rabbinic Judaism and Christianity. Scripture speaks of the offense of the gospel (see Matt. 11:6; Rom. 9:33). Some believe that our evangelism is a denigration of Judaism. However, Christianity's affirmation of Jesus is no more a denigration of Judaism than Judaism's denial of Jesus is a denigration of Christianity. You might ask your Jewish friend, "What is it about Jesus that makes you so angry?"

- *Identity.* The question of whether a Jewish person can believe in Jesus and still be Jewish is important, but a better question is whether Jesus is who He claimed to be. If Jesus is the Messiah of Israel, the fulfillment of Hebrew prophecy, and the crown jewel of the Torah, faith in Him cannot make anyone less Jewish. Jewish people believe that Christians want them to become Gentiles, but the New Testament forbids Jewish Christians to forsake their Jewishness (see 1 Cor. 7:18,20). Your Jewish friends will remain Jewish, but what kind of Jewish people will they be—those who have personal relationships with the God of Abraham, Isaac, and Jacob or those whose sin separates them from God?

- *Guilt.* Horrible things have been done during the past two thousand years in the name of Jesus, including the Crusades, Spanish Inquisition, and Holocaust. But it is unfair to equate medieval Roman Catholics with evangelical Christians today. Baptists played a key role in bringing religious liberty to the United States, and few

Step 4 (10 mins.)

Direct participants to turn to page 59 in their Journals and to fill in the blanks as you present the key points in Witnessing to Jewish People. Use the computer presentation or the overhead cel.

Witnessing to Jewish People

groups have benefited more than Jewish people. As it is unjust to blame Jewish people today for complicity in Jesus' crucifixion, it is unjust to blame evangelical Christians for horrific deeds in the past.

2. Rely on ___prayer___.

Prayer and dependence on the Holy Spirit are crucial in evangelism, but prayer is particularly appropriate for the salvation of Jewish people. The Old Testament admonishes prayer for the spiritual well-being of the people of Israel (see Ps. 122:6-9), and one of the New Testament references to specific prayer for the lost, Romans 10:1, describes Paul's prayer for the salvation of the Jewish people.

3. Be ___humble___.

The pride and arrogance of Christians throughout Jewish history and the sensitivities Jewish people developed as a minority among a Christian majority make it important to approach them with an absence of pride. We are Christians not because we are smarter, more obedient, or better than they are but because of God's amazing grace.

4. Cultivate genuine ___friendships___.

God uses the normal patterns of personal relationships as bridges for the gospel. Be a friend to your Jewish acquaintances. Send an appropriate card or small gift for the Jewish holidays. Be sure that your friendships are genuine. It is dishonest to condition a friendship on the acceptance of Jesus. Nevertheless, do not compromise your willingness to discuss the gospel with your friend in order to preserve your friendship.

5. Exercise ___cultural___ ___sensitivity___.

Learn about Jewish customs and terms. Stress the Jewishness of faith in Jesus by using Jesus' Hebrew name, *Yeshua*, and by speaking of *Messiah* rather than *Christ*. Use *believer in the Messiah* instead of *Christian*. Use *the Messiah's return* instead of *Christ's second coming*. Avoid church words like *conversion* and *convert*. Use *congregation of believers* instead of *church*. Use *good news* instead of *gospel*. Gentiles have often spoken the word *Jew* with an edge. Instead, say *Jewish people, person, man, woman*, and so on.

6. Use Scripture to point to the ___Messiah___.

God has promised to bless His Word. Ask your Jewish friends to join you and other friends for a brief Bible study from the Jewish Bible, that is, the Old Testament. Ask whether your friends would accept the gift of a New Testament. An edition that highlights the fulfillment of messianic prophecy would be ideal. As you use the FAITH gospel presentation with Jewish people, use Old Testament Scriptures like the ones suggested in the FAITH Tip on pages 66–67. Also share Scriptures like the following to show ways Jesus fulfilled messianic prophecy.

MESSIANIC PROPHECY	VERSE(S)	FULFILLMENT
To be the Son of God	Psalm 2:7	John 3:16-17
To be born of the tribe of Judah	Genesis 49:10	Hebrews 7:14
To be born in Bethlehem	Micah 5:2	Matthew 2:1-6
To be a descendant of David	Isaiah 9:6-7	Luke 1:32-33
To die for the sins of His people	Isaiah 53:5-8	1 Corinthians 15:3-4
To die by crucifixion	Psalm 22:13-18	Luke 23:33
To sit at God's right hand	Psalm 110:1	Mark 16:19

7. *Speak with* _____confidence_____.

When you speak with Jewish people, speak with confidence in the gospel, confidence in the Scripture, and confidence that God is speaking to them. Explain that the most urgent issue anyone faces is alienation from God. Because Jesus is the answer to this alienation, He is the most deeply relevant issue in life. "What have you done with Jesus?" is much more important than the Jewish person's good deeds.

Visitation Time

Do It

1. Assign specific responsibilities to your Team Learners. Ask one to share a Sunday School or evangelistic testimony. Ask one to be the navigator to arrange the visitation schedule. Suggest that this person start with the prospect's home that is farthest away. Then work your way back toward the church. Assign another Team Learner to gather age-appropriate materials for your visit. This procedure will save time and will provide good training for Learners.
2. Pray before you go.
3. Review in the car. Share your evangelistic testimony and ask Learners to share what they would like to include in theirs.
4. Debrief each visit. Facilitate by asking specific questions.

Celebration Time

Share It

1. Hear reports and testimonies.
2. Complete Evaluation Cards.
3. Complete Participation Cards.
4. Update visitation forms with the results of visits.

STUDY IT

Step 5 (5 mins.)

Overview Home Study Assignments for session 3.

Transition to assemble with FAITH Teams to prepare for home visits. (5 mins.)

DO IT (110 MINS.)

SHARE IT (30 MINS.)

Home Study Assignments

Home Study Assignments reinforce this session by helping you apply what you have learned.

Your Discipleship Journey

Journaling activities in Your Discipleship Journey are an important part of your development as a Great Commission Christian through FAITH training.

1. Match the following to learn how the New Testament Scriptures on the left fulfill Old Testament prophecies about the Messiah on the right.

    ___ 1. Matthew 1:1   a. Would be betrayed by a friend (Ps. 41:9)

    ___ 2. Matthew 1:18   b. Would be seen as a prophet (Deut. 18:15)

    ___ 3. Matthew 2:1   c. Would be the seed of a woman (Gen. 3:15)

    ___ 4. Mark 14:10   d. Would be born of a virgin (Isa. 7:14)

    ___ 5. Mark 15:1-37   e. Would be rejected by His own (Isa. 53:3)

    ___ 6. Luke 24:1-7,36-39   f. Would descend from Abraham (Gen. 18:18)

    ___ 7. John 1:11   g. Would rise from the dead (Ps. 16:10)

    ___ 8. John 6:14   h. Would be born in Bethlehem (Mic. 5:2)

    ___ 9. Acts 3:25-26   i. Would be heir to David's throne (Isa. 9:7)

    ___ 10. Galatians 4:4   j. Would suffer and die for others (Isa. 53:4-6,12)

2. In Judaism people are seen as basically good because they bear God's image. Therefore, Jewish people do not see the need for a Redeemer. Read the following verses and summarize the way they respond to this false belief.

    Psalm 51:5-6; 53:3: _____

    _____

    Isaiah 1:18-20: _____

    _____

    Isaiah 41:14; 43:11: _____

    _____

    Isaiah 59:20-21: _____

    _____

3. How do the verses on the following page support the truth that Jesus is Redeemer and Savior?

Jeremiah 50:44: _____

Romans 3:24: _____

1 Peter 1:18-19: _____

_____

Titus 2:13: _____

Revelation 1:17-18; 2:8: _____

_____

Growing as a Life Witness

Growing as a Life Witness reminds you of your responsibility to witness and minister to others during the week.

1. Talk or meet with your accountability partner and share ways you have cultivated a lost person or have witnessed or ministered on occasions other than FAITH visits.
2. Discuss ways you can apply the session 3 content.
3. Pray for lost persons by name and for each other.

Prayer Concerns	Answers to Prayer
_____	_____
_____	_____
_____	_____
_____	_____

Your Weekly Sunday School Leadership Meeting

A FAITH participant is an important member of Sunday School. Encourage Team members who are elected Sunday School leaders to attend this weekly meeting. Use this section to record ways your FAITH Team influences the work of your Sunday School class or department. Use the information to report during weekly Sunday School leadership meetings. Identify actions that need to be taken through Sunday School as a result of prayer concerns, needs identified, visits made by the Team, and decisions made by the persons visited. Also identify ways you can disciple others in your Sunday School class or department and in your church.

1. Share results of visits. Suggest opportunities to minister to persons who were visited.

_____

2. List ways your class or department can minister to or assimilate new members.

_____

_____

3. Evaluate last week's Bible-study session. Discuss ways to make Sunday's lesson applicable to life. Indicate anyone visited by a FAITH Team who is likely to attend on Sunday.

_____

4. Periodically consider actually making follow-up phone calls to prospects and new members during this meeting. (If this is not possible, make assignments.) In the calls communicate excitement about guests' participation in Sunday School.

5. In receiving the new list of absentees, share any information that can help in follow-up. Does this member need a Sunday School ministry visit? If so, by what date and by which FAITH Team?

_____

6. Pray specifically for Sunday School plans and leaders this week.

Discipling Your Team Members

This weekly feature suggests actions the Team Leader can take to support Team members, prepare for Team Time, and improve visits. This work is part of the Team Leader's Home Study Assignments. Add any actions suggested by your church's FAITH strategy.

Support Team Members
❏ Call Team members and talk with them about their participation during the class training and visits. Discuss any observations they made during the visits and particularly about sharing their Sunday School testimonies.
❏ Discuss ways to prepare and share their evangelistic testimonies without revealing the answer to the Key Question.
❏ Encourage them as they memorize all of *Preparation* in the FAITH Visit Outline.

Prepare to Lead Team Time
❏ Preview Leading Team Time at the beginning of session 4.

Prepare to Lead Visits
❏ Review the FAITH Visit Outline in order to model the entire process for Team members.
❏ Be prepared to model a visit in which Team member(s) are asked to lead in sharing Sunday School and evangelistic testimonies.
❏ Be prepared to model the use of the Opinion Poll in making visits.
❏ Be prepared to lead your Team to participate during Celebration Time.

Link with Sunday School
❏ Participate in your weekly Sunday School leadership meeting. Share pertinent information in this meeting, using Your Weekly Sunday School Leadership Meeting (pp. 63–64) and FAITH-visit results.
❏ Take every opportunity to communicate Christ's true identity as the Messiah through Sunday School lessons and contacts with visitors who need His salvation.

For Further Growth: The Deity of Jesus Christ, Part 1
For Further Growth may include additional reading or activities that will enhance your growth as a disciple and a discipler of others. These assignments are intended to be long-term projects and do not have to be completed during this semester of study.

1. Jesus Christ is eternal God. Study these Scriptures from the Gospel of John and note how they verify Jesus' deity: John 1:1; 5:18; 10:30; 14:8.
2. Read one or more of the following resources.
   • Millard J. Erickson, *Christian Theology*, part 7, "The Person of Christ," chapter 32, "The Deity of Christ" (Grand Rapids: Baker, 1985), 683–704.
   • Josh McDowell, *Evidence That Demands a Verdict*, chapters 6–8 (San Bernardino: Here's Life, 1979), 89–140.
   • C. S. Lewis, *Mere Christianity*, chapters 4–5 (New York: Scribners, 1952), 42–51.
3. Read the FAITH Tips on pages 66–68.

---

[1]Israel V. Berman, trans. and ed., *The Talmud*, vol. 3, *Tractate Bava Metzia*, part 3 (New York: Random House, 1990), 59b.
[2]Michael Medved, "What Do American Jews Believe? A Symposium," *Commentary*, 102:2 (Aug. 1996): 70–71.

Answers to matching activity on page 62: 1. i, 2. d, 3. h, 4. a, 5. j, 6. g, 7. e, 8. b, 9. f, 10. c

FAITH TIP

Old Testament References for FAITH

When you have opportunities to present the gospel to Jewish people, it may be helpful to substitute the following Old Testament passages for the Scriptures in the *Presentation* portion of the FAITH Visit Outline.

F is for FORGIVENESS

We cannot have eternal life and heaven without God's forgiveness.
"If You, Lord, should mark iniquities,
O Lord, who could stand?
But there is forgiveness with You,
that You may be feared"—Psalm 130:3-4, NASB.

A is for AVAILABLE

Forgiveness is available. It is—

AVAILABLE FOR ALL

" 'To the Lord our God belong compassion and forgiveness, for we have rebelled against Him' "—Daniel 9:9, NASB.

BUT NOT AUTOMATIC

" 'Many of those who sleep in the dust of the ground will awake, these to everlasting life, but the others to disgrace and everlasting contempt' "—Daniel 12:2, NASB.

I is for IMPOSSIBLE

It is impossible for God to allow sin into heaven.

GOD IS—

• LOVE

" 'The Lord, the Lord God, compassionate and gracious, slow to anger, and abounding in lovingkindness and truth; who keeps.lovingkindness for thousands, who forgives iniquity, transgression and sin' "—Exodus 34:6-7, NASB.

• JUST

" 'He will by no means leave the guilty unpunished' "—Exodus 34:7, NASB.

MAN IS SINFUL

"Your iniquities have made a separation between you and your God, And your sins have hidden His face from you so that He does not hear"—Isaiah 59:2, NASB.

Question: But how can a sinful person enter heaven, where God allows no sin?

T is for TURN

Question: If you were driving down the road and someone asked you to turn, what would he or she be asking you to do? (change directions)
Turn means *repent*.

TURN from something—sin and self

" 'Say to them, "As I live!" declares the Lord God, "I take no pleasure in the death of the wicked, but rather that the wicked turn from his way and live. Turn back, turn back from your evil ways! Why then will you die, O house of Israel?" ' "—Ezekiel 33:11, NASB.

TURN to Someone; trust God's Messiah only

(Scripture tells us that Messiah) *"was pierced through for our transgressions,*
He was crushed for our iniquities;
The chastening for our well-being fell upon Him,
And by His scourging we are healed.
All of us like sheep have gone astray,
Each of us has turned to his own way;
But the Lord has caused the iniquity of us all
To fall on Him"—Isaiah 53:5-6, NASB.

" 'Turn to Me and be saved, all the ends of the earth;*
For I am God, and there is no other' "—Isaiah 45:22, NASB.

H is for HEAVEN

Heaven is eternal life.

HERE

"You will make known to me the path of life;
in Your presence is fullness of joy"—Psalm 16:11, NASB.

HEREAFTER

"In Your right hand there are pleasures forever"—Psalm 16:11, NASB.
"God will redeem my soul from the power of Sheol,
For He will receive me"—Psalm 49:15, NASB.

HOW

How can a person have God's forgiveness, heaven and eternal life, and His Messiah as personal.Savior and Lord?

"He [Abraham] believed in the Lord; and He reckoned it to him
as righteousness"—Genesis 15:6, NASB.
" 'The righteous will live by his faith' "—Habakkuk 2:4, NASB.*
" 'It will come about that whoever calls on the name of the Lord*
Will be delivered' "—Joel 2:32, NASB.

FAITH TIP

Messianic Congregations

The first local church was a messianic congregation. All of the members were Jewish believers in Jesus (Hebrew, *Yeshua*), and this first congregation was planted on the Temple Mount in Jerusalem (see Acts 5:12).

How times have changed! The Al Aksa Mosque now occupies the site of that first messianic congregation, and the vast majority of the churches that have been planted around the world since then have been Gentile, both in membership and in cultural expression. We rejoice in these Gentile congregations of every tribe, nation, and tongue that have come to salvation through Israel's Messiah.

What is a messianic congregation? For those of us who believe that Jesus is the Messiah, *messianic* is synonymous with *Christian*. *Messiah* is based on the Hebrew word (and *Christ* on the Greek word) for *the Anointed One*. When reference is made to a messianic congregation, the Hebrew origin is emphasized, just as Hebrew culture is expressed in the life of the congregation.

Messianic congregations offer Jewish believers the following benefits.

1. They are natural expressions of faith and worship for Jewish believers within their own cultural heritage.
2. They provide an appropriate context in which to present the claims of the New Testament to Jewish seekers and to meet the needs of mixed marriages.
3. They allow Jewish believers in Jesus to preserve their cultural heritage for their children and grandchildren.

Usually, messianic congregations meet on Friday evenings or Saturday mornings. They may utilize worship elements found in traditional Jewish synagogues unless they contradict biblical teaching. Usually, the Shema (Deut. 6:4) is sung. Traditional songs of praise are sung, along with choruses bearing testimony to the congregation's faith in Yeshua as the Messiah. As in the synagogue, the weekly Scripture portion from the Torah may be read, followed by either a brief homily or an entire sermon based on that text. The teaching and preaching usually include insights from a Hebraic perspective but always point to faith in Messiah. The services are usually followed by an *oneg*, or a fellowship, which includes a *nosh*, or snack, and time for visiting and fellowship.

Messianic congregations observe Jewish holidays and festivals, but Jesus is central in them all. For example, at Passover He is the Passover Lamb; at Hanukkah He is the Light of the world.

Islam

N. S. R. K. RAVI

In this session you will—

CHECK IT by engaging in Team Time activities;

KNOW IT by reviewing content from session 3;

HEAR IT by examining Islamic beliefs and by learning ways
   to witness to Muslims;

SEE IT by viewing a video segment;

STUDY IT by overviewing Home Study Assignments;

DO IT by leading your Team in making visits;

SHARE IT by celebrating.

IN ADVANCE
- Overview content.
- Preview teaching suggestions. Prepare key points. Decide whether to use the session 4 computer presentation or the overhead cels.
- Prepare the room for teaching.
- Cue the videotape to the session 4 segment.
- Pray for participants and for Teams as they prepare to visit.
- As Teaching Time begins, direct participants to open their Journals to page 72.

If the computer presentation is used, display the agenda frame for Team Time. Add other points as needed.

CHECK IT agenda:
✔ FAITH Visit Outline
✔ Evangelistic Testimony
✔ Sunday School Testimony
✔ Other Home Study Assignments/Session 3 Debriefing
✔ Help for Strengthening a Visit

Leading Team Time

All Team members participate in Team Time. They are primarily responsible for reciting the assigned portion of the FAITH Visit Outline and for discussing other Home Study Assignments.

As you direct this important time of CHECK IT activities with your Team, keep in mind that Learners look to you as a role model, motivator, mentor, and friend. Team Time activities can continue in the car as the Team travels to and from visits.

Lead CHECK IT Activities

✔ FAITH Visit Outline
❑ Listen as each Learner recites the appropriate portion of the FAITH Visit Outline (all of **Preparation**, adding the Key Question and Transition Statement, plus key words for **Presentation** and **Invitation**).
❑ Indicate your approval by signing each Learner's Journal.
❑ Involve an Assistant Team Leader in this part of Team Time, if you have this Team member.

✔ Evangelistic Testimony
❑ Review the first draft of written evangelistic testimonies, due this session. Use the criteria from the session 3 FAITH Tip in *A Journey in FAITH Journal*. Explain why you are making your suggestions. Indicate that most testimonies undergo revisions. Be sensitive in helping Team members develop their testimonies, keeping their stories intact. As a reminder, these are the criteria Learners have used to develop their testimonies:
  • Define a specific event before (preconversion) and after your conversion (benefits).
  • Do not answer the Key Question in your testimony.
  • Keep your testimony brief (three minutes or less).
  • Do not give too many unnecessary details; instead, concisely reflect your experience.
  • Conclude your testimony with the assurance that you are going to heaven.

✔ Sunday School Testimony
❑ If possible, provide time for Team members to practice their Sunday School testimonies. Review of the evangelistic testimony, however, should be your priority.

✔ Other Home Study Assignments/Session 3 Debriefing

❏ Answer other questions Learners may have from session 3 or as a result of their Home Study Assignments.

✔ Help for Strengthening a Visit

❏ Identify ways Team members can improve sharing their evangelistic testimonies in a visit.

❏ Help your Team, especially Learners, know how to handle the following issues.

- Dialogue with someone who answers the Key Question with a faith answer by discussing his or her journey of faith in Christ.
- Briefly explain to a person who answers the Key Question with a works answer that many people feel that doing good things gets them into heaven. Discuss the various ways such a response might be verbalized.
- Look for opportunities to ask permission to share what the Bible says about how a person goes to heaven.
- Look for ways to get clarification or explanation if someone shares an unclear response to the Key Question.
- Prayerfully look for ways to talk with a person who indicates no opinion about the Key Question.

Notes

_____

_____

_____

Actions I Need to Take with Team Members This Week

_____

_____

_____

_____

Transition to classrooms for instruction on the content of the session. (5 mins.)

TEACHING TIME

KNOW IT

Step 1 (5 mins.)

Direct participants to locate A Quick Review on page 72 in their Journals and to complete the activities. Then give the answers, using the computer presentation or the overhead cel.

A Quick Review

HEAR IT

Step 2 (5 mins.)

Direct participants to fill in the blanks as you summarize A Religion of Hopelessness and Fear. Use the computer presentation or the overhead cels.

A Religion of Hopelessness and Fear

A Quick Review

Last week you examined the Jewish religion. Test your knowledge of Jewish beliefs by marking each statement T for *true* or F for *false*.

F 1. A plurality of gods is worshiped in Judaism.
T 2. Scripture is inferior to tradition.
F 3. Tradition is inferior to Scripture.
T 4. Jesus' messiahship is denied.
T 5. Salvation must be earned.
T 6. There is only one God.
F 7. Jewish people acutely realize the need for a Redeemer.
F 8. Judaism teaches salvation by grace alone.
T 9. Observing the law, the Sabbath, festivals, and feasts is essential.
T 10. Humanity is basically good.

To identify ways to witness to Jewish people, select the correct words or phrases below that complete the numbered statements.

Messiah • humble • prayer • cultural sensitivity
defensive tactics • friendships • confidence

1. Anticipate _____**defensive**_____ _____**tactics**_____.
2. Rely on _____**prayer**_____.
3. Be _____**humble**_____.
4. Cultivate genuine _____**friendships**_____.
5. Exercise _____**cultural**_____ _____**sensitivity**_____.
6. Use Scripture to point to the _____**Messiah**_____.
7. Speak with _____**confidence**_____.

A Religion of Hopelessness and Fear

Muslims (literally, *submitted ones*), who make news more frequently than any other religious group, are usually portrayed by the media as fanatical, militant terrorists. As a result, Americans associate Muslims with international incidents of terrorism. The atrocities committed by a small group of terrorists overshadow the fact that the vast majority of Muslims condemn terrorism and quietly practice the religious faith known as Islam, which means _____**submission**_____ to _**God**_.

Islam is the youngest of the world's three monotheistic faiths. It was born through the prophet _____**Muhammad**_____ in Arabia nearly 1,300 years ago in the midst of Arab idolatry and animistic polytheism. Muhammad was born in 570 into the Quraish tribe of _**Mecca**_ in what is present-day Saudi Arabia. Muslim tradition says that at age 40, while Muhammad was meditating in a cave near Mecca, the archangel Gabriel revealed to him a series of messages and told him to recite them. These messages became the Islamic holy book, the **Qur'an**.

Muslims believe Muhammad to be the last and greatest prophet of God—"the seal of the prophets." In the beginning his message encompassed two main points: there is one God to whose will people must submit, and there will be a day of judgment when all people will be judged. Muhammad considered himself the supreme seer of God because the Qur'an was dictated to him. When his message was met with rejection and hostility, Muhammad was forced to flee from Mecca to Medina in 622. Muslims date their calendar from this date, known as *hijrah*. In 630 Muhammad entered Mecca with an army and destroyed all idols and images. There he established the Islamic faith and became the sole prophet and leader of the Arabian people. Muhammad died in 632.

From Medina Islam spread to Palestine and the entire Middle East. Through its invading armies Islam then traveled to North Africa, Spain, Persia, India, and parts of China. With its missionary zeal Islam spread by traders into sub-Saharan Africa, Indonesia, and Malaysia. Islam faced periods of stagnation but eventually reached all six continents.

Today Islam has more than **one billion** followers around the globe. About 58 percent of its adherents live in south and southeast Asia. Indonesia is the largest Islamic country, followed by Pakistan and India. More than 28 percent of Muslims live in Africa. Only about 15 percent live in the Middle East. More than 500,000 Muslims live in Canada, and in the United States estimates of the Muslim population range from **6.5** to **8 million**. The two major sects of Islam are Sunnis (around 85 percent) and Shiites (close to 15 percent).

Islam is the second largest religion in the world, but it is the **fastest-growing** religion in North America. In the United States Islam is growing in three major ways: through immigration; through conversion, especially among African Americans; and through native-born Islamic Americans. The United States is the home to more than 1,250 Islamic centers or mosques.

Islamic Beliefs

Islam is both a world religion and a political system and claims to be the final restoration of the original monotheism and truth revealed to humankind. Thus, it boasts to be superior to both Judaism and Christianity in its message and monotheistic faith. It is considered one of the least complicated world religions to practice, governing all aspects of its adherents' lives.

Step 3 (15 mins.)

Direct participants to turn to page 74 in their Journals and to fill in the blanks as you summarize Islamic Beliefs. Use the computer presentation or the overhead cel.

Islamic Beliefs

1. There is no god but ___Allah___.

Islam teaches that there is only one God. Allah, the Arabic name for God, is the sole and sovereign ruler of the universe. There is no one like Allah. He knows everything and has the ability to do anything. He is everywhere. Allah is the giver of good and evil. He does not share His divinity with any others. He is numerically and absolutely one. He has no wife and no son, and He is not triune. He is beyond human understanding. Muslims claim that it is impossible to know Allah's nature, personality, or character, but it is possible to know the attributes or "beautiful names" of Allah. The Qur'an includes 99 names for God. He is confessed as the merciful and compassionate one.

Christians also believe that God is one but has revealed Himself in the plural form *Elohim* (see Gen. 1:26). The Bible clearly reveals that God's oneness comprises three persons—Father, Son, and Holy Spirit (see Matt. 28:19). God's triune nature is part of His mystery and greatness. It helps us understand Him as truly personal and capable of expressing His nature in a variety of ways. God's work in accomplishing salvation is through the person of Jesus Christ.

2. Jesus was a lesser ___prophet___.

Muslims believe that prophets are special messengers of Allah sent to redeem humanity from infidelity, idolatry, and superstition. Thousands have been sent, but only about 25 are mentioned in the Qur'an. They include Adam, Noah, Abraham, Moses, Jesus, and Muhammad. Jesus is accepted as a prophet but not as God's Son. The Qur'an affirms Jesus' virgin birth, life of miracles, and compassion but not His crucifixion. Muslims believe that God took Jesus from the cross and substituted Judas or someone who looked like Jesus. Jesus was then taken to heaven, where He is alive and from where one day He will return. Muslims believe that Muhammad was prophesied in the Bible (see Deut. 18: 18-19; John 14:16; 15:26; 16:7). Unlike Jesus, who was sent only to the Jews, Muhammad was sent to all people; he is the last prophet of Allah.

The Bible affirms that Jesus is much more than a prophet. He was supernaturally conceived by the Holy Spirit and was born of the virgin Mary. Jesus was God's unique Son. During His earthly ministry He carried out His Father's will. He died on a cross as the sacrifice for the sins of the world, was raised from the dead, and is exalted at the right hand of the Father in heaven. Jesus provides salvation for all who repent of their sins and confess Him as Lord.

3. The Qur'an is the Muslim's source of ___authority___.

The Qur'an is the most holy book of Islam and its highest authority. As a record of Allah's exact words, the Qur'an is believed to completely reveal His will. It is the source of an individual's faith and practice, as well as a guide to society. It is considered to be the earthly version of a heavenly book. Muslims believe that the Qur'an maintains its fullest and authoritative message only in the Arabic tongue, having been dictated to Muhammad in that language. Therefore, Muslims consider it a religious obligation to learn, read, and recite the Qur'an in Arabic.

The Qur'an is about the length of the New Testament and is divided into 114 chapters called *surahs*. Each chapter is divided into verses called *ayat*. The chapters are arranged by length, from the longest chapter to the shortest. The Qur'an contains many references to the Torah, the psalms of David, and the four Gospels. However, the Qur'an emphatically claims to be the final source of authority.

Christians do not believe that the Qur'an is a divinely revealed book, because it contains contradictory messages. For example, the Qur'an confirms Jewish and Christian Scriptures; yet it contradicts them by claiming that the Bible is corrupted. The Qur'an accepts Jesus' miraculous birth as sinless; yet it rejects His divinity and His death on the cross.

Christians believe that the Bible is the perfect record of God's revelation of Himself to humanity. The Scriptures are divinely inspired and preserved and are therefore completely true and trustworthy (see 2 Tim. 3:16-17; 1 Pet. 1:25; 2 Pet. 1:19-21).

4. Humankind is born without a __sinful__ __nature__.

According to Islam, humankind is born pure. However, we are weak, fragile, and forgetful; therefore, we commit sin. Muslims believe that people did not inherit original sin from Adam and Eve. Adam and Eve were forgiven of their sin, so no sin remained in them. Thus, we as their children are not basically sinful. People are religious and long to worship Allah. They are slaves to Allah and superior to angels. Islam's central demand of followers is submission to Allah's will.

Christians believe that people are made in God's image (see Gen. 1:27), but because all people inherit a sinful nature, all commit sin (see Rom. 3:23; 5:12,19). However, when people repent of their sin and accept Jesus Christ, they are declared sinless through Christ's shed blood (see Rom. 3:24-26).

5. Sin is breaking Allah's __law__ and not doing His __will__.

Islam does not affirm the fallen state of humankind. Rather, humankind is born sinless and without a sinful nature. In Islam sin is an error and is the result of weakness. Sin is breaking Allah's law and not doing His will. When a person commits sin, it harms him only. The Qur'an even teaches that Allah created humans' evil deeds, so humans must do them. Sin does not grieve Allah. However, Allah does not love the sinner. Allah, at His will, decides whom to punish and whom not to punish. People can increase their good deeds to gain Allah's favor and to earn forgiveness of their sins. The most serious sin that can be committed is that of shirk, or considering Allah as more than one.

After presenting point 6, show the session 4 video segment. Briefly make the following points.

- James, the father of Yolanda's son, wants to reinvolve himself in their lives because of his conversion to Islam.
- Yolanda has not yet made a profession of faith and is confused about James's beliefs and his desire to be a faithful husband and father. She wisely seeks the advice and prayers of Christian friends.
- Stella provides Yolanda some material that compares Islamic and Christian beliefs.
- Marsha emphasizes that Yolanda's most urgent decision is about Christ, not James.
- Because of her study, Yolanda is able to refute James's attacks on Christianity and to confront him about Islamic beliefs that promote violence and discord.
- God uses the message of the Christmas play to highlight Jesus' identity as God's Son and to bring Yolanda to a point of commitment to Him.
- James leaves but is obviously affected by his son's quoting John 3:16.

The Bible teaches that sin is missing the mark, that is, missing God's set standard. People miss God's mark by rebelling against God (see Ps. 51:4), by breaking the law (see 1 John 3:4). All people have sinned and are guilty before God (see Rom. 3:23). Human sin grieves God (see Ps. 78:40). It breaks fellowship between the person and God and between the person and others (see Isa. 59:2-3; 1 John 1:3,6-7). The Bible teaches that God hates sin but loves the sinner (see Rom. 5:6-8). God forgives the sins of those who repent and trust in Jesus (see 2 Cor. 5:19-21). Good works do not earn forgiveness, which is a free gift (see Eph. 2:8-9).

6. Salvation requires adherence to the   Five   Pillars .
In Islam salvation is not ensured for anyone but is determined by God's will. The hope of salvation is pursued by declaring faith in Allah's existence, acknowledging that Muhammad is His prophet, obeying the Qur'an, and compiling good deeds in conformity to the Five Pillars. The following essential disciplines are practiced to satisfy the will of Allah.

1. *The confession.* The fundamental creed of Islam, "There is no God but Allah, and Muhammad is the prophet of Allah," expresses the belief in absolute monotheism that is crucial to Islam. All that is necessary to become a Muslim is sincerity in repeatedly voicing the confession. This confession of faith consumes the Muslim's life from birth until death. This is the first step on the road to the hope of salvation.

2. *Prayer.* Prayer expresses obedience to Allah's will. Each Muslim is to perform ritual prayers five times a day: before sunrise, at noon, in mid-afternoon, at sunset, and before sleep. These prayers are preceded by ceremonial washing of hands, face, and feet. Muslims are required to say these prayers facing the city of Mecca in Saudi Arabia. The prayers are formal rituals that combine postures and recitations in Arabic from the Qur'an. In addition to these formal prayers, Islam allows informal prayers that come from individuals' hearts in their own language.

3. *Fasting.* Fasting is required during Ramadan, the ninth month of the Islamic lunar calendar. It is believed that Muhammad received his first revelations during that month. To commemorate this event, Muslims are required to abstain from all food, drink, and sexual relations during daylight hours—from sunrise to sunset.

4. *Almsgiving.* The Qur'an commands Muslims to practice regular charity. They are expected to give 2½ percent of their capital wealth to the causes of the poor and for the propagation of Islam.

5. *Pilgrimage.* A pilgrimage to Mecca is required of every Muslim, if economically and physically possible, at least once. Each pilgrim must walk seven times around the *kaabah*—the shrine of the sacred black stone—and kiss it. Muslims believe that the *kaabah* was the original place of worship for Adam and for Abraham; thus, it is the holiest site of Islam. On the 10th day sheep and goats are sacrificed, and a huge festival is celebrated to commemorate Abraham's sacrifice of an

animal as a substitute for his son Ishmael (not Isaac as recounted in the Bible).

One of the most controversial practices in Islam is holy war or *jihad*. *Jihad* means *holy struggle for Allah*. *Jihad* is popularly interpreted as the act of fighting against pagans and infidels. However, *jihad* represents both internal spiritual struggle and external war against adversaries of Islam. Paradise is promised for those who die fighting in the cause of Islam.

Muslims who perform good deeds and obey the Five Pillars and the Qur'an will enter paradise. Lacking assurance of salvation, Muslims live in uncertainty and fear.

The Bible teaches that salvation is available to all who repent of sin and accept Jesus Christ as Savior and Lord. Salvation is a gift from God through faith in Jesus Christ (see Eph. 2:8-10). It is impossible to earn salvation by good works (see Titus 3:1-7) or by religious deeds and exercises (see Matt. 7:22-23; Rom. 9:32; Gal. 2:16). Those who accept Christ as Savior and Lord have assurance of salvation and the hope of personal fellowship with God for eternity (see John 14:2-3; 1 John 2:17,24-25).

Witnessing to Muslims

1. Be confident and diligent in ___prayer___.
Pray with confidence by name for your Muslim friends and acquaintances. The Bible clearly states God's concern for the lost and the power of prayer (see 2 Cor. 4:4-5; 2 Pet. 3:9; 1 John 4:4-5). Prayer is an essential evangelistic strategy for Muslims.

2. Demonstrate Christian ___love___.
Believers are challenged by the spread of Islam, but we are not at war with Muslims. Our attitude must be love and acceptance, because God accepts and loves people as they are and wants them to enter a relationship with Him (see 2 Pet. 3:9). Against love there is no defense. Therefore, be sure that the love of Christ is your motive in reaching Muslims with the gospel (see John 3:16; Acts 17). Ministry is an excellent way to express the love of Jesus. Jobs, literacy programs, and child care are examples of specific ways you can share His love.

3. Be sensitive to Muslim ___culture___.
Be aware that many Muslims believe that all Americans are Christians. Because American society is immoral, they believe that all Christians are immoral. Your Christlike lifestyle can prove otherwise. Be sensitive to Muslim cultural teachings. For example, a Muslim man may resist a witness from a woman. Muslims may be uncomfortable attending a Bible study if pictures of Jesus are on the walls.

HEAR IT

Step 5 (5 mins.)

Direct participants to turn to page 77 in their Journals and to fill in the blanks as you present the key points in Witnessing to Muslims. Use the computer presentation or the overhead cel.

Witnessing to Muslims

4. Cultivate _____relationships_____.

When you approach Muslims, be very friendly and encourage them to talk first. Show genuine interest in their beliefs. Be familiar with Islamic beliefs and ask Muslims to show you passages from the Qur'an that you can examine together. Ask questions like these: Will Islam guarantee the forgiveness of sins? Will it provide assurance of salvation? Be patient and do not argue. You may win the argument but lose a soul forever.

5. Establish the _____authority_____ of the Bible.

Explain why the Bible can be trusted as the inspired Word of God (see 2 Tim. 3:16-17; 1 Pet. 1:24-25). Provide prophetic evidence that Jesus is the Messiah (see Ps. 22:13-18; 110:1; Isa. 9:6-7; 53:5-8; Mic. 5:2). Show Islamic evidence of the Bible's truth (see Surah 5:43-44,46; 5:68; 10:64).

6. Clarify biblical teachings about ___God___.

Explain that Christians also believe in one God, who has revealed Himself in three ways: as Father, Son, and Holy Spirit (see John 14: 16-17; Rom. 1:3-4; 1 Cor. 8:6). State that Christians do not limit God by saying that He cannot reveal Himself as three in one. Clarify that the Trinity is not the Father, Son, and Mary or three different gods.

7. Build on ___respect___ for Jesus.

Muslims have great respect for Jesus as a prophet of God. He is mentioned 97 times in the Qur'an, which affirms His supernatural birth, life of miracles, compassion, and ascension to heaven. However, Muslims do not accept Jesus as the Son of God. Explain Jesus' eternal nature and sonship, emphasizing that He was conceived by the Holy Spirit without physical relations with Mary. As God in the flesh, He died on the cross to pay for humanity's sin and rose from the dead in power and victory.

8. Present the ___good___ ___news___.

Give a personal testimony of your Christian experience and use the FAITH gospel presentation to share the good news of salvation in Jesus Christ. Explain that Christ is sufficient for salvation (see Rom. 5:8-9,17; Eph. 2:13; Col. 1:20; Heb. 9:22; 10:19; 1 Pet. 1:18-20). Explain that salvation is a free gift from God and cannot be earned (see Eph. 2:8-9). Explain that we can have assurance of salvation (see 1 John 5:13). Stress that salvation by faith does not mean that a holy lifestyle is not necessary. Rather, faith makes a holy lifestyle possible through the indwelling power of Christ. When Muslims are ready to accept Christ, do not ask them to do so in front of other Muslims but to pray with you in private so that they will not fear a violent reaction from their Muslim associates.

9. Provide _____follow-up_____.

When Muslims accept Christ, nurture them in the faith through intentional discipleship and through involvement in Bible study. The Muslim community emphasizes strong brotherhood, so provide opportunities for Christian fellowship. Offer love, care, and friendship by involving converts in Sunday School. Encourage other Christians to provide spiritual support. Continually pray for new believers.

Visitation Time

Do It

1. Your visitation assignments will include evangelistic prospects, recent guests who visited the church and are already believers, and absentees from Sunday School. Approach evangelistic visits with the expectation that you will ask the Key Question. If the person gives a strong faith answer, your Team will have an opportunity for practice. If the prospect does not respond in faith, you as the Team Leader will have an opportunity to demonstrate how to present the gospel. Remember that you are there to fulfill God's divine purpose, whether in an evangelistic or a ministry role. Remember 2 Timothy 2:2.
2. Pray before you go.
3. Use the time in the car to review, allowing Learners to ask questions. Because they studied ministry visits in this session, ask them what ministry visits they think the Sunday School class needs. Remind them to listen to prayer requests and other discussions in Sunday School that might reveal ministry needs.
4. After each visit allow Learners to debrief it. Facilitate the debriefing by asking specific questions: What were their feelings about the visit? How could the visit have gone more smoothly? How does this visit compare with the previous week's visits?

Celebration Time

Share It

It is important that everyone attend Celebration Time. Emphasize this as an important part of the FAITH process. This is an opportunity to rejoice for decisions that were made. Demonstrate for your Team Learners how to do the following.
1. Hear reports and testimonies.
2. Complete Evaluation Cards.
3. Complete Participation Cards.
4. Update visitation forms with the results of visits.

STUDY IT

Step 6 (5 mins.)

Overview Home Study Assignments for session 4.

Transition to assemble with FAITH Teams to prepare for home visits. (5 mins.)

DO IT (110 MINS.)

SHARE IT (30 MINS.)

Home Study Assignments

Home Study Assignments reinforce this session by helping you apply what you have learned.

Your Discipleship Journey

Journaling activities in Your Discipleship Journey are an important part of your development as a Great Commission Christian through FAITH training.

1. A fundamental difference between Christianity and Islam is our belief in the Bible as the complete Word of God. How do the following verses illustrate this belief?

   2 Timothy 3:16-17: _____

   _____

   2 Peter 1:19-21: _____

   _____

   Jude 3: _____

   _____

2. Followers of Islam believe that by strict adherence to the Qur'an, they can achieve a hope of salvation. Match the following verses with their teachings about salvation.
   ____ 1. Matthew 11:28-29   a. Jesus died for our sins once for all.
   ____ 2. John 3:16   b. Jesus promises rest because His yoke is easy.
   ____ 3. Ephesians 2:8-9   c. God gives eternal life through His Son.
   ____ 4. 1 Peter 3:18   d. Salvation is by grace through faith, not
   ____ 5. 1 John 5:11-13   by works
           e. Whoever believes in Jesus has eternal life.

3. Building bridges to Muslims is essential to reaching them with the gospel. Read the following verses and match the references with the persons to whom Jesus built bridges.
   ____ 1. Matthew 8:1-4   a. The Samaritan woman
   ____ 2. Matthew 9:35-38   b. The Canaanite woman
   ____ 3. Matthew 15:21-28   c. The leper
   ____ 4. Luke 7:1-10   d. The Centurion
   ____ 5. John 4:7-14   e. The distressed and downcast

4. Read 1 Corinthians 9:19-22. To reach the lost who were not like him, what was Paul willing to do?

_____

Growing as a Life Witness

Growing as a Life Witness reminds you of your responsibility to witness and minister to others during the week.

1. Talk or meet with your accountability partner and share ways you have cultivated a lost person or have witnessed or ministered on occasions other than FAITH visits.
2. Discuss ways you can apply the session 4 content.
3. Pray for lost persons by name and for each other.

Prayer Concerns	Answers to Prayer
_____	_____
_____	_____
_____	_____
_____	_____
_____	_____

Your Weekly Sunday School Leadership Meeting

A FAITH participant is an important member of Sunday School. Encourage Team members who are elected Sunday School leaders to attend this weekly meeting. Use this section to record ways your FAITH Team influences the work of your Sunday School class or department. Use the information to report during weekly Sunday School leadership meetings. Identify actions that need to be taken through Sunday School as a result of prayer concerns, needs identified, visits made by the Team, and decisions made by the persons visited. Also identify ways you can disciple others in your Sunday School class or department and in your church.

1. Share results of witnessing and ministry visits. Have Teams made Opinion Poll visits yet? Suggest opportunities to minister to persons who were visited.

_____

_____

_____

2. Give or receive information appropriate for future FAITH Team assignments. Are additional prospect-discovery activities needed to keep FAITH assignments up-to-date?

_____

_____

_____

3. Pray specifically for Sunday School plans this week. As a team, evaluate the previous session and discuss ways Sunday's Bible-study lesson can involve members and guests in transformational Bible study and discipleship.

_____

_____

_____

Discipling Your Team Members

This weekly feature suggests actions the Team Leader can take to support Team members, prepare for Team Time, and improve visits. This work is part of the Team Leader's Home Study Assignments. Add any actions suggested by your church's FAITH strategy.

Support Team Members

❑ Call Team members and talk with them about their participation in class training and visits. Discuss any observations they made during the visits and particularly about sharing their Sunday School testimonies.

❑ Discuss ways to prepare and share their evangelistic testimonies without revealing the answer to the Key Question.

❑ Encourage them as they memorize all of *Preparation* in the FAITH Visit Outline.

Prepare to Lead Team Time

❑ Preview Leading Team Time at the beginning of session 5.

❑ Be prepared to evaluate Team members' written evangelistic testimonies, using these criteria:

  • Define a specific event before (preconversion) and after your conversion (benefits).

  • Do not answer the Key Question.

  • Keep your testimony brief (three minutes or less).

  • Do not give unnecessary details; instead, concisely relate your experience.

  • Conclude your testimony with the assurance that you are going to heaven.

Prepare to Lead Visits

❑ Review the FAITH Visit Outline in order to model the entire process for Team members.

❑ Be prepared to model visits in which Team member(s) are asked to lead in sharing Sunday School and/or evangelistic testimonies.

❑ Be prepared to model the use of the Opinion Poll in making visits.

❑ Be prepared to lead your Team to participate during Celebration Time.

Link with Sunday School

❑ Participate in your weekly Sunday School leadership meeting. Share pertinent information in the meeting, using Your Weekly Sunday School Leadership Meeting (pp. 81–82) and FAITH-visit results.

❑ When Sunday School lessons address salvation, emphasize biblical teachings that believers can have assurance of salvation for eternity.

For Further Growth: The Deity of Jesus Christ, Part 2

For Further Growth may include additional reading or activities that will enhance your growth as a disciple and a discipler of others. These assignments are intended to be long-term projects and do not have to be completed during this semester of study.

1. In Mark 14:61 the high priest asked Jesus a question, which Jesus answered in verse 62. What are the implications of both the question and the answer?

2. Read Colossians 2:9. How much of God dwells in the person of Jesus Christ?

3. Read Hebrews 1:1-3. Whose likeness do we see in Jesus?

4. Read Revelation 1:8; 22:12-13. What does it mean to be the Alpha and Omega?

5. Read one or more of the following resources.
   • Millard J. Erickson, *Christian Theology*, part 7, "The Person of Christ," chapter 32, "The Deity of Christ" (Grand Rapids: Baker, 1985), 683–704.
   • Josh McDowell, *Evidence That Demands a Verdict*, chapters 6–8 (San Bernardino: Here's Life, 1979), 89–140.
   • C. S. Lewis, *Mere Christianity*, chapters 4–5 (New York: Scribners, 1952), 42–51.

Answers to matching activities on page 80:
Activity 2: 1. b, 2. e, 3. d, 4. a, 5. c
Activity 3: 1. c, 2. e, 3. b, 4. d, 5. a

FAITH AT WORK

About 30 years ago seminary student Gary Javens saw an evangelist lead a young man to pray to receive Christ. Javens's response was "Wow! I can do that!" Ever since, Javens, now the pastor of Clifton Park Baptist Church in Silver Springs, Maryland, has made it his habit to go out one night a week specifically to visit people, share his faith, and lead them to the Lord.

Not surprisingly, Javens eagerly led Clifton Park to adopt FAITH as the backbone of the church's evangelism efforts. Javens's FAITH Team recently visited a Muslim family whose three children were involved in the church's missions activities. After being welcomed, the pastor asked about the children, who had been absent for several weeks. The father, Abdul, courteously told Javens that he didn't want the children to be involved at the church any longer. He said: "We are Muslims and are teaching the children from the Qu'ran. We don't want them to be confused hearing one thing here and something else at your church."

Being respectful of the man's words, Javens told Abdul that was certainly his right as the children's father and commended him for taking an interest in his children's religious teaching. But then he asked Abdul the Key Question. When Abdul said he believed that someone who followed the Five Pillars of Islam would go to heaven, Javens readily listed them. Abdul seemed surprised but honored that Javens knew that much about Islam. After a brief discussion of the Five Pillars, Javens asked if he could share what the Bible says about what it takes to get to heaven. "I will always listen when someone speaks about God," Abdul replied. Javens gave the FAITH presentation and asked if Abdul would like to turn to Christ. Although Abdul declined to accept Christ, Javens said: "At least now I know Abdul has heard the gospel and can think about what we talked about. The seeds have been planted."

The evening's second FAITH visit was to a man named Noah, who had recently visited the church. When the Team knocked on the door, Noah's wife, Michelle, answered and was crying. Javens introduced himself and the FAITH Team. Noah was not home, but the pastor asked if the Team could do anything for Michelle. She invited the Team in, explaining that she had just learned that her grandmother had died. "God has just sent you here," Michelle sobbed.

The Team listened as Michelle shared some memories about her grandmother. Talking seemed to help her feel better. Before leaving, everyone joined hands and prayed for Michelle and her family. One Team member hugged Michelle and promised that she would pray for her.

"You never know what you're going to walk in on," Javens said on the way back to the church. "You just have to be ready for anything."

Polly House
LifeWay Christian Resources
of the Southern Baptist Convention
Nashville, Tennessee

The Baha'i Faith

CKY CARRIGAN

In this session you will—

CHECK IT by engaging in Team Time activities;

KNOW IT by reviewing content from session 4;

HEAR IT by examining Baha'i beliefs and by learning ways

to witness to Baha'is;

SAY IT by practicing the *Presentation* portion of the FAITH Visit Outline;

STUDY IT by overviewing Home Study Assignments;

DO IT by leading your Team in making visits;

SHARE IT by celebrating.

IN ADVANCE
- Overview content.
- Preview teaching suggestions. Prepare key points. Decide whether to use the session 5 computer presentation or the overhead cels.
- Prepare the room for teaching.
- Pray for participants and for Teams as they prepare to visit.
- As Teaching Time begins, direct participants to open their Journals to page 88.

If the computer presentation is used, display the agenda frame for Team Time. Add other points as needed.

CHECK IT agenda:
- ✔ FAITH Visit Outline
- ✔ Evangelistic Testimony
- ✔ Key Question/Transition Statement
- ✔ Other Home Study Assignments
- ✔ Session 4 Debriefing
- ✔ Help for Strengthening a Visit

Leading Team Time

All Team members participate in Team Time. They are primarily responsible for reciting the assigned portion of the FAITH Visit Outline and for discussing other Home Study Assignments.

As you direct this important time of CHECK IT activities with your Team, keep in mind that Learners look to you as a role model, motivator, mentor, and friend. Team Time activities can continue in the car as the Team travels to and from visits.

Lead CHECK IT Activities

✔ *FAITH Visit Outline*
❏ Call on each Learner to recite the assigned portion of the FAITH Visit Outline (all of **Preparation**, plus key words in **Presentation** and **Invitation**).
❏ Indicate your approval by signing each Learner's Journal. Be prepared to answer any questions Learners may have. Make suggestions for improvement.

✔ *Evangelistic Testimony*
❏ Call for final written copies of Learners' evangelistic testimonies. Congratulate Team members for achieving another important milestone.
❏ Make sure any revisions include criteria discussed in sessions 3 and 4. Ask for permission to print these testimonies in church materials that publicize the FAITH strategy or that encourage persons to share their faith.
❏ Emphasize to Team members the importance of sharing their testimonies naturally, in their own words, in actual visits.

✔ *Key Question/Transition Statement*
❏ Practice the Key Question/Transition Statement, helping Learners comfortably use their hands to spell the word *FAITH*.

✔ *Other Home Study Assignments*
❏ Look over Learners' Home Study Assignments. Are Learners on track? Clarify or emphasize key points from FAITH Tips and/or *Evangelism Through the Sunday School: A Journey of FAITH* as needed.

✔ *Session 4 Debriefing*
❏ Review the importance of and approach for making Sunday School ministry visits. Help Team members understand how such visits reconnect many inactive members to church life. Highlight ministry

visitation assignments and indicate why certain comments are made during different types of ministry visits (to absentees, nonattenders, members with ministry needs). As inactive members return to Sunday School or church, remind Team members they had a part.

❑ Ask any questions you feel would solidify Learners' understanding of session 4, including questions that will appear on the final written review (ses. 16).

✔ Help for Strengthening a Visit

❑ Be prepared to discuss ways to strengthen a visit, based on what has been discovered in previous sessions.

❑ Be prepared to model an Opinion Poll visit during Visitation Time.

❑ Identify which Team member(s) will take the lead in sharing a Sunday School testimony. Ask another Team member to be prepared to share his or her evangelistic testimony. With sensitivity to Learners and person(s) being visited, be prepared to resume the visit after Team members have shared.

Notes

_____

_____

_____

_____

_____

Actions I Need to Take with Team Members This Week

_____

_____

_____

_____

Transition to classrooms for instruction on the content of the session. (5 mins.)

KNOW IT

Step 1 (5 mins.)

Direct participants to locate A Quick Review on page 88 in their Journals and to complete the activities. Then give the answers, using the computer presentation or the overhead cel.

A Quick Review

SAY IT

Step 2 (10 mins.)

Ask accountability partners to practice sharing the **Presentation** portion of the FAITH Visit Outline with each other.

HEAR IT

Step 3 (5 mins.)

Ask participants to fill in the blanks as you summarize The Religion of World Unity. Use the computer presentation or the overhead cels.

The Religion of World Unity

A Quick Review

Last week you examined Islam. Identify Islamic beliefs by underlining the correct word or words that complete each sentence.
1. There is no god but (Jesus Christ, <u>Allah</u>, the Trinity).
2. Jesus was a lesser (high priest, deity, <u>prophet</u>).
3. The Qur'an is the Muslim's source of (pain, <u>authority</u>, magic).
4. Humankind is born without a (<u>sinful nature</u>, respect for Allah, clue).
5. Sin is breaking Allah's (word, resolve, <u>law</u>) and not doing His (<u>will</u>, homework, laundry).
6. Salvation requires adherence to the (Great Manifestation of God, <u>Five Pillars</u>, Eightfold Path).

Check effective ways to witness to Muslims.
- ☑ 1. Be sensitive to Muslim culture.
- ☑ 2. Build on respect for Jesus.
- ☐ 3. Repay hostility with vengeance.
- ☑ 4. Establish the authority of the Bible.
- ☑ 5. Present the good news.
- ☐ 6. Affirm the Muslim's good works as a valid way to get to heaven.
- ☑ 7. Provide follow-up.
- ☑ 8. Clarify biblical teachings about God.
- ☑ 9. Be confident and diligent in prayer.
- ☐ 10. Explain that it is not necessary to recognize Jesus as God's Son.
- ☑ 11. Cultivate relationships.
- ☐ 12. Concede that the Christian God is actually three different gods.
- ☑ 13. Demonstrate Christian love.

The Religion of World Unity

The Baha'i Faith is a young, widely distributed, fast-growing world religion that promotes the oneness of God, the oneness of religion, the oneness of humanity, and social activism. Baha'i began in 19th-century Iran, but its roots extend back to the time of Muhammad. When Muhammad died in 632, he left no son as heir and made no provision for a successor. The majority of his followers selected Abu Bakr as *caliph* or successor. This sect of Muslims is known as Sunnis. A smaller group of Muhammad's followers contended that the prophet's successors must be chosen by God and must be literal descendants of Muhammad. This sect was called Shi'ite, meaning *separatist*. They followed Ali, Muhammad's cousin and son-in-law, as the first __**imam**__, or leader.

Ali and the next 10 *imams* suffered violent deaths. The 12th *imam* disappeared during childhood immediately following the death of his father in 873. Shi'ites believe that the 12th *imam* is still alive in a mysterious city and will return again as the messiah, or *mahdi*, to bring justice to the earth. The 12th *imam* communicated with his followers through four **babs**, or gates, for 69 years. But after the death of the fourth *bab* in 941, the communication ceased. Then in the early 1800s several Shi'ites claimed to be *babs* and heightened interest in the return of the *mahdi*. One of these Shi'ites was a 24-year-old wool merchant, who announced in 1844 that he was the *bab*. Shortly before his execution for apostasy in 1850, the *bab* began to claim that he was the expected *imam*, not merely the *bab*. Some of his followers even claimed that he was a new prophet who took the place of Muhammad.

Prior to his death, the *bab* named Mirza Yahya, also called Subh-i-Azal, as his successor. Nineteen-year-old Subh-i-Azal had few leadership abilities, so administrative responsibilities fell to his older half-brother, Mirza Husayn Ali, who gradually assumed full leadership.

Taking the name Baha'u'llah, Mirza Husayn Ali ignored the *bab*'s claim to be a new prophet, and Subhi-i-Azal, the *bab*'s rightful successor, announced in 1863 that Baha'u'llah was the new prophet or **Manifestation** of God. Most of the *bab*'s followers accepted Baha'u'llah's claim and became known as Baha'is. Baha'is have rewritten this period of their history and claim that Subh-i-Azal attempted to poison their leader.

Baha'u'llah, whose name means **glory** of **God**, was exiled in 1868 to Akka, now in Israel, where he died in 1892. Prior to his death, he dictated more than one hundred books and letters, which were recorded word for word and are considered the word of God.

Baha'u'llah's successor was Abbas Effendi, also known as Abdu'l-Baha, his eldest son. When Abdu'l-Baha died, his grandson, Shoghi Effendi, led the Baha'is until his death in 1957. Because Shoghi Effendi had no heir and appointed no successor, a nine-member Universal House of Justice was elected to govern Baha'i affairs from the international headquarters in Haifa, Israel.

The Baha'i Faith was introduced to the United States in 1892. However, most Bahai's point to **1912** as the beginning of the movement in America, when Abdu'l-Baha came for a seven-month tour and dedicated the grounds for the Baha'i House of Worship in Wilmette, Illinois. Today there are about **six** **million** Baha'is from about two thousand ethnic groups in about two hundred countries of the world.[1] The Baha'i Faith is the second most widely distributed religion in the world behind Christianity.[2] The Baha'i Faith enjoys a faster **growth rate** than Christianity, Islam, Judaism, Hinduism, and Buddhism.[3] About **300,000** Baha'is reside in the United States.[4]

Many Baha'is in the United States are professional people who have carefully thought about their religious choices and tend to be heavily

PRONUNCIATION GUIDE

Abbas Effendi: *ah-BAHS ef-IN-dee*
Abdu'l Baha: *ob-DOOL bah-HAH*
Abu Bakr: *AH-boo BAH-ker*
bab: *bob*
Baha: *bah-HAH*
Baha'i: *bah-HIGH*
Baha'u'llah: *bah-HA-oo-LAH*
caliph: *ka-LEEF*
imam: *i-MAHM*
mahdi: *MAH-dee*
Mirza Husayn Ali: *meer-ZA hoo-SANE ah-LEE*
Mirza Yahya: *meer-ZAH YAH-yu*
Shi'ite: *SHEE-ite*
Subh-i-Azal: *SOOB-i-uh-ZAHL*
Sunni: *SOO-nee*

involved in social and political causes like civil rights, world peace, and poverty issues. Because the Baha'i Faith is a relatively new religion, Baha'is usually join this religion deliberately. Rarely do Baha'is in the United States join the Baha'i Faith only on the basis of their association with the Baha'i culture. Most people become Baha'is because they are attracted to the teachings of the Baha'i Faith and reject the exclusive claims of Christianity, Islam, or another world religion.[5]

Baha'i Beliefs

1. God is ____unknowable____.

Baha'u'llah taught that there is one God, who is the eternal Creator. The greatest name of the one God is Baha, which means *glory*, *splendor*, or *light*. Shoghi Effendi described God as the one eternal, omniscient, omnipresent, and almighty being but unknowable and inaccessible. Baha is essentially unknowable because a human's finite mind cannot comprehend the infinite God.

Baha manifests himself from time to time through divine messengers, called Great Manifestations. They are believed to appear in every age to act as God's mouthpiece on earth and are the founders of the world's great religions. Baha'u'llah taught that the Great Manifestations in history include Abraham, Krishna, Moses, Zoroaster, Buddha, Muhammad, Ali Muhammad (also known as the *bab*), and Baha'u'llah himself. Jesus Christ is regarded by Baha'is as only one of these Great Manifestations, not as unique. Although Baha'is consider God unknowable, they can reflect on his nature by meditating on his 99 names as revealed through his various Manifestations.

Christians agree that there is only one God (see Deut. 6:4), but He is personal and knowable. He eternally exists as three divine persons: the Father, Son, and Holy Spirit (see Matt. 28:19; 1 Cor. 12:4-6). God's ultimate and final written revelation is found in the Holy Bible (see 2 Tim. 3:15-17; 2 Pet. 1:9-21). His only manifestation in human form was in His Son, Jesus Christ, who came to earth as a man; lived a perfect, sinless life; died on the cross as an atonement for humanity's sin; and rose in victory over death (see Phil. 2:6-11; Col. 2:9; Heb. 1:1-2).

2. Baha'u'llah was the last Great ____Manifestation____ of God.

The most fundamental belief of the Baha'i Faith is that Baha'u'llah was the last Great Manifestation of God. Baha'u'llah taught that each Great Manifestation of God provided the divine manifestation for his own time and culture. These Manifestations were divine, sinless, infallible persons who reflected God's attributes, such as love, mercy, justice, and power, through their lives and teachings. Their purpose was to change thoughts,

Step 4 (15 mins.)

Direct participants to turn to page 90 in their Journals and to fill in the blanks as you present the key ideas in Baha'i Beliefs. Use the computer presentation or the overhead cels.

Baha'i Beliefs

morals, and character in their eras through education. Because human needs change and people grow spiritually, new Manifestations are needed for different eras. When a new Manifestation appears, he is the only way, replacing and superseding all previous Manifestations. Believers must accept the Manifestation's teachings and submit to them.

Baha'is believe that Baha'u'llah is the Manifestation of God for this era, which will last for one thousand years. Baha'u'llah is "the one promised in all the scriptures of the past, the 'Desire of nations,' the 'King of Glory.' To Judaism He is 'Lord of hosts'; to Christianity, the Return of Christ in the glory of the Father; to Islam, the 'Great Announcement'; to Buddhism, the Maitreya Buddha; to Hinduism, the new incarnation of Krishna."[6] Baha'u'llah also taught that his divine teachings were the end of a prophetic cycle and constituted eternal truth, but he also acknowledged the eventual necessity of a future Great Manifestation to maintain the complete body of the true teachings he set forth.

While Bahai's see Jesus as one of nine Manifestations of God, Christianity affirms the absolute uniqueness of Christ (see John 1:1-14; 3:16). Baha'is believe that Christ was great because He was perfect; Christians believe that Christ was perfect because He was the divine Son of God. Baha'is speak of Christ as a great educator who came to enlighten the people of His age; Christians believe in Christ as the Savior who literally died on the cross for the sins of humankind. The Bible teaches that Christ, not Baha'u'llah, is the agent of world unity who will bring all things under His rule at the end of time (see Rev. 11:15).

3. Baha'u'llah's ____writings____ are authoritative.

The principles of the Baha'i Faith are derived from the extensive writings of Baha'u'llah and the interpretations of his son and grandson. The most important Baha'i scripture is *The Most Holy Book*, written by Baha'u'llah in 1872 or soon after. It is about the size of the Gospel of Mark. *The Most Holy Book* prescribes regulations for worship and fasting, gives the law of inheritance, provides for the House of Justice, and gives ethical and social teachings. Baha'u'llah's teachings are also found in *The Book of Certitude* and *The Hidden Words*.

In addition, Baha'is misinterpret events in the Bible to attempt to prove the Manifestation of the *bab* in 1844. Such interpretations are unsupported by correct principles of biblical interpretation. Christians believe that only the Scriptures of the Old and New Testaments, which were divinely inspired and preserved by God, accurately and consistently reveal the ways of God and His instruction for humankind (see 2 Tim. 3:16-17). The focus of Scripture is not Baha'u'llah but Jesus Christ.

4. Baha'is teach the ____oneness____ of humankind.

Baha'is believe that humanity is one racial stock. They regard ethnic, linguistic, racial, and national divisions as arbitrary and destructive.

World unity is seen as the final stage of humanity's growth. The oneness of humankind is the central spiritual principle to be learned. Baha'is are encouraged to worship together and to work toward the unification of all humankind. Interracial and interethnic marriages are encouraged as solutions to humanity's divisions.

Christians agree that humanity is all of one human stock. The Bible teaches that we are all descendants of one man, Adam (see Acts 17:26). However, the Bible indicates that human unity and peace are not possible except through Christ and will ultimately occur only at His return (see Matt. 5:9; Rev. 21:1-4).

5. Baha'i is the common __foundation__ of all religions.

Baha'is believe that all genuine religions are based on the teachings of a Great Manifestation of God. Each Great Manifestation taught his perspective on the divine reality, but the pure truth of his teachings became corrupted by ritual and superstition. Therefore, every religion should set aside its nonessential teachings and unite with the Baha'i Faith on the basis of common, essential beliefs held by all religions. The standard for the pure truth to which all religions should conform is the teachings of Baha'u'llah.

Christians reject the belief that all religions teach the same principles and stem from the same divine source (see Rom. 1:18-32). The Bible teaches that only in Christ can humankind find salvation. Christians see Baha'u'llah as a false prophet (see Matt. 24:4-5; Mark 13:5-6; John 14:6).

6. Salvation is living a moral __lifestyle__.

The Baha'i code of conduct promotes honesty, trustworthiness, compassion, and justice. It affirms monogamous and chaste marriages and prohibits homosexual behavior. It forbids abortion on demand as a measure of birth control and the consumption of alcoholic beverages and narcotics. Baha'is are required to observe daily prayers, holy days, and an annual 19-day fast during daylight hours. They are required to obey the laws of the state and are encouraged to vote in general elections.

The high moral principles espoused by Baha'is are commendable. Yet the Bible teaches that salvation is not a result of good works. Based on God's grace, salvation is provided by the atoning death and resurrection of Jesus Christ. We receive salvation by repenting of sin and placing faith in Him as personal Savior and Lord. Baha'u'llah and other Baha'i religious leaders never made such a sacrifice for sin, nor did they rise from the dead (see John 3:16; Rom. 5:18; 1 Cor. 15:1-8; Eph. 2:8-10).

7. Heaven is a state of __being__.

Baha'is affirm that every person has a soul or spirit, which is created immortal and progresses toward God after death. Because there is only one force in the universe, the all-powerful and all-good God, evil is seen as lesser good or the absence of good. If people do evil, it is because their animal nature is in control. People can overcome the animal nature by developing the spiritual nature. This is accomplished by obeying God's commands as taught by Baha'u'llah.

For Baha'is, heaven and hell are not places of reward and punishment but states of being. Baha'is refer to the Paradise of God, but it is not a clearly delineated concept. Heaven is nearness to God; hell is remoteness from God. They are states in this life as well as after death. Advancement toward God after death depends on the efforts we make on earth. Progress toward perfection in the afterlife is endless and limitless.

The Bible teaches that people do evil because of their sinful nature (see Jer. 17:9). Only Jesus Christ can deliver us from the power of sin and can change our sinful human nature so that our thoughts and actions conform to His mind and character (see Rom. 12:2).

The Bible also indicates that those who put their faith and trust in Jesus Christ as Savior and Lord are assured of eternal life in heaven with God. Those who die without Him will suffer in hell for eternity, separated from God (see Matt. 18:8-9; 25:41-46; Mark 9:43-48; 2 Thess. 1:9).

8. Baha'i envisions a utopian __theocracy__.

Baha'is believe that Baha'u'llah came to unify all of the world's religions by renewing and purifying the religious and social teachings of all of the previous Manifestations. Through the unity of all religions, world peace will come. The following principles serve as a blueprint for a utopian theocracy under the guardianship of the Baha'i Faith.

1. *The independent investigation of* __truth__. Everyone should have equal access to the truth, and no one should be compelled by any authority to embrace a particular belief.
2. *The essential harmony of* __science__ *and* __religion__. The proper use of reason supports religion and is not the enemy of religion.
3. *The* __equality__ *of men and women.* The full equality of the two genders is an essential component of worldwide progress.
4. *The elimination of* __prejudice__. The unity of humanity and the equality of the sexes eliminate racial, political, and religious prejudice.
5. *Universal, compulsory* __education__. Since the greatest threat to worldwide unity and peace is ignorance, every child must be educated.
6. __Spiritual__ __solutions__ *to economic problems.* The extremes of poverty and wealth can be eliminated if the wealthy give to the poor as a spiritual act of worship.
7. *A universal, auxiliary* __language__. The world must adopt a universal language called Esperanto in order for the entire human race to function as a unified people. All people should learn to speak this universal, auxiliary language in addition to their native tongues.
8. *Universal* __peace__ *upheld by a world federation.* A central, worldwide authority must maintain world peace, human unity, and universal

justice. As humankind's organizations evolve, Baha'i will be recognized as the world's unifying faith. The seat of this world federation will be at its International House of Justice in Haifa, Israel.

As Christians, we should work to establish moral and just societies, fight prejudice and racism, and work for peace among nations. Nevertheless, the Bible teaches that those goals will not be fully accomplished by human efforts (see Isa. 64:6; Eph. 2:8-10). Only the love of Christ can transform an individual and a society. Only when He returns and establishes His kingdom will humanity realize true and eternal peace and harmony under His rule in a new heaven and a new earth (see Acts 1:11; 1 Thess. 4:14-18; Rev. 20—22).

Witnessing to Baha'is

1. Capitalize on Baha'is' ____curiosity____.
Most Baha'is are very curious about religious matters. They are eager to discuss their religion and religion in general.

2. Be ____prepared____.
The Baha'i Faith encourages the study of other religions. Most Baha'is know more about other religions than most evangelicals do. Be well prepared if you intend to challenge the Baha'i claim that it is the authentic culmination of all world religions.

3. Build on beliefs that complement biblical ____truths____.
To establish a relationship and to begin dialogue with Baha'is, affirm beliefs and practices that directly or indirectly correspond to Christianity. For instance, commend their commitment to moral character and behavior, to the fundamental equality of all humanity, to religious liberty, to universal education, and to the freedom to investigate religious claims without coercion. Commend their belief that reason is not necessarily an enemy of religion and that a spiritual solution may solve social problems. As you develop the relationship, you will be free to introduce the difference Christ makes in these areas of life.

4. Keep the discussion ____low-key____.
Most Baha'is will disengage if the discussion becomes too aggressive or generates too much passion. Baha'is are forbidden to be aggressive in religious discussions and will reject aggressive behavior on your part.

5. Show ____compassion____.
Most Baha'is expect Christians to be narrow-minded bigots with little interest in issues of poverty, racial equality, and social justice. Jesus

---

Step 5 (5 mins.)

Direct participants to turn to page 94 in their Journals and to fill in the blanks as you summarize Witnessing to Baha'is. Use the computer presentation or the overhead cel.

Witnessing to Baha'is

repeatedly spoke of the importance of meeting the social and physical needs of people (see Matt. 15:29-38; 25:35-46). Emphasize Christians' concern for human need. Listen a lot and show compassion for " 'the least of these' " (Matt. 25:45, NIV). Express concern for Baha'is who have been persecuted by the Shi'ite Muslim majority in Iran. Assure Baha'is that Baptists support religious freedom and abhor persecution.

6. Emphasize that God is _____personal_____ and _____knowable_____.

The God of the Baha'i Faith is an unknowable, unreachable, unfamiliar God who does not relate directly or personally to individuals. If Baha'is fully conform to Baha'i teachings on the nature of God, they can know nothing of the intimacy and personal relationship that can be experienced with the God of Christianity. If they claim to have a personal relationship with God, it may be because they have unwittingly ignored Baha'u'llah teachings on this point and have imported a concept of God from Judaism or Christianity. Ask your Baha'i friends if they conceive of God and attempt to relate to Him as personal and knowable. Some will agree that they do. Then ask why they remain in a religious system that fundamentally rejects this concept of God. State that Christianity alone offers a personal, intimate relationship with God through Jesus Christ. Then explain the nature of your relationship with God.

7. Emphasize humanity's _____sinful_____ _____nature_____.

Explain that sin, not a lack of education, is the cause of human suffering and separation from God. The sin problem is not solved by human effort or social action but by the transforming presence of Christ in an individual's heart. Only repentance of sin and acceptance of Christ bring fellowship with God and true peace.

8. Present the true identity of _____Christ_____.

Baha'is see Jesus only as a great educator, not as the unique Son of God, the Savior of the world, and the agent of world unity. Be prepared to explain the true identity of Christ as " 'the way and the truth and the life' " (John 14:6, NIV), who reconciled humankind to God (see Rom. 5:6-10). Discuss what it means to believe in Christ and to be delivered from the power of sin. When the Baha'i is open, use the FAITH gospel presentation to explain the way to salvation.

9. Offer _____assurance_____ of life after death.

The Baha'i Faith offers no assurance or security about life after death. Like Muslims, Baha'is cannot be certain that they will be delivered from judgment and enter the Paradise of God. Entrance into the Paradise of God is based purely on merit. If Baha'is submit to the teachings of Baha'u'llah to an acceptable, though undisclosed, degree, they may enter

STUDY IT

Overview Home Study Assignments for session 5.

Transition to assemble with FAITH Teams to prepare for home visits. (5 mins.)

DO IT (110 MINS.)

SHARE IT (30 MINS.)

Paradise. In contrast, Christians can be certain that we will be in God's presence after death and forever. Ask your Baha'i friends if they would like to know with certainty that they will experience God's presence and immeasurable blessings in eternity after death. Use the FAITH gospel presentation to show that Christianity offers security and peace of mind about life after death.

10. Be willing to invest your ___time___.
If Baha'is convert to biblical faith, it will almost certainly involve a lengthy process of discussion. Be patient and be prepared to make your appeal over a lengthy period of time.

Visitation Time

Do It

1. Pray for God to lead your Team to a divine appointment. If someone is not home, go next door. It just may be God's divine appointment.
2. Use the time in the car to review, allowing Learners to ask questions. This week they have heard the full gospel presentation. Begin preparing them to share the outline in a few weeks. How do they feel about that?
3. Choose one letter in the FAITH Visit Outline and ask Learners how that concept applied to them when they came to Christ.
4. After each visit allow Learners to debrief it. Facilitate the debriefing by asking specific questions.

Celebration Time

Share It

1. Share a divine appointment.
2. Not every Opinion Poll results in a profession of faith, but celebrate all attempts made. Highlight decisions made, prospects discovered, and other outcomes that would encourage and motivate other Teams.
3. Rejoice with other reports.
4. Complete Evaluation Cards.
5. Complete Participation Cards.
6. Update visitation forms with the results of visits.

Home Study Assignments

Home Study Assignments reinforce this session by helping you apply what you have learned.

Your Discipleship Journey

Journaling activities in Your Discipleship Journey are an important part of your development as a Great Commission Christian through FAITH training.

1. Baha'u'llah claimed to be the last and greatest Manifestation of God, which is a claim to be the returned Christ. Summarize what the following Scriptures teach about false prophets and antichrists.

   Matthew 24:23-27: _____

   _____

   1 John 4:1-4: _____

   _____

2. Match the following verses with the teachings they present about a personal relationship with God.

   ____ 1. Ephesians 1:5   a. Fellow heirs of the promise
   ____ 2. Ephesians 2:4-6   b. Beloved children of God
   ____ 3. Ephesians 2:19   c. Alive with Christ
   ____ 4. Ephesians 3:6   d. Members of God's household
   ____ 5. Ephesians 4:4-6   e. Members of the body of Christ
   ____ 6. Ephesians 5:1-2   f. Adopted as sons

3. A follower of Baha'i has no assurance or security about life after death. How would you offer someone assurance of salvation in Jesus Christ, using the following verses?

   John 10:27-30: _____

   _____

   John 14:1-6: _____

   _____

   John 20:31: _____

Romans 8:37-39: _____

Growing as a Life Witness

Growing as a Life Witness reminds you of your responsibility to witness and minister to others during the week.

1. Talk or meet with your accountability partner and share ways you have cultivated a lost person or have witnessed or ministered on occasions other than FAITH visits.
2. Discuss ways you can apply the session 5 content.
3. Pray for lost persons by name and for each other.

Prayer Concerns	Answers to Prayer
_____	_____
_____	_____
_____	_____
_____	_____
_____	_____

Your Weekly Sunday School Leadership Meeting

A FAITH participant is an important member of Sunday School. Encourage Team members who are elected Sunday School leaders to attend this weekly meeting. Use this section to record ways your FAITH Team influences the work of your Sunday School class or department. Use the information to report during weekly Sunday School leadership meetings. Identify actions that need to be taken through Sunday School as a result of prayer concerns, needs identified, visits made by the Team, and decisions made by the persons visited. Also identify ways you can disciple others in your Sunday School class or department and in your church.

1. If you do not have a weekly meeting, meet with your class or department. Consider inviting the Sunday School leadership team from your class or department to your home after church on a Sunday evening. Excitedly share with the leadership team the results of weekly FAITH visits. Ask for additional names of persons you will need to make a ministry or evangelistic visit. Close with prayer. Consider conducting these meetings regularly until a weekly team prayer meeting is begun.

2. Discuss ways Sunday's Bible-study lesson can involve members and guests in transformational Bible study and discipleship.

3. Make assignments for follow-up calls to prospects and new members, communicating excitement about their participation in Sunday School. Share and receive information about absentees. Make assignments to follow up.

_____

4. Share highlights that reflect the Holy Spirit's leadership and presence in FAITH visits thus far. Include actual visit results, an extraordinary sense of God's presence during visits, divine appointments, and so forth.

_____

5. Pray for FAITH Teams, the pastor and church staff, and Sunday School department directors and teachers.

Discipling Your Team Members

This weekly feature suggests actions the Team Leader can take to support Team members, prepare for Team Time, and improve visits. This work is part of the Team Leader's Home Study Assignments. Add any actions suggested by your church's FAITH strategy.

Support Team Members
❑ Pray for and personally follow up on any Learner who may need personal encouragement.
❑ Contact Team members during the week to remind them that you are praying for them and to discuss their participation in FAITH. Seek to encourage Learners.
❑ Remember, Learners have overviewed the entire gospel presentation in session 5 and may have questions about their role in making a visit. Respond to specific needs and concerns.
❑ Think of appropriate ways to involve an Assistant Team Leader, if assigned to your Team.

Prepare to Lead Team Time
❑ Preview Leading Team Time for session 6.
❑ In a review of session 5 be prepared to overview the entire gospel presentation.

Prepare to Lead Visits
❑ Review the FAITH Visit Outline.
❑ Think about: Do you need to begin gently pushing some Learners out of their comfort zones during evangelistic visits? Some may be hesitant to participate fully without some encouragement.
❑ Be prepared to model a visit in which a Team member is asked to lead in a visit up to asking the Key Question. Think about who might be ready for

this opportunity or to share an evangelistic or Sunday School testimony.
- ❏ Pray for sensitivity as you involve different members in visits and pick up your part of the presentation appropriately and naturally.
- ❏ Prepare to lead your Team during Celebration Time.

Link with Sunday School
- ❏ Participate in your weekly Sunday School leadership meeting. Share pertinent information in this meeting, using Your Weekly Sunday School Leadership Meeting (pp. 98–99) and FAITH-visit results.
- ❏ Provide opportunities for Sunday School members and visitors to learn about and experience the personal nature of God and His plan for peace on earth.

For Further Growth: The Virgin Birth of Jesus Christ

For Further Growth may include additional reading or activities that will enhance your growth as a disciple and a discipler of others. These assignments are intended to be long-term projects and do not have to be completed during this semester of study.

1. In Genesis 3:15 what is characteristic of the Person who will bruise the head of the serpent?
2. According to Isaiah 7:14, what is the sign the Lord Himself will give?
3. Micah 5:2 speaks of the coming Messiah. Where will this Ruler be born?
4. Matthew 1:18-25; Luke 1:26-37; 2:1-7 recount Jesus' conception and birth. Do the events recorded in these Gospels correspond to the Old Testament teachings you studied in questions 1–3?
5. How does Galatians 4:4-5 bring together the Old and New Testament Scriptures you studied in questions 1–4?
6. Read one or more of the following resources.
   - Millard J. Erickson, Christian Theology, part 7, "The Person of Christ," chapter 35, "The Virgin Birth" (Grand Rapids: Baker, 1985), 739–60.
   - R. C. Sproul, Essential Truths of the Christian Faith, part 4, "Jesus Christ," chapter 29, "The Virgin Birth" (Wheaton: Tyndale, 1992), 85–86.
   - Philip Yancy, The Jesus I Never Knew (Grand Rapids: Zondervan, 1995), 27–46.
7. Read the FAITH Tip on page 101.

¹The Baha'i Faith in the World Community (Wilmette: The Baha'i Publishing Trust, 1999).
²The Baha'i (New York: Baha'i International Community, 1992), 14.
³Ibid.
⁴Winfried Corduan, Neighboring Faiths: A Christian Introduction to World Religions (Downers Grove: InterVarsity, 1998), 269.
⁵Ibid., 276.
⁶Shoghi Effendi, God Passes By (Wilmette: The Baha'i Publishing Trust, 1987), 94–96, as quoted in Baha'u'llah (New South Wales, Australia: Baha'i Publications Australia, 1991), 57.

Answers to matching activity on page 97: 1. f, 2. c, 3. d, 4. a, 5. e, 6. b

FAITH TIP

Creating a Crisis of Belief

You can create uncertainty about the truthfulness of the Baha'i Faith. The most vulnerable claims of Baha'i are two of its core beliefs: the identity of Baha'u'llah as a Great Manifestation of God and the unity of all religions.

A hypothesis is a claim for truth only until evidence is presented to substantiate it. The proposition that Baha'u'llah is the messenger of true religion for this age is only a claim for truth, a hypothesis. Most Baha'is can offer little or no strong evidence to substantiate this belief. This deficiency has implications for the two Baha'i principles of the essential harmony of reason and religion and the individual right to freely and independently investigate truth.

Also ask your Baha'i friends if they have a reasonable explanation for the very short term of the *bab* (20 years) as a Great Manifestation of God. Ask them how they account for Baha'u'llah's identity as a Great Manifestation of God in light of the *bab*'s prediction that the next Manifestation would follow him in 15 to 20 centuries, not in 15 to 20 years. The *bab*'s very short term as a Great Manifestation of God in the same geographical region with Baha'u'llah presents a very serious challenge to the claim that Baha'u'llah and the *bab* were both authentic Great Manifestations of God.

You can also challenge the Baha'i claim to be the unity of all religions. Baha'is believe that their faith is composed of teachings common to all major world religions and that all present teachings of the world religions are not the authentic teachings of their founders. Ask Baha'is to provide evidence for their claim that the present teachings of the world religions are not the authentic teachings of their founders. More importantly, ask them to provide supporting evidence for their claim that the present teachings of evangelical Christianity are not the authentic teachings of Abraham, Moses, and Jesus. Most Baha'is hold this position wholly on the basis that Baha'u'llah taught it, not on the basis of any independent evidence to support it. Such evidence does not exist.

You can also ask Baha'is if they are aware of the mutually exclusive differences between world religions. For example, Vedantic Hinduism is polytheistic (many noncreating gods), Bhakti Hinduism is henotheistic (devotion to one noncreating incarnation of God among many gods), and Buddhism is atheistic (no God, no creator, no creation). Islam is monotheistic (one creator God who is so transcendent that He cannot become in-fleshed), and Christianity is a Trinitarian-monotheistic religion (one God who is three eternal persons and one essential being, one of these persons becoming in-fleshed). All of these various teachings on the number and nature of God exclude all others.

In addition, in Buddhism, Ultimate Reality or God is described as "no thing" (nonexistent or nonbeing). In Hinduism, Ultimate Reality or God is "one thing" or "some thing" (Brahman). Whatever Ultimate Reality or God may be, it cannot both exist and not exist.

FAITH AT WORK

It's one thing to learn the FAITH Visit Outline, go to a complete stranger's home, share unashamedly, lead in the sinner's prayer, and walk away blessed, encouraged, and secure in the fact that you will never see that person again in this life. It's another thing to turn to the husband of your daughter and say, "Son, I have something to talk with you about."

I'm not a timid man, but there's something about sharing the plan of salvation with someone who's going to see you again tomorrow that makes a man's blood run a little cooler. Maybe it was the fear of rejection. Maybe it was the fear that my own life didn't show enough of Christ for me to be a credible witness.

You would think that FAITH would have helped, that I would have been more confident, more prepared, more relaxed. I was. The Scripture I had learned was powerful. The changes I saw in my own life—a new boldness, a quickness to pray, a guarding of my tongue—made me feel closer to God than I ever had. But they also made the burden I felt for my son-in-law even greater. Talk about spiritual warfare! I prayed: "God, You've guided my actions and my words, and I've seen so many come to a saving knowledge of You. They have been complete strangers. Please give me the strength I need to share now with this loved one."

The opportunity finally came. The Scriptures and presentation I had memorized calmed my spirit as I began to share. God had prepared me for this moment, and I praise Him that I was ready. I shared from my heart, and my son-in-law prayed to receive Christ. God answered my prayer. I stand in awe of His power and love.

Mike Horne
Immanuel Baptist Church
Highland, California

SESSION 6

Hinduism

N. S. R. K. RAVI

In this session you will—

CHECK IT by engaging in Team Time activities;

KNOW IT by reviewing content from session 5;

HEAR IT by examining Hindu beliefs and by learning ways
to witness to Hindus;

STUDY IT by overviewing Home Study Assignments;

DO IT by leading your Team in making visits;

SHARE IT by celebrating.

IN ADVANCE
- Overview content.
- Preview teaching suggestions. Prepare key points. Decide whether to use the session 6 computer presentation or the overhead cels.
- Prepare the room for teaching.
- Pray for participants and for Teams as they prepare to visit.
- As Teaching Time begins, direct participants to open their Journals to page 106.

TEAM TIME

If the computer presentation is used, display the agenda frame for Team Time. Add other points as needed.

CHECK IT agenda:
- ✔ FAITH Visit Outline
- ✔ Other Home Study Assignments
- ✔ Session 5 Debriefing
- ✔ Help for Strengthening a Visit

Leading Team Time

All Team members participate in Team Time. They are primarily responsible for reciting the assigned portion of the FAITH Visit Outline and for discussing other Home Study Assignments.

As you direct this important time of CHECK IT activities with your Team, keep in mind that Learners look to you as a role model, motivator, mentor, and friend. Team Time activities can continue in the car as the Team travels to and from visits.

Lead CHECK IT Activities

✔ FAITH Visit Outline
❏ Listen while each Learner recites all of *Preparation*, *Presentation* through the Forgiveness statement and verse (Eph. 1:7a), as well as other key words in *Presentation* and *Invitation*.
❏ Indicate your approval by signing or initialing Journals. Encourage Learners.

✔ Other Home Study Assignments
❏ Check to see whether Learners shared their evangelistic testimonies with two different believers. Briefly discuss how these two believers responded to the testimonies.
❏ Discuss benefits Learners are discovering from assigned reading material in *Evangelism Through the Sunday School* and in the FAITH Tip "Nurturing a New Christian" in *A Journey in FAITH Journal*.
❏ Make sure Learners are writing in Your Journey in Faith (their journaling section).

✔ Session 5 Debriefing
❏ Learners have heard the entire gospel presentation by viewing the videotape, hearing the presentation during visits, and overviewing it in session 5. Ask Learners to share how comfortable they are becoming with understanding the significance of sharing the complete gospel presentation.
❏ Remind Learners that although the gospel presentation is built on the letters in FAITH, *A Step of Faith* is used to help lead a person to make a commitment to Christ and enroll in Sunday School. Indicate that each of the following six sessions will focus on a letter of the gospel presentation and on how to use the leaflet in leading a person to make a decision to follow Christ.

✔ Help for Strengthening a Visit

❑ Encourage Learners to be constantly in prayer for one another and for persons being visited. Emphasize the importance of looking for opportunities to build bridges that allow us to share the gospel while, at the same time, being sensitive to the needs of the person being visited. Call attention to the fact that many times a Team might inadvertently close a door to receptivity to the gospel because they come across as pushy.

❑ Remind Team members of the importance of being available to the Holy Spirit and of relying on Him to prepare someone for the gospel. We are to be prepared to share and to know how to compassionately lead someone to make the commitments that will change his or her life forever.

Notes

_____

_____

_____

_____

Actions I Need to Take with Team Members This Week

_____

_____

_____

_____

_____

Transition to classrooms for instruction on the content of the session. (5 mins.)

TEACHING TIME

KNOW IT

Step 1 (5 mins.)

Direct participants to locate A Quick Review on page 106 in their Journals and to complete the activities. Then give the answers, using the computer presentation or the overhead cel.

A Quick
Review

A Quick Review

Last week you studied the Baha'i Faith. Identify Baha'i beliefs by marking the following statements T for *true* or F for *false*.

F 1. Baha'is believe that we can know God intimately.

T 2. Baha'is claim that Baha'u'llah was the last Great Manifestation of God.

T 3. Baha'is regard Baha'u'llah's writings as authoritative.

F 4. Baha'is teach the importance of maintaining distinct ethnic, linguistic, racial, and national differences.

T 5. Baha'is believe that their faith is the common foundation of all religions.

F 6. Baha'is teach salvation by grace through faith in Jesus Christ.

F 7. The Baha'i concept of heaven is a place much like the biblical picture of heaven in Revelation 21—22.

T 8. Baha'i envisions a utopian theocracy.

Check the appropriate principles for witnessing to a follower of the Baha'i Faith.

☑ 1. Capitalize on Baha'is' curiosity.

❏ 2. Ask how a rational person can believe in Baha-what's-his-name.

☑ 3. Be prepared.

☑ 4. Build on beliefs that complement biblical truths.

❏ 5. State that world unity is a dream that Christians do not support.

☑ 6. Keep the discussion low-key.

☑ 7. Show compassion.

❏ 8. Tell Baha'is that the path they are on will lead them straight to hell.

☑ 9. Emphasize that God is personal and knowable.

☑ 10. Emphasize humanity's sinful nature.

☑ 11. Present the true identity of Christ.

❏ 12. Admit that Baha'u'llah is quite possibly the returned Christ.

❏ 13. Express your conviction that social action will bring Baha'is into fellowship with God.

☑ 14. Offer assurance of life after death.

☑ 15. Be willing to invest your time.

A Faith That Spans the Ages

Hinduism, which has been called the world's oldest living religion, is the product of five thousand years of development. Prehistoric Hinduism dates to around **2500** B.C. in India. In 1500 B.C. the Aryans, or noble ones, from Persia invaded India and brought the Vedas, or holy scriptures. The term *Hindu* refers to the people who lived in the Indus River Valley in ancient India. The name originated around A.D. 1200, when invading Muslims wanted to distinguish the faith of the Indian people from their own. Hinduism is the most **complex** and **diverse** religion in the world, including almost any form of religion from simple animism to elaborate philosophical systems. Hinduism has no founder, no prophet, no organizational structure, and no creed. The emphasis is on a way of living rather than a way of thought. The only common ingredient in Hinduism is the **Indian** origin of its adherents.

Christian missionaries and merchant seamen first brought reports of India and Hinduism to the United States soon after the Revolutionary War. The first Hindu guru (religious teacher), P. C. Mozoomdar, came to the United States in **1883**. Later, Swami Vivekananda founded the first Hindu movement in the United States, the Vedanta Society. Several other gurus followed, and Americans adopted Hindu teachings and formed study groups. Hindu guru Maharishi Mahesh Yogi arrived in California in 1959, and his **Transcendental Meditation** movement met with almost immediate success. Thousands of Americans purchased mantras and meditated for 20 minutes twice a day.

A change in American immigration policy in 1963 opened the door for Asians to immigrate to the United States in large numbers. In the 1960s and '70s professional people from India immigrated to this country, bringing Hinduism with them. A. C. Bhaktivedanta came to the United States in 1965 with his devotional form of Hinduism, called **Hare Krishna**. In the 1980s and '90s many American universities were dominated by students from India. At the same time, Indians took over many hotel and motel businesses. Today they own more than 50 percent of all hotel and motel establishments in this country. The computer industry also opened additional doors to Indians.

We have also seen Hinduism's influence in literature, movies, and music. Today Hindu words like *karma* and ideas like reincarnation are often heard. Cults like Christian Science have borrowed many teachings from Hinduism. The **New Age** movement is firmly rooted in Hinduism.

In its orthodox form Hinduism is not a missionary-minded religion. According to orthodox Hinduism, to be a Hindu, a person must be born

HEAR IT

Step 2 (5 mins.)

Ask participants to turn to page 107 in their Journals and to fill in the blanks as you present the key ideas in A Faith That Spans the Ages. Use the computer presentation or the overhead cels.

A Faith That Spans the Ages

to Hindu parents. However, in recent years reform sects in Hinduism have attempted to proselytize former Hindus as well as Western converts. Reformers are aggressively propagating Hindu beliefs and practices in the Western world under various packages and labels.

At the 2000 Parliament of World Religions, hundreds of religious movements were represented that are influenced by Hinduism. In the United States Hindu philosophies may be seen in such movements as the Ramakrishna Mission, Vedanta Societies, the Arobindo Society, the International Society for Krishna Consciousness (Hare Krishna), Transcendental Meditation, Eckankar, New Age philosophies, the teaching of Deepak Chopra, and many others.

The number of Hindus around the world ranges from __825__ to __850__ million. About 780 million of these live in India, with the rest distributed throughout Bangladesh, Nepal, Indonesia, Sri Lanka, Pakistan, Fiji, Guyana, Mauritius, Surinam, Trinidad and Tobago, and Africa. More than 500,000 Hindus reside in Canada. In the United States estimates range from __1.5__ to __2__ __million__.

Hindu Beliefs

Hinduism is a mystical religion that leads a devotee to personally experience the truth within, which finally leads to a state of consciousness in which a person and God become one. This is achieved through the pursuit of *dharma*, a person's duty in life. *Dharma* means *to hold*. What humans hold on to is the inner law, which leads from ignorance to truth. Hinduism teaches that all souls ultimately realize the truth of their divinity and reach a state of oneness with God.

Hinduism is a vast religion. Because no founder and no commonly accepted final truth or revelation are claimed by Hinduism, beliefs and practices vary. However, a general set of beliefs can be identified.

1. *God is* _____**impersonal**_____ *and* _____**unknowable**_____.
Hindus accept the concept of God but do not always agree about His nature and His relationship to humankind. Some Hindus believe in an impersonal god; others worship a personal god like Krishna or an animal or human incarnation of an impersonal god; some do not believe in a god at all. Others are heavily influenced by tradition, superstition, magic, and spiritualism. Some Hindus elevate their guru to almost godlike status. Still others, secular Hindus, are indifferent to all religious practices and beliefs. Many Hindus worship one or two gods but believe that millions of gods exist from whom to choose.

In general, Hindus believe that all is one, a teaching called monism. The impersonal god, Brahman, created the universe by expanding

Step 3 (20 mins.)

Direct participants to turn to page 108 in their Journals and to fill in the blanks as you summarize Hindu Beliefs. Use the computer presentation or the overhead cel.

Hindu
Beliefs

himself to become the universe. The teaching identifying God with the universe is called pantheism. Even Hindus who worship personal gods accept the idea of an impersonal god, Brahman, beyond the personal ones. However, Brahman is essentially unknowable.

Hindus may personalize Brahman as Brahma, the creator; Vishnu the preserver, the god of stability and control; and Shiva, the destroyer, the god of endings. Hinduism teaches that God incarnates Himself in mythical forms such as Krishna and Rama. Hindus worship these different gods on special occasions, along with family and/or individual deities. There are 330 million gods in Hinduism.

The Bible teaches that there is only one God (see Deut. 6:4,13; Jer. 10:10; 1 Cor. 8:6). God is personal and is described in Scripture as having personal attributes. He talks, rebukes, feels, becomes angry, is jealous, laughs, loves, and has a personal name (see Gen. 1:29-30; 6:6; Ex. 3:14-15; 20:5; Lev. 20:23; Ps. 2:4; 59:9; Zeph. 3:17). The Bible also warns against all forms of idolatry (see Gen. 35:2; Ex. 20:3-4; 23:13; Josh. 23:7; Ps. 96:5; Ezek. 20:7). No idol can represent the true God. Scripture also rejects a belief in pantheism. Although God created the universe, He is distinct and separate from His creation (see Rom. 1:22-23).

2. The human soul is _____divine_____.

Hinduism teaches that a person's soul contains a divine spark because it is part of Brahman. All things are God; therefore, a person is also God. A person's problem is ignorance of his divinity. Hindus have no concept of rebellion against a holy God or of original sin. The solution to humanity's problem is to discover that the human soul is part of Brahman. Knowledge is required to overcome ignorance and discover the truth of our divine nature. The body has no ultimate worth.

In contrast, the Bible teaches that humanity's problem is not ignorance but sin—willful rebellion against God and His commandments (see Eccl. 7:20; Rom. 1:28-32; 2:1-16; 3:23; Gal. 3:22; 1 John 1:8-10). Although God created people in His image (see Gen. 1:27), they inherit a sinful nature and choose to sin against Him (see Rom. 3:23; 5:12). The Bible does not teach that we are part of God. A Christian can pray to God but can never become God. We are acceptable to Him only if we repent of our sin and accept the atoning work of Jesus Christ for our sin (see Rom. 3:24-26). Because God created our physical bodies, they have worth as the temple of His Holy Spirit (see Rom. 12:1; 1 Cor. 3:16-17), and they have the potential to honor God (see 1 Cor. 6:19-20).

3. Salvation is escaping _____karma_____ and becoming one with _____God_____.

Hinduism teaches that the human soul is mysteriously trapped in a physical body. The soul can be liberated from the physical body only through a cycle of births or reincarnations. Reincarnation is the belief that the souls of the dead successively return to earth in new bodies or forms. An individual's present life is determined by the law of *karma*, the moral law of cause and effect. This law teaches that the state a person is in today was determined by deeds, words, and thoughts from a previous lifetime. Actions, words, and thoughts in this life determine what a person will be in a future life. People experience many reincarnations until *karma* has been completely satisfied and true knowledge of their divinity is learned. Then the soul is removed from the body and is reabsorbed into Brahman. According to Hinduism, there is no eternal hell.

Works of righteousness are said to satisfy the law of *karma*. Evil thoughts and deeds are said to add to the cycle of reincarnation. Hindus have gurus who teach them the special knowledge necessary to discover their divinity. Hindus recognize three possible paths to union with God.

1. *Karma Marge* is the way of ___**works**___ or the performance of religious ___**duties**___. This path teaches that bad *karma* can be overcome and liberation obtained by fulfilling familial and social duties.
2. *Jnana Marge,* the way of ___**spiritual**___ ___**knowledge**___, appeals to those with an intellectual curiosity to reason and analyze. Salvation can be achieved by meditating on and studying Hindu scriptures, which leads to a state of intellectual enlightenment or spiritual intuition by which the person fully realizes oneness with Brahman.
3. *Bhakti Marge* satisfies the longing for an ___**emotional**___ and ___**personal**___ approach to religion. It requires self-surrender to a personal god and goddess of Hinduism. Devotion is expressed through acts of worship at the temple or in the home, through participation in the festivals in honor of the god, or through a pilgrimage.

Hinduism accepts all spiritual paths to God. Each soul is free to find its own way, whether by devotion, austerity, meditation, or selfless service. Emphasis is placed on temple worship, scriptures, and the guru-disciple tradition. Festivals, pilgrimages, the chanting of holy hymns, and worship are common practices. Many Hindus practice yoga. *Yoga,* a Sanskrit word meaning *to yoke together* or *to unite,* refers to a spiritual discipline for achieving knowledge of and union with God. It may include postures and exercises, breath control, diet, and concentration.

The concepts of reincarnation and *karma* contradict biblical teachings. They rob the Almighty of mercy and deny Christ's sacrifice on the cross and His shedding of blood as atonement for sin (see 1 Pet. 2:24). The Bible declares, "Just as man is destined to die once, and after that to face judgment, so Christ was sacrificed once to take away the sins of many people" (Heb. 9:27-28, NIV). The Bible teaches the resurrection of the physical body and stresses that it is eternal (see John 2:18-22; 1 Cor. 15).

According to Hinduism, escape from the cycle of reincarnation is achieved by our own efforts, whether through good works, meditation, or devotion to a deity. However, the Bible teaches that our basic needs are deliverance from sin and restoration of eternal life, which is provided to anyone who accepts God's grace. Salvation is a gift from God through faith in Jesus Christ (see Eph. 2:8-9). It is impossible to earn salvation by good works (see Titus 3:1-7). Religious deeds and exercises do not provide salvation (see Matt. 7:22-23; Rom 9:32; Gal. 2:16; Eph. 2:8-9). All believers in Christ look forward not to an impersonal absorption into God but to a conscious existence after death, as well as personal fellowship with God forever (see Matt. 22:32; 2 Cor. 5:8; Phil. 1:23). Acceptance or rejection of Jesus Christ as Savior and Lord determines a person's eternal destiny (see John 3:36; Rom. 10:9-10).

4. The Veda is sacred _____scripture_____.

Hindu scripture is called the *Veda,* a Sanskrit word meaning *knowledge* or *wisdom.* The Veda, written around 1500 B.C., is divided into four Vedas, which are collections of hymns, chants, and other teachings about God and nature.

1. The Rig-Veda (the Royal Veda) reveals three gods: Varuna (principal), Indra (war), and Agni (fire).
2. The Yajur-Veda specifies sacrifices to gods.
3. The Sama-Veda includes chants for worship.
4. The Atharva-Veda gives magic spells and healing methods.

The Veda is also broadly classified into three main categories: Smriti, meaning *heard;* Shruti, meaning *remembered;* and Nyaya, meaning *logic.* Smriti writings are considered to be the most authoritative scriptures in Hinduism because Hindus believe that gods directly revealed them to spiritual seers.

Other Hindu scriptures include the Brahmanas (hymns), Aranyakas (interpretations), and Vedanta (the Upanishhads, which are metaphysical dialogues). These scriptures are considered Shruti writings (written from memory, remembered) and therefore less authoritative than Smriti writings. The most read and well-known scripture in Hinduism is the *Bhagavad Gita* (the Song of God), which is a portion of the *Mahabaratha,* a Hindu epic.

Because Hindu scriptures were written over a period of several centuries, they may teach different, even contradictory, ideas. Hindus choose the scriptures with which they agree, since all paths lead to God. Hindus are expected to venerate and recite the Veda more than they are expected to practice exactly what the scripture commands.

Christians reject Hindu writings as divine or authoritative. Only the Bible is the revealed Word of the one true God to all humankind. Divinely inspired and preserved by God, the Bible contains perfect instruction and truth (see Ps. 19:7-10; 2 Tim. 3:15-17; 2 Pet. 1:19-21). It is the only written authority that is binding on humans because it alone shows the only way to God through His Son, Jesus Christ (see Matt. 5:17-18; Luke 24:44-46).

Step 4 (10 mins.)

Direct participants to turn to page 112 in their Journals and to fill in the blanks as you summarize Witnessing to Hindus. Use the computer presentation or the overhead cel.

Witnessing to Hindus

1. Demonstrate God's ___love___.

We are challenged by the spread of Hindu philosophies, but we are not at war with Hindus. Our attitude must be one of love. Remember that God accepts and loves Hindus, and we can open the door to a witness by showing that love. As a relationship develops, you may be able to share Christ's love for every person (see Luke 15; 19:1-10; John 3:16; 1 John 4:9-10).

2. Demonstrate high ___morals___.

Hindus try to maintain very high morals and expect high morals from others. A Christlike lifestyle will show Hindus the image of Christ in the flesh. Praise the Hindu's self-discipline and moral lifestyle in preparation for a discussion of the reason you value these as a Christian.

3. Build on respect for the ___Bible___.

Hindus respect sacred writings. Many Hindus will attentively listen to an explanation of the teachings of the Bible. Use this openness to present biblical truth about God, Jesus, and salvation.

4. Emphasize the ___personal___ ___nature___ of God.

Clarify God's personal nature and love (see 1 John 4:7-21). Explain that God has revealed Himself throughout human history in personal ways, most significantly in the incarnation of His Son, Jesus Christ.

5. Emphasize Christ's ___uniqueness___.

In contrast to Hindu belief in multiple gods, Christ is unique, and His incarnation was sufficient for all time (see Heb. 10:1-18). He was God in the flesh (see John 1:1-18). Demonstrate His authority and power over nature, sickness, physical need, and evil spirits (see Matt. 14:13-21; 20:29-34; Mark 4:35-41; John 5:1-15; 11:1-44).

6. Promise freedom from ___reincarnation___.

Christ's triumph over sin means that Hindus who accept Him can be free of the cycles of reincarnation caused by *karma*. Share with the Hindu Christ's triumph over sin and His taking on Himself the penalty of humankind's sins (see Mark 10:32-45; John 8:1-11; Rom. 8:1-17). Through Christ we can be free from the guilt that results from our actions. God initiates the purification process in our lives, not ourselves. Christ's presence brings inward changes that motivate outward actions.

7. Offer hope for <u>peace</u>.

The Hindu quest for peace and bliss can be met in Christ, the author and giver of peace, with the promise of heavenly blessings and eternal fellowship with God (see John 6:35-40; 14:1-7; Rom. 5:1-11). Explain that Jesus broke the power of death and that believers go to be with Him when they die.

8. Use FAITH to lead the Hindu to <u>salvation</u>.

Your FAITH gospel presentation clearly explains the only way to enjoy a relationship with God and to be free of the consequences of sin. Follow the Holy Spirit's direction as you use this gospel message to reach the heart and mind of your Hindu friend.

Visitation Time

Do It

1. Learners have completed the letter *F*. Ask whether any of them are ready to lead the visit through *Preparation* and the Key Question. If so, instruct them: "After the Key Question is asked and the person responds with a work, unsure, or unclear answer, you can say, 'Would you mind if [name of Team Leader] shares with you how the Bible answers that question?'"
2. Use the time in the car to review, allowing Learners to ask questions.
3. After each visit allow Learners to debrief it. Facilitate the debriefing by asking specific questions.

Celebration Time

Share It

1. Ask a Team member to take the lead in sharing reports.
2. Hear reports and testimonies.
3. Complete Evaluation Cards.
4. Complete Participation Cards.
5. Update Visitation Forms with the results of visits.

STUDY IT

Step 5 (5 mins.)

Overview Home Study Assignments for session 6.

Transition to assemble with FAITH Teams to prepare for home visits. (5 mins.)

DO IT (110 MINS.)

SHARE IT (30 MINS.)

Home Study Assignments

Home Study Assignments reinforce this session by helping you apply what you have learned.

Your Discipleship Journey

Journaling activities in Your Discipleship Journey are an important part of your development as a Great Commission Christian through FAITH training.

1. Hindus believe that a person experiences a series of incarnations until the soul is absorbed into the Brahman. The Bible teaches that we live one life-time, after which we face judgment and eternal destiny in heaven or hell. Match the following Scriptures with the correct teachings about heaven.

   ____ 1. Luke 10:20
   ____ 2. John 14:3
   ____ 3. 2 Corinthians 5:6-8
   ____ 4. Philippians 1:21-23
   ____ 5. Revelation 22:3-5

   a. To be away from the body is to be at home with the Lord.
   b. We will serve God in His presence and will reign with Him forever.
   c. Our names are written in heaven.
   d. Dying means being with Christ.
   e. Jesus will take us to a place He has prepared for us in heaven.

2. Match the following Scriptures with the correct teachings about hell.

   ____ 1. Matthew 8:11-12
   ____ 2. Matthew 25:41,46
   ____ 3. Mark 9:42-48
   ____ 4. Luke 12:5
   ____ 5. 2 Peter 2:4-9
   ____ 6. Revelation 20:11-15

   a. It is a place of eternal fire and punishment.
   b. Those who have been condemned await judgment in the gloomy, dark prison of hell.
   c. Hell is a place to fear.
   d. The fire never goes out.
   e. There will be weeping and gnashing of teeth.
   f. Those whose names are not in the book of life will be thrown into the lake of fire.

3. Hindus hope to attain salvation through works of righteousness. Read the following verses and record what they teach about the way a person comes into fellowship with God.

   John 1:12-13: _____

   John 3:3: _____

   John 3:15-16: _____

   John 6:40: _____

John 7:37-38: _____

John 10:1-11: _____

John 11:25-26: _____

John 14:6: _____

Growing as a Life Witness

Growing as a Life Witness reminds you of your responsibility to witness and minister to others during the week.

1. Talk or meet with your accountability partner and share ways you have cultivated a lost person or have witnessed or ministered on occasions other than FAITH visits.
2. Discuss ways you can apply the session 6 content.
3. Pray for lost persons by name and for each other.

Prayer Concerns	Answers to Prayer
_____	_____
_____	_____
_____	_____
_____	_____
_____	_____

Your Weekly Sunday School Leadership Meeting

A FAITH participant is an important member of Sunday School. Encourage Team members who are elected Sunday School leaders to attend this weekly meeting. Use this section to record ways your FAITH Team influences the work of your Sunday School class or department. Use the information to report during weekly Sunday School leadership meetings. Identify actions that need to be taken through Sunday School as a result of prayer concerns, needs identified, visits made by the Team, and decisions made by the persons visited. Also identify ways you can disciple others in your Sunday School class or department and in your church.

1. Highlight FAITH needs/reports that affect your class/department or age group. Among persons contacted through FAITH this week, who is likely to attend on Sunday? Ask specific class members to take specific actions to make guests feel welcome. For some ministry visits, is follow-up needed by the class/department?

_____

_____

2. Share relevant information about persons who will be the focus of future FAITH assignments so that visits can be especially personal and meaningful. Are some people the focus of continuing cultivation by your FAITH Team? Are additional prospect-discovery activities needed?

_____

_____

3. Participate in evaluating last week's Bible-study session and discuss ways Sunday's lesson can involve members and guests in transformational Bible study and discipleship.

_____

_____

4. Record prayer requests for your teacher and department director.

_____

_____

5. Forgiveness is a significant theme in the gospel and in the FAITH gospel presentation. Is your class/department characterized by a forgiving, loving spirit? List and discuss ways to further cultivate an atmosphere of acceptance and reconciliation.

_____

_____

Discipling Your Team Members

This weekly feature suggests actions the Team Leader can take to support Team members, prepare for Team Time, and improve visits. This work is part of the Team Leader's Home Study Assignments. Add any actions suggested by your church's FAITH strategy.

Support Team Members

❑ Contact Team members during the week. Remind them that you are praying for them. Discuss prayer concerns and answers to prayer.

❑ This week Learners are memorizing the FAITH presentation through FORGIVENESS. Encourage them to meditate on the significance of forgiveness in their personal lives.

❑ Learners have a significant amount of reading this week. Encourage them in this. It is important that they grasp the basic concepts in the reading material.

❑ Pray for specific needs and concerns shared by Team members.

Prepare to Lead Team Time
❑ Review Team members' Home Study Assignments.
❑ Preview Leading Team Time for session 7.

Prepare to Lead Visits
❑ Review the FAITH Visit Outline.
❑ Be prepared to explain the significance of God's forgiveness.

Link with Sunday School
❑ Participate in your weekly Sunday School leadership meeting. Share pertinent information in this meeting, using Your Weekly Sunday School Leadership Meeting (pp. 115–16) and FAITH-visit results.

❑ When appropriate, take opportunities during Sunday School lessons to teach the biblical doctrines of God, sin, and humanity.

For Further Growth: The Humanity of Jesus Christ

For Further Growth may include additional reading or activities that will enhance your growth as a disciple and a discipler of others. These assignments are intended to be long-term projects and do not have to be completed during this semester of study.

1. Read the following Scriptures and note how they verify Jesus' humanity: Matthew 4:1-11; 9:36; Luke 22:44; John 1:14; 11:35; 19:28; Philippians 2:5-8.

2. Read one or more of the following resources.
   • Millard J. Erickson, The Word Became Flesh, chapters 15–16 (Grand Rapids: Baker, 1991), 383–430.
   • Josh McDowell, Evidence That Demands a Verdict, chapter 5, "Jesus— A Man of History (San Bernardino: Here's Life, 1979), 81–87.
   • J. I. Packer et al., Exploring the Christian Faith, chapter 6, "Who Was Jesus?" (Nashville: Thomas Nelson, 1992), 40–56.

Answers to matching activities on page 114:
Activity 1: 1. c, 2. e, 3. a, 4. d, 5. b
Activity 2: 1. e, 2. a, 3. d, 4. c, 5. b, 6. f

FAITH AT WORK

I really began to appreciate the Key Question in the FAITH presentation when on a recent FAITH visit we met a couple who had been traveling and visiting churches for more than 10 years. They had experienced different churches, denominations, cultures, and communities, but they had not experienced Jesus.

We went to their home after they had visited our church on a Sunday morning. When we arrived, it appeared to be a bad time, and the husband was about to send us away when we heard his wife calling from the other room, "Who's at the door?"

"Just some people from the church."

"Please let them in. We need to talk."

As we began getting to know this young family, we found out that they were not Christians even though they had both grown up in church. They had never settled things with God. And although they had visited several churches in our area, we were the first church members to pay them a visit.

They had a small child and were starting to feel those pangs of guilt: "We need to get our lives in order so that we can set the right example for our son." They were full of questions, and the FAITH presentation seemed to fan the flame. God was definitely moving. Then we asked that question. Yes, that intrusive, uncomfortable question: "Understanding what we have shared, would you like to receive this forgiveness by trusting in Christ as your personal Savior and Lord?" In 10 years, through two childhoods, no one had ever asked them that question. Maybe they were waiting for a more convenient time. Maybe they didn't want to offend. Maybe they were trying not to be annoying. Maybe they didn't know how.

I am thankful to God that someone asked me. And I'm thankful that we asked them. What a joy to see this sweet couple, who loved their child so much, reaching out to God for forgiveness, love, and help. They knelt on their living-room floor and received Christ as their Savior and Lord. I wonder what the past 10 years of their life together would have been like if someone had been courageous enough to ask the question earlier. That's what FAITH is about: having the courage to knock, perhaps to offend, possibly to annoy, and most assuredly to ask whether a lost soul wants to join the kingdom of God.

Tom Boggs
Immanuel Baptist Church
Highland, California

Buddhism

N. S. R. K. RAVI

In this session you will—

CHECK IT by engaging in Team Time activities;

KNOW IT by reviewing content from session 6;

HEAR IT by examining Buddhist beliefs and by learning ways

to witness to Buddhists;

STUDY IT by overviewing Home Study Assignments;

DO IT by leading your Team in making visits;

SHARE IT by celebrating.

IN ADVANCE

• Overview content.
• Preview teaching suggestions. Prepare key points. Decide whether to use the session 7 computer presentation or the overhead cels.
• Prepare the room for teaching.
• Pray for participants and for Teams as they prepare to visit.
• As Teaching Time begins, direct participants to open their Journals to page 122.

If the computer presentation is used, display the agenda frame for Team Time. Add other points as needed.

CHECK IT agenda:
- ✔ FAITH Visit Outline
- ✔ Other Home Study Assignments
- ✔ Session 6 Debriefing
- ✔ Help for Strengthening a Visit

Leading Team Time

All Team members participate in Team Time. They are primarily responsible for reciting the assigned portion of the FAITH Visit Outline and for discussing other Home Study Assignments.

As you direct this important time of CHECK IT activities with your Team, keep in mind that Learners look to you as a role model, motivator, mentor, and friend. Team Time activities can continue in the car as the Team travels to and from visits.

Lead CHECK IT Activities

✔ FAITH Visit Outline
❑ Listen while each Learner recites all of **Preparation;** all of F and A, FORGIVENESS and AVAILABLE; the key words for I, T, and H in **Presentation;** and the key outline words in **Invitation.**
❑ Indicate your approval by signing or initialing Journals. Encourage Learners.
❑ Give Learners an opportunity to practice reciting the portion of the FAITH Visit Outline they have learned to this point.

✔ Other Home Study Assignments
❑ Check to see whether Learners listed two or three persons who might have a particular interest in knowing that God's forgiveness is available for them. Discuss how your FAITH Team can impact their lives with the gospel and with ministry. Also discuss the assigned reading material. Encourage Learners to continue writing in Your Journey in Faith (their journaling section).

✔ Session 6 Debriefing
❑ Learners are beginning to learn the gospel presentation. God's forgiveness becomes the foundation on which the rest of the gospel is shared. It is vital to understand that God's forgiveness is based on the free gift of grace that God gives because of Jesus' sacrificial death. As part of the gospel presentation, each letter is accompanied by at least one verse.

✔ Help for Strengthening a Visit
❑ Many people will not be aware of the free gift of forgiveness that God offers. Some are living with guilt and remorse because of sin in their lives. Others are insensitive to the fact that they are sinners who reject God's love and rebel against Him. The message of forgiveness may be an unfamiliar one to them. Emphasize the importance of showing compassion and understanding with each person being

visited. It helps to remember that your Team is not going to be judgmental but to share that real hope exists because God provides forgiveness through faith in Jesus.

❏ Have Learners had opportunities to practice parts of the gospel presentation in home visits? When they visit a Sunday School class member or fellow Christian, sometimes practice is a good option.

❏ Have Learners seen someone come to know Christ in a home visit?

Notes

_____

_____

_____

_____

_____

_____

_____

Actions I Need to Take with Team Members This Week

_____

_____

_____

_____

_____

_____

_____

Transition to classrooms for instruction on the content of the session. (5 mins.)

TEACHING TIME

KNOW IT

Step 1 (5 mins.)

Direct participants to locate A Quick Review on page 122 in their Journals and to complete the activities. Then give the answers, using the computer presentation or the overhead cel.

A Quick Review

A Quick Review

Last week you studied Hinduism. As you read the statements below, write *H* beside those that represent Hindu beliefs and *C* beside those that represent Christian beliefs.

C 1. God is intimate and personal.
H 2. God is impersonal and unknowable.
C 3. There is only one God.
C 4. Humanity's problem is sin.
H 5. The human soul is divine.
C 6. People inherit a sinful nature.
H 7. Salvation is escaping *karma* and becoming one with God.
C 8. Salvation is being delivered from sin and receiving eternal life by God's grace through faith in Jesus Christ.
C 9. Only the Bible is the revealed Word of God.
H 10. The Veda is sacred scripture.

Check appropriate principles for witnessing to Hindus.
☑ 1. Demonstrate God's love.
❑ 2. Thoroughly understand the vast range of Hindu philosophies.
❑ 3. Point out everything that is wrong with the Hindu religion.
☑ 4. Demonstrate high morals.
☑ 5. Build on respect for the Bible.
❑ 6. Look down on them and be prepared to argue.
☑ 7. Emphasize the personal nature of God.
❑ 8. State that a belief in reincarnation is stupid.
☑ 9. Emphasize Christ's uniqueness.
☑ 10. Promise freedom from reincarnation.
❑ 11. Condemn the Hindu's good works and religious practices.
☑ 12. Offer hope for peace.
☑ 13. Use FAITH to lead the Hindu to salvation.
❑ 14. Explain that because of bad *karma*, the Hindu's condition is hopeless.

The Middle Way

One Saturday morning while reading the newspaper, I heard a heated discussion between my son and his friend. My son's friend, a Laotian immigrant, asked: "If my religion is not true, why does Coach Phil Jackson follow it? Why is it the cover story in *Time* magazine? Why are movies being made about Buddhism? Why is the Dalai Lama invited to American universities to lecture on Buddhism?" As I thought about his questions, I began to realize the influence of Buddhist beliefs in America today. Many music lovers are influenced by the Buddhist chants of musicians like Tina Turner or by the rock band Bush with its song "Everything Is Zen." The film actor Richard Gere, through close contacts with the Dalai Lama, has created more interest in Buddhist causes than any other individual. Buddhist stories in Hollywood movies not only generate profits at the box office but also create sympathy around the country for Buddhist aspirations. Hundreds of Buddhist Web sites advocate Buddhist teachings and concepts and promote Eastern practices like meditation, chanting, yoga, philosophical debates, and mystical experiences. These reminders of the growing influence of Buddhism should convince evangelical Christians to look at Buddhism closely and learn ways to minister to Buddhists' immense spiritual needs.

Buddhism is both a philosophy and an ethical system that is considered the Middle Way between religion and nihilism. It is based on the idea of refraining from evil and doing good actions. Buddhism is one of the oldest and most continuous missionary religions. Across the world Buddhist philosophy and practices, with special appeal to the human mind, are highly respected. The combination of curiosity and a search for inner peace drives many people to seek enlightenment through Buddhist teachings and practices.

Many Buddhist practices are rooted in Vedic Hinduism, though they now differ significantly in form and practice. Buddhism traces its beginning to ___**Siddhartha**___ ___**Gautama**___ (560–480 B.C.). Reared in a rich family in northern India, Gautama was protected from witnessing any kind of suffering during his early life. At the age of 29 Gautama experienced suffering for the first time when he saw a sick man, an old man, a hermit, and a corpse. He abandoned his family and became a wandering monk to seek the cause of human ___**suffering**___.

Six years later, while sitting under a *bodhi* tree, Gautama decided that ___**desire**___ is the cause of suffering. This led to his enlightenment, and he became the ___**Buddha**___, which means *the enlightened one*. Gautama spent the remainder of his life traveling and teaching the way to enlightenment.

During the centuries following Buddha's death, his teachings spread to many parts of Asia, especially Southeast Asia, his teachings blending

HEAR IT

Step 2 (5 mins.)

Ask participants to turn to page 123 in their Journals and to fill in the blanks as you present the content in The Middle Way. Use the computer presentation or the overhead cel.

The
Middle Way

with the traditional beliefs of many recipient countries. During the 20th century many Buddhists greatly suffered from the effects of communism and consumerism. Nonetheless, today nearly __six__ __hundred__ __million__ Buddhists live in the world. This figure includes cultural Buddhists—those who are influenced by Buddhist ethics and lifestyles. The vast majority live in Burma, China, Cambodia, India, Indonesia, Japan, Korea, Mongolia, Nepal, Malaysia, Sri Lanka, Singapore, Thailand, Tibet, and Vietnam.

In America the first Chinese Buddhists arrived in California in the __1840s__, and the first Chinese Buddhist temple was built in 1852 in San Francisco. Beginning in 1875, the Theosophical Society promoted Buddhism as a viable religion throughout America. An upsurge of interest in Buddhism occurred after World War II because American service personnel stationed in Japan had developed an interest in it.

In recent years a large number of people with Buddhist backgrounds came to the United States from China and Japan because of wars or the spread of communist ideologies in their nations. Many refugees from Cambodia, Laos, and Vietnam also made their way to this nation. Today more than eight hundred well-established and well-funded Buddhist temples and institutions are registered across the United States, where the number of Buddhists is estimated to be __1.5__ __million__.

Buddhist Beliefs

Buddhism consists of three main branches.
1. Mahayana (the great vehicle) believes that Buddha was not unique and that individual practitioners can become Buddhas. In other words, anyone can attain enlightenment. It consists of liberal elements and seeks to be relevant to the life of the world. Today Mahayana Buddhism is practiced in China, Japan, Korea, and Vietnam. Zen, popular in the West, is a school of Mahayana Buddhism.
2. Theravada (the doctrine of the elders) teaches that only elders and monks are capable of the discipline necessary for enlightenment. This branch of Buddhism claims to be closest to the beliefs of the original followers of Buddha. Conservative in nature, Theravada Buddhism seeks to preserve the true teaching of Buddha and concentrates on meditation and monastic practices. Today Theravada Buddhism is practiced in Myanmar (Burma), Cambodia, Laos, Sri Lanka, and Thailand.
3. Vajrayana (the diamond vehicle), also known as tantric or esoteric Buddhism, is characterized by the practice of elaborate rituals, mandalas (round or many-sided diagrams representing cosmic and spiritual relationships), mantras (spiritually powerful words), meditation,

Step 3 (20 mins.)

Direct participants to turn to page 125 in their Journals and to fill in the blanks as you summarize Buddhist Beliefs. Use the computer presentation or the overhead cel.

Buddhist Beliefs

and mudras (physical gestures). Vajrayana Buddhism spread to Tibet and then to Mongolia. In Tibet it assumed distinctive forms that are usually called Lamaism, since the monks are called lamas. The present Dalai Lama claims that he was the priestly ruler of Tibet until he fled the Communist Chinese in 1959.

The different schools of Buddhism explain their teachings in different ways with different words, but certain ideas are commonly held by most Buddhists.

1. There is no ___God___.

Buddhism is mostly atheistic. It does not speculate about the existence of God or any form of supreme being. Buddha made no claims to divinity, believing that a supreme deity was unnecessary for enlightenment. A Theravada Buddhist prays for his own mental discipline, while a Mahayana Buddhist prays to Buddha, whom he sees as a compassionate savior. In addition, relics of Buddha or other deities may also be worshiped. There is no concept of creation in Buddhism. Jesus Christ, to Buddhists, was nothing more than an enlightened man.

The Bible teaches that God is real and personal. He is the Creator, Redeemer, Preserver, and Ruler of the universe. He is holy, righteous, loving, perfect, all-powerful, and all-knowing. God reveals Himself to us as Father, Son, and Holy Spirit. Jesus Christ is God's unique Son, who came to earth in the flesh (see John 1:14). He carried out the Father's will, died as an atonement for human sin, and rose again from the dead (see 1 Cor. 15:1-8).

2. Humans are bound by the law of ___karma___.

According to Buddhism, a human being does not have a soul or spirit. Like everything in the universe, humans are composed of many individual elements that are in a constant state of flux. These elements, which include such diverse individual characteristics and universal physical laws as the senses, emotions, power of reasoning, fame, beauty, riches, sexuality, sleep, hunger, illness, growing, aging, and dying, are always dissolving and combining with one another in new ways. In humans these elements rearrange themselves according to the law of *karma*, a concept borrowed from Hinduism. *Karma* is the law of cause and effect determining the quality of a person's reincarnated state of being. Good works bring about a good rebirth, bad works a bad rebirth.

Because of Buddhists' view of humanity, they reject a belief in self. The concept of *I* or *my* has no meaning. Although it seems that a human being is an independent unit, this is an illusion. A person is a flowing stream of elements, which continually change and rearrange themselves after death to form a new individual. This teaching contrasts with Hinduism, which holds that the self remains constant through the cycle of reincarnation.

Rather than denying self-worth, Christians believe that each person is a special creation and is made in God's image (see Gen. 1:27). Each person has an immortal soul (see Gen. 2:7) and an eternal destiny (see 1 John 5:11). Jesus valued people so much that He sacrificed His life so that all who trust Him can have eternal life (see John 3:16; Rom. 5:8).

The Bible denies the law of *karma* and the concept of reincarnation. People live one life on earth and then face God's judgment (see Heb. 9:27-28). After death Christians enjoy fellowship with Christ in heaven (see John 14:3; 2 Cor. 5:8).

3. *Salvation is attaining* _____nirvana_____.

Buddhists believe that people have no sin, but they have cravings that create desire. Desire leads to suffering. Buddha set forth his teachings on suffering in the Four Noble Truths.

1. Suffering in life is inevitable.
2. The cause of suffering is desire or craving.
3. Suffering can be removed by overcoming desire.
4. The way to overcome desire is through the Eightfold Path, which is a guide to wisdom, morality, and mental discipline:
   * Right understanding—that truth is the guide
   * Right thought—to be calm at all times and not to harm any living creature
   * Right speech—never to lie, slander, or use coarse or harsh language
   * Right action—never to steal, kill, or do anything you may regret or be ashamed of
   * Right livelihood—never to choose a bad occupation
   * Right effort—always to strive for what is good and to avoid what is evil
   * Right mindfulness—of the Four Noble Truths in calmness and detachment
   * Right concentration—will then follow and lead to the path of perfect peace

Buddhism views life as an endless cycle of continuous suffering. A person's goal is to attain enlightenment, which can be reached in three phases: (1) the state of wisdom, (2) the state of boundless compassion, and (3) the state of total liberation from all energies of mind and body, known as *nirvana*. *Nirvana*, which means *blown out* or *extinct*, is a state of pure bliss and happiness in which a person is no longer subject to desire, no longer suffers, and is no longer bound by the law of *karma*. *Nirvana* is attained by following the Eightfold Path. Most Buddhists would agree that it is impossible to attain *nirvana* in one lifetime.

According to the Bible, humanity's primary problem is not suffering but sin. Sin is missing God's set standard. People miss God's mark by rebelling against God (see Ps. 51:4) and by breaking His law (see 1 John 3:4). All humankind is sinful by nature and guilty before God (see Rom.

3:23). However, those who trust in Jesus Christ are forgiven of their sin (see 2 Cor. 5:19-21). Good works do not earn forgiveness. Forgiveness is a free gift of God's grace through Jesus Christ (see Eph. 2:8-9).

Those who trust Christ have spiritual resources for dealing with suffering. God participates in our suffering by helping us in our weakness (see Rom. 8:26), by giving us the Holy Spirit to intercede for us (see Rom. 8:26-27), by working in every situation for our good (see Rom. 8:28), and by promising that nothing can separate us from Him (see Rom. 8:35-39). A Christian also has the hope of a future life free of suffering. A Christian's hope for the afterlife is not extinction but conscious, meaningful, eternal fellowship with Christ in heaven (see 2 Cor. 4:18; Phil. 1:23), free of suffering and pain (see Rev. 21:4).

4. Buddha's __teachings__ are authoritative scripture.

After Buddha's death in 480 B.C., his followers passed down his teachings orally. It was 253 B.C. before monks began checking, completing, and classifying the traditions that had been passed down. Finally, the first Buddhist scriptures were written down in the first century B.C. This collection of writings is called the Pali canon, after the language in which it was written. It forms the main body of teachings for conservative Theravada Buddhists. This canon is popularly known as the Tripitaka, or triple basket, because it consists of three parts that were originally written on palm leaves and preserved in baskets.

1. The first part recounts Buddha's life, describes the origin of the monastic community, and outlines rules of discipline for monks.
2. The second part gives teachings of Buddha and the monks and includes stories of Buddha's previous existences.
3. The third part is a collection of advanced teachings written in an academic style.

In addition to the Pali canon, there are many Buddhist writings. Mahayana Buddhists recognize many more texts as authoritative than Theravada Buddhists do. Some of these writings are geared to practical piety; others are more philosophical. Various schools of Buddhism developed around *sutras*, or manuals of teachings. Teachers then wrote *shastras*, or teaching books, to ground followers in Buddhism and interpret Buddhist teachings in the *sutras*.

Christians reject the authority of Buddhist teachings because they do not conform to biblical truth. Only the Old and New Testament Scriptures can be relied on to be the true and perfect record of God's revelation to humanity and of salvation through His Son, Jesus Christ (see 2 Tim. 3:15-17).

In addition, the Old and New Testament Scriptures are the best-attested and documented of all ancient documents. In contrast to Buddha's teachings, which were not written down until almost four hundred years after his death, Paul's earliest letters were written between

A.D. 48 and 60. The four Gospels were written between A.D. 60 and 100 by followers of Jesus who were eyewitnesses to the events they describe. All of the New Testament books were written within a century after Christ's death, resurrection, and ascension.

Witnessing to Buddhists

1. *Address Buddhists' concern with* __suffering__.
Buddhists are occupied with overcoming suffering. The Bible teaches that suffering is caused by sin, human carelessness, and natural events. Help the Buddhist understand that as serious as the problem of suffering is, the basic problem in life is sin against a holy God (see Rom. 3:23; 1 John 1:8; 3:1-9). Christ faced suffering on the cross and overcame it (see John 16:33). By trusting Jesus Christ, people can gain forgiveness of their sin, can be victorious in suffering in this life (see John 10:10; Rom. 8:37), and can have definite hope and assurance of a future life without suffering (see 1 John 5:13; Rev. 21:4).

2. *Offer hope for the* __future__.
Karma is an oppressive law of cause and effect that lacks mercy and offers no means of escape except an unceasing effort at self-perfection. The hope of *nirvana* is no hope at all—only death and extinction. Christians know that the moral force governing the universe is a personal God who has mercy on those who repent and who works for the good of those who follow Christ (see Rom. 8:28). Those who place their trust in Jesus Christ are assured of eternal life in a new heaven and new earth.

3. *Introduce the truth of the personal* __God__.
Buddhists reject the idea of a personal God. Because they believe in and fear spirits, they burn incense or offer food at home altars for protection. Share with them that God is a personal God who is always near, always around us, and always in us (see Jas. 4:8). Explain that God gives His followers real peace (see Phil. 4:7).

4. *Explain the futility of trying to gain* __merit__.
Buddhists constantly struggle to earn merit by doing good works, hoping to collect enough merit to break free from the sufferings of life. Jesus Christ, who has unlimited merit (righteousness), offers His unlimited merit as a free gift to anyone who becomes His follower (see Eph. 2:8-9).

5. *Point out contradictory teachings about* __desire__.
Buddhists seek to overcome suffering by eliminating desire, but at the same time they desire self-control, a life of good works, and *nirvana*.

Step 4 (10 mins.)

Direct participants to turn to page 128 in their Journals and to fill in the blanks as you summarize Witnessing to Buddhists. Use the computer presentation or the overhead cel.

Witnessing
to Buddhists

Christianity offers a consistent attitude toward desire. We seek to reject evil desires and cultivate good desires with the power of the Holy Spirit according to the standard of Christ (see 2 Tim. 2:22).

6. *Share your personal* _____**testimony**_____.

Buddhists emphasize the importance of personal experience rather than doctrine. Share your personal testimony, emphasizing the change Christ has brought in your life. State what it means to have a personal relationship with Jesus, being sure to point out your freedom from guilt and assurance of heaven. Use the FAITH gospel presentation to explain that only through a relationship with Christ are we made righteous before God. This is good news to a Buddhist who is struggling to break the cycles of *karma* and reincarnation. As you discuss salvation, avoid terms like *new birth, rebirth,* and *born again.* Instead, use *endless freedom from guilt and sin; new power for living a holy life; promise of eternal life without suffering;* and *gift of unlimited merit.*

Visitation Time

Do It

1. Pray for sensitivity to the situations the Team will encounter in these visits. Always be open to enrolling someone in Sunday School.
2. During the INTRODUCTION listen for opportunities for you, your Sunday School class, or your church to minister. Be ready to develop a friendship and to offer to meet a need.
3. All Team members should know the FAITH presentation through A is for AVAILABLE. While visiting, invite Team members to support you up to the letter A.

Celebration Time

Share It

1. Ask a Team member to take the lead in sharing the report.
2. Hear reports and testimonies.
3. Complete Evaluation Cards.
4. Complete Participation Cards.
5. Update visitation forms with the results of visits.

STUDY IT

Step 5 (5 mins.)

Overview Home Study Assignments for session 7.

Transition to assemble with FAITH Teams to prepare for home visits. (5 mins.)

DO IT (110 MINS.)

SHARE IT (30 MINS.)

Home Study Assignments

Home Study Assignments reinforce this session by helping you apply what you have learned.

Your Discipleship Journey

Journaling activities in Your Discipleship Journey are an important part of your development as a Great Commission Christian through FAITH training.

1. Most Buddhists do not believe in God and eternal judgment; therefore, they do not see a need for salvation. Study Acts 17:24-31 and complete the statements that reveal the truth about God and humanity.

   God does not live in temples built by humans because (see v. 24)

   _____

   God does not need humans to serve Him because (see v. 25)

   _____

   God made all people and determined their courses so that they (see vv. 26-28)

   _____

   God is not (see v. 29) _____

   _____

   God commands all people to (see v. 30) _____

   One day God will judge the world through (see v. 31) _____

2. The Buddha wrote: "Rely upon yourself: do not depend upon anyone else. Make my teachings your light. Rely upon them: do not depend upon any other teaching."[1] Discover a biblical response by matching the following verses with their teachings.
   ___ 1. Proverbs 2:6   a. Don't scorn instruction but respect a command.
   ___ 2. Proverbs 3:5-6   b. The ways that seem right to people lead to death.
   ___ 3. Proverbs 13:13   c. God gives wisdom.
   ___ 4. Proverbs 14:12   d. There is more hope for a fool than for a man
   ___ 5. Proverbs 26:12   who considers himself wise.
                            e. Don't depend on your own understanding
                                but seek God's direction in all things.

Growing as a Life Witness

Growing as a Life Witness reminds you of your responsibility to witness and minister to others during the week.

1. Talk or meet with your accountability partner and share ways you have cultivated a lost person or have witnessed or ministered on occasions other than FAITH visits.
2. Discuss ways you can apply the session 7 content.
3. Pray for lost persons by name and for each other.

Prayer Concerns	Answers to Prayer
_____	_____
_____	_____
_____	_____
_____	_____
_____	_____

Your Weekly Sunday School Leadership Meeting

A FAITH participant is an important member of Sunday School. Encourage Team members who are elected Sunday School leaders to attend this weekly meeting. Use this section to record ways your FAITH Team influences the work of your Sunday School class or department. Use the information to report during weekly Sunday School leadership meetings. Identify actions that need to be taken through Sunday School as a result of prayer concerns, needs identified, visits made by the Team, and decisions made by the persons visited. Also identify ways you can disciple others in your Sunday School class or department and in your church.

1. Highlight needs that surfaced in FAITH visits and discuss ways these reports affect the ministry of your class/department or age group. Especially discuss ways to keep assimilation of newcomers a priority for the group.

_____

_____

_____

2. How does preparation for Sunday need to consider the varying needs of families/individuals represented by selected FAITH visits?

_____

_____

_____

3. Participate in evaluating last Sunday's Bible-study session. Discuss ways Sunday's lesson can involve members and guests in transformational Bible study and discipleship.

_____

_____

_____

4. Record prayer requests for your teacher and department director.

_____

_____

_____

Discipling Your Team Members

This weekly feature suggests actions the Team Leader can take to support Team members, prepare for Team Time, and improve visits. This work is part of the Team Leader's Home Study Assignments. Add any actions suggested by your church's FAITH strategy.

Support Team Members
❑ Contact Team members during the week. Remind them that you are praying for them. Discuss prayer concerns and answers to prayer.
❑ Record specific needs and concerns of Team members.

_____

_____

_____

Prepare to Lead Team Time
❑ Review Team members' Home Study Assignments.
❑ Preview Leading Team Time for session 8.

Prepare to Lead Visits
❑ Review the FAITH Visit Outline.
❑ Be prepared to explain the significance of God's forgiveness being available
for all but not automatic.

Link with Sunday School
❑ Participate in your weekly Sunday School leadership meeting. Share
pertinent information in this meeting, using Your Weekly Sunday School
Leadership Meeting (pp. 131–32) and FAITH-visit results.
❑ When you have opportunities in Sunday School discussions, emphasize
the hope Christianity offers for people who feel trapped and for those
who are suffering.

For Further Growth: The Sinless Perfection of Jesus Christ

For Further Growth may include additional reading or activities that will
enhance your growth as a disciple and a discipler of others. These assignments
are intended to be long-term projects and do not have to be completed during
this semester of study.

1. Read the following verses and note what they have to say about Jesus'
sinlessness: John 14:30; 2 Corinthians 5:21; Hebrews 4:15; 1 Peter 2:22;
1 John 3:5.
2. Also examine what others said about Jesus' sinless life. Read Matthew
27:4,19; Luke 23:41,47; John 19:4.
3. Read one or more of the following resources.
   • R. C. Sproul, *Essential Truths of the Christian Faith*, part 4, "Jesus Christ,"
   chapter 28, "The Sinlessness of Christ" (Wheaton: Tyndale House, 1992),
   83–84.
   • Millard J. Erickson, *Christian Theology*, part 7, "The Person of Christ,"
   chapter 33, "The Humanity of Christ—The Sinlessness of Jesus" (Grand
   Rapids: Baker, 1985), 718–20.
4. Read the FAITH Tip on page 134.

---

[1]Jack Kornfield and Gil Fronsdal, eds., *The Teachings of Buddha*, rev. ed. (Boston: Shambhala, 1995), 18.

Answers to matching activity on page 130: 1. c, 2. e, 3. a, 4. b, 5. d

FAITH TIP

The Eightfold Path: A Christian View

Buddhists believe that a good life consists of following the Eightfold Path set forth by Buddha. When you talk with Buddhists who are willing to listen, present the following biblical responses to the eight points.

1. Right understanding
Jesus is the way, the truth, and the life (see John 14:6). Salvation is found in no one else (see Acts 4:12).

2. Right thought
Fights and quarrels come from selfish desires and wrong motives (see Jas. 4:1-3). Right desires and motives honor God (see 1 Cor. 10:31).

3. Right speech
Jesus said, " 'The mouth speaks out of that which fills the heart' " (Matt. 12:34, NASB). A day of judgment is coming when God will hold people accountable for every careless word they have spoken (see Matt. 12:36).

4. Right action
Those who love Jesus must obey Him (see John 14:21). Those who live by God's wisdom produce good fruit (see Jas. 3:17).

5. Right livelihood
God cares for those who put Him first (see Matt. 6:31,33). All work must be done for God's approval (see Eph. 6:6-7; 2 Tim. 2:15).

6. Right effort
Like runners in a race, followers of Christ must throw off every hindrance in order to give Him their best efforts (see Heb. 12:1-2).

7. Right mindfulness
The sinful mind cannot submit to God's law (see Rom. 8:7). Disciples of Christ must submit to God as Jesus did (see Phil. 2:5).

8. Right concentration
The secret of true success, inner peace, self-control, and salvation is submission to Jesus Christ as Savior and Lord. Set your heart and mind on things above, where Jesus now sits in glory, waiting to bring the present order of sin and suffering to an end (see Col. 3:1-4).

The New Age Movement, Part 1

BILL GORDON

In this session you will—

CHECK IT by engaging in Team Time activities;

KNOW IT by reviewing content from session 7;

HEAR IT by examining New Age beliefs and by learning ways

to witness to New Age followers;

SEE IT by viewing a video segment;

STUDY IT by overviewing Home Study Assignments;

DO IT by leading your Team in making visits;

SHARE IT by celebrating.

IN ADVANCE

- Overview content.
- Preview teaching suggestions. Prepare key points. Decide whether to use the session 8 computer presentation or the overhead cels.
- Prepare the room for teaching.
- Cue the videotape to the session 8 segment.
- Pray for participants and for Teams as they prepare to visit.
- As Teaching Time begins, direct participants to open their Journals to page 138.

CHECK IT (15 MINS.)

If the computer presentation is used, display the agenda frame for Team Time. Add other points as needed.

CHECK IT agenda:
- ✔ FAITH Visit Outline
- ✔ Session 7 Debriefing/Other Home Study Assignments
- ✔ Help for Strengthening a Visit

Leading Team Time

All Team members participate in Team Time. They are primarily responsible for reciting the assigned portion of the FAITH Visit Outline and for discussing other Home Study Assignments.

As you direct this important time of CHECK IT activities with your Team, keep in mind that Learners look to you as a role model, motivator, mentor, and friend. Team Time activities can continue in the car as the Team travels to and from visits.

Lead CHECK IT Activities

✔ FAITH Visit Outline
- ❏ Listen while each Learner recites all of **Preparation**; all of the outline points for the letters *F* (FORGIVENESS), *A* (AVAILABLE), and *I* (IMPOSSIBLE); key words for the letters *T* (TURN) and *H* (HEAVEN); and key words for the **Invitation**.
- ❏ Indicate your approval by signing or initialing Journals. Encourage Learners.
- ❏ Provide an opportunity for Learners to practice reciting the portions of the FAITH Visit Outline they have learned to this point.

✔ Session 7 Debriefing/Other Home Study Assignments
- ❏ God's forgiveness is available for everyone. Even the most hardened criminal or the most unloving person is the target of God's love and forgiveness. John 3:16 reminds us of the scope of God's love and forgiveness ("God so loved the world … that whoever"). This same verse introduces us to the fact that God's forgiveness is not automatic ("whoever believes in Him"). This passage also focuses on the consequences of not accepting God's forgiveness ("perish"). It is important to remember that many persons you visit will not understand that God's forgiveness is available to them, but it is not automatic.

✔ Help for Strengthening a Visit
- ❏ Many persons you seek to visit will indicate that they do not have much time for a lengthy visit. Some persons may not allow your Team to enter the house because of time or personal constraints. Your primary jobs are to seek to build relationships with people and to introduce them to the idea of enrolling in your Sunday School class or department. Indeed, you look for opportunities to ask the Key Question, hear responses, and share the FAITH gospel presentation. But also look for opportunities to build bridges with the person through Sunday School enrollment. God may be using you to plant a seed. He may also be using you and your Team members to nurture

relationships on His behalf and to prepare the harvest. Be sensitive to opportunities God is providing for you in the midst of visits.

Notes

_____

_____

_____

_____

_____

_____

_____

Actions I Need to Take with Team Members This Week

_____

_____

_____

_____

_____

_____

_____

_____

Transition to classrooms for instruction on the content of the session. (5 mins.)

TEACHING TIME

KNOW IT

Step 1 (5 mins.)

Direct participants to locate A Quick Review on page 138 in their Journals and to complete the activities. Then give the answers, using the computer presentation or the overhead cel.

A Quick Review

HEAR IT

Step 2 (5 mins.)

Ask participants to turn to page 139 and to fill in the blanks as you present the key points in The Quest for Self-Enlightenment. Use the computer presentation or the overhead cel.

The Quest for Self-Enlightenment

A Quick Review

Last week you studied the Buddhist religion. Match each Buddhist belief in the left column with a Christian response in the right column.

<u>f</u> 1. Jesus Christ was an enlightened man.

<u>b</u> 2. There is no God.

<u>h</u> 3. A human being does not have a soul or spirit.

<u>c</u> 4. Humans are bound by the law of *karma.*

<u>g</u> 5. Humanity's problem is suffering.

<u>a</u> 6. Salvation is attaining *nirvana.*

<u>e</u> 7. *Nirvana* is extinction.

<u>d</u> 8. Buddha's teachings are authoritative Scripture.

a. Salvation is God's gift of grace through faith in Jesus Christ.

b. God is real and personal, revealing Himself as Father, Son, and Holy Spirit.

c. People live one life on earth and then face God's judgment.

d. The Bible is the perfect record of God's revelation.

e. The afterlife is conscious, eternal fellowship with God in heaven.

f. Jesus Christ is the Son of God.

g. Humanity's problem is sin.

h. Each person has an immortal soul and an eternal destiny.

To identify ways to witness to Buddhists, select the correct words below that complete the numbered statements.

merit • desire • future • God • suffering • testimony

1. Address Buddhists' concern with _____**suffering**_____.
2. Offer hope for the _____**future**_____.
3. Introduce the truth of the personal _____**God**_____.
4. Explain the futility of trying to gain _____**merit**_____.
5. Point out contradictory teachings about _____**desire**_____.
6. Share your personal _____**testimony**_____.

The Quest for Self-Enlightenment

A few years ago the Interfaith Evangelism Team of the North American Mission Board set up a booth at a New Age convention to share the gospel with those attending. One worker returned from witnessing with a shocked look on his face. He had asked someone attending the meeting what he would do if he were standing before God and God asked him, "Why should I let you into My heaven?" The New Ager answered, "I am God and would not ask myself that question." The frustrated Christian worker asked, "How do you witness to people who think they are God?"

The New Age movement is composed of diverse groups of individuals and organizations who share the view that humanity is on the verge of a new age of self-enlightenment, harmony, and worldwide transformation through which the world's social, political, and economic problems will be solved through the release of unlimited human potential. The New Age movement finds "truth" in all religions, but it is primarily rooted in **Hindu** and **occult** philosophies. Hindu concepts have been modified to make them acceptable to Westerners. New Age occult beliefs include astrology, spiritualism (communicating with alleged spiritual teachers of the past), and fortune-telling.

The New Age movement has no central leader or organization but consists of thousands of different groups and gurus. It has no official membership. Many in the movement do not even consider New Age a religion but a philosophy of life or a scientific view.

Although the beginning of the New Age movement dates to the late **1960s**, its historical roots in American society began much earlier. The **transcendentalism** of the early 19th century prepared the way for the coming of the New Age movement. Transcendentalist writers like Henry David Thoreau (1817–62) and Ralph Waldo Emerson (1803–82) stressed the mystical unity of nature. Emerson was strongly influenced by Swedish mystic Emanuel Swedenborg (1688–1772). The grandmother of New Age is the **Theosophical Society**, founded in **1875**. Theosophy was greatly influenced by Hindu writings and teachings. The Theosophical Society first introduced Americans to Westernized Hindu concepts. The first World Parliament of Religions, held in Chicago in 1893, also helped introduce Eastern religious concepts to Westerners. Only one year after the World Parliament of Religions, the Hindu Vedanta Society was founded in New York.

The influence of Eastern religious concepts on American society increased in the 20th century. In 1931 **Edgar Cayce** (1877–1945) founded the Association for Research and Enlightenment. Cayce, an active psychic healer from 1901 to 1944, helped popularize belief in **reincarnation** in North America. The 1960s and '70s witnessed an explosion of interest in Eastern religious concepts. Many in the counterculture movement embraced New Age beliefs and practices.

New Age Beliefs

Although New Age is composed of a diversity of beliefs and practices, certain common New Age beliefs can be articulated.

1. All is **God**.
A fundamental belief of the New Age movement is pantheism, the belief that everything is either God or a part of God. In pantheism God is not

Step 3 (15 mins.)

Direct participants to fill in the blanks as you summarize New Age Beliefs. Use the computer presentation or the overhead cel.

New Age Beliefs

the personal being worshiped by Christians but an impersonal energy, power, or consciousness that emanated itself into the universe. Impersonal terms like *Mind, Light, Love,* and *Truth* are used to describe God.

The Bible denies the teaching of pantheism and affirms that God is not impersonal but personal (see 1 Tim. 4:10), relating to humans as Father (see Matt. 6:9), Son (see John 8:36), and Holy Spirit (see Gen. 1:2; John 14:26). God possesses personal qualities of love (see 1 John 4:7), mercy (see Ps. 143:1), grace (see Col. 1:6), righteousness (see Rom. 1:17), goodness (see Ps. 106:1), faithfulness (see 1 Thess. 5:23-24), wisdom (see Ps. 147:5), and justice (see Ps. 33:5). The Bible denounces those who confuse God with His creation: "Although they claimed to be wise, they became fools and exchanged the glory of the immortal God for images made to look like mortal man and birds and animals and reptiles" (Rom. 1:22-23, NIV). Although humanity was created in God's image, we are not and never will be God (see Gen. 1:26-27; Isa. 43:10).

2. All is __one__.

New Agers have also adopted the Hindu teaching called monism, the belief that there is only one ultimate reality and that we are one with that reality. New Agers speak of being one with Mother Earth, the universe, or God. According to monism, all distinctions are illusions. Monism and pantheism go hand in hand, for if everything is God, then logically, everything must be one.

Monism contradicts the biblical teaching that God's creation is distinct from Him and really exists. Genesis 1 teaches that the beings God created were separate and distinct from one another. Verse 4 indicates that God "separated the light from the darkness" (NIV). Furthermore, different things were created on different days—plants and vegetation on the third (see vv. 11-13), sea animals and birds on the fifth (see vv. 20-23). Distinctions are also emphasized within the plant and animal kingdoms (see vv. 12,25). Humans are distinguished from plants and animals because only we are created in God's image (see v. 27).

Later, the Bible makes another important distinction that refutes monism. Genesis 9:3 teaches that Noah and his descendants were to eat vegetation and were given permission to kill and eat animals. However, verse 6 prohibits taking the life of a human being:

> "Whoever sheds the blood of man,
>   by man shall his blood be shed;
> for in the image of God
>   has God made man" (NIV).

This passage reveals that humans and not animals were made in God's image, underscoring humanity's uniqueness.

3. Humans are ___divine___.

Because everything is God, New Age followers believe that people are also part of God and are therefore divine. It follows that people are basically good, but they are ignorant of the divine within themselves. Because ignorance is humanity's basic problem, knowledge is the solution and, according to New Agers, can be learned or discovered in many ways. Eastern meditation, yoga, martial arts, past-life regression, divination, astrology, and consciousness-raising seminars are some of the methods New Agers use to become enlightened about their inner divinity. Others discover this knowledge by studying under one or more spiritual teachers. Different New Age groups may speak of this enlightenment as God-realization or God-consciousness, self-realization, cosmic consciousness, nirvana, or at-one-ment. As individuals become aware of their divinity, new potential emerges.

The Bible presents a different view of humanity. Although we are made in God's image, we are not divine (see Gen. 1:27). Nor are we basically good. We inherit a sinful nature and consistently rebel against God (see Rom. 5:12). Therefore, our basic problem is not ignorance of divinity but sin against Holy God (see Rom. 3:23). The solution to this problem is not knowledge or self-awareness but forgiveness of sin, which is available to all who repent and come to God through Christ's atoning work on the cross (see Luke 13:3; Rom. 10:9). Instead of placing faith in Christ, New Agers seek a shift in consciousness. Many consciousness-altering techniques used by New Agers are occult and forbidden by the Bible. God condemns the use of divination, sorcery, witchcraft, magical spells, mediums, and spiritualists (see Deut. 18:9-12).

4. Morality is ___relative___.

One implication of monism is the idea that all distinctions are illusions, including the distinctions between good and evil and between right and wrong. To New Agers, there is no ultimate truth. Each person must choose for himself what he believes is correct, both in lifestyle and belief. Different religions are different paths to the same goal of self-enlightenment. People have no moral absolutes or standards by which to be held accountable and judged. The only wrong is saying that someone is wrong.

The New Age insistence that there is no difference between good and evil and between right and wrong defies universal human experience. God has built this understanding into the human heart and mind. To maintain this belief, New Agers must deny their own conscience (see Ps. 34:14; Eccl. 12:14; Amos 5:15). In addition, their position denies clear biblical teachings on the distinction between good and evil, right and wrong. James 1:13 teaches that God is not the source of evil. The Bible also teaches that "God is light; in him there is no darkness at all" (1 John 1:5, NIV). Isaiah 5:20 warns,

Step 4 (10 mins.)

Show the session 8 video segment. Briefly make the following points.

- Vernon travels with Zack to New England to execute his great-uncle's will.
- Through a series of mysterious gifts and letters left by his great-uncle, Vernon discovers a legend surrounding the lighthouse. Several New Age followers, believing that the lighthouse holds special powers, have moved into the area.
- Vernon meets Robbie, who claims to sense vibrations from the lighthouse and to be the reincarnation of Argyle Farris.
- This situation will be resolved in the session 9 video segment.

HEAR IT

Step 5 (5 mins.)

Direct participants to turn to page 142 in their Journals as you summarize Witnessing to New Age Followers. Use the computer presentation or the overhead cel.

Witnessing to New Age Followers

Woe to those who call evil good and good evil (NIV).

5. Jesus was only a great ___teacher___.
Many New Agers separate the man Jesus from His Christ Consciousness or Christ Spirit—the self-realization of personal divinity. They do not believe that Jesus and Christ are the same person or that Jesus is the only Christ. Rather, He was one of several great teachers who obtained the Christ Spirit. Other teachers like Krishna and Buddha are also claimed to have become fully aware of their divinity and to have taught others the way to reach enlightenment.

Some New Age followers also claim that the Christian church has corrupted the teachings of Jesus. They believe that Jesus traveled to India and studied Hinduism before beginning His public ministry. He was rejected and crucified because of His Hindu teachings.

When New Agers use the term *Christ* to refer to the self-realization of deity, they give the term a meaning very different from the one used in the New Testament. The word *Christ* is a Greek term that means *Anointed One*. It is the equivalent of the Hebrew word *Messiah*, which also means *Anointed One*. When the New Testament writers used the term *Christ* to refer to Jesus, they were indicating that Jesus was the promised Messiah of the Old Testament. The New Age claim that Jesus is not the only Christ fulfills Jesus' prophecy in Matthew 24:24-25: " 'False Christs and false prophets will appear and perform great signs and miracles to deceive even the elect—if that were possible' " (NIV). The New Age view of the Christ Consciousness or Christ Spirit is a false Christ. The New Testament declares that Jesus is the unique Son of God: " 'God so loved the world that he gave his one and only Son, that whoever believes in him shall not perish but have eternal life' " (John 3:16, NIV). The phrase "one and only" is a translation of the Greek term meaning *unique, one of a kind*. Jesus is the only Christ, and we can have a personal relationship with Him through faith.

In session 9 you will continue your study of New Age beliefs.

Witnessing to New Age Followers

1. Point out ___contradictions___ in New Age beliefs.
Although most New Agers believe in pantheism and monism, they do not live as if these concepts are true. For example, New Agers value the teaching of pantheism because it means that they are God. But this teaching loses appeal when you point out that a rat rummaging through garbage is also God, according to pantheism. For that matter, so is garbage. Ask whether the follower really believes that everything is divine.

Another problem with pantheism is that God is seen as an impersonal consciousness or power. Therefore, New Agers must value the impersonal more than the personal. However, New Age followers live as though they value the personal more than the impersonal. They obviously value animals more than rocks and their families more than plants. Point out that the New Ager is actually living by biblical truth—that the personal has greater value than the impersonal.

New Age followers also do not live as though monism were true. They experience themselves as different from other people. They perceive and treat their children differently from the offspring of other people. And they treat their mates differently than they do someone else's spouse. Use this tension between what New Agers believe and the way they live to introduce biblical truth about the differentiation between components of God's creation and between individual humans.

2. Discover the person's ___beliefs___.
The New Age movement encompasses a great diversity of beliefs. Not all New Agers agree on every point. Find out what the person believes about God and Christ and begin your witness from those positions.

3. Emphasize the ___personal___ ___nature___ of God.
Introduce the New Ager to the fact that God is a living person, not an impersonal force. Share His qualities of love, mercy, grace, righteousness, goodness, faithfulness, wisdom, and justice. Point out that each person was created for a personal relationship with God.

4. Assert the ___uniqueness___ of Jesus Christ.
Stress the uniqueness of Jesus as the only Christ. He is not one religious teacher among many. He is God incarnate, the one and only Son of God. Testify about your personal relationship with Jesus Christ and the difference He makes in your life. Make sure your life also testifies to the change that has taken place because of your faith in Christ.

5. Answer objections to the ___gospel___.
Many New Agers take offense with the gospel message that faith in Jesus Christ is the only way of salvation. They claim that there is no right or wrong way to God and that we are wrong to claim that there is. Ask, "If there is no right or wrong way to God, how can you claim that our gospel is wrong?" Lovingly point out that their position is illogical.

6. Direct the person to the ___New___ ___Testament___.
Be prepared to cite and explain biblical texts that deal specifically with New Age issues. Encourage the person to read the New Testament, particularly the Gospels, to witness the life of Christ. Faith comes by hearing the Word of God (see Rom. 10:17).

Step 6 (5 mins.)

Overview Home Study Assignments for session 8.

Transition to assemble with FAITH Teams to prepare for home visits. (5 mins.)

DO IT (110 MINS.)

SHARE IT (30 MINS.)

7. *Present the biblical plan of* _____salvation_____.
Many New Age followers do not accept Christ the first time they hear the gospel. Do not become frustrated but trust the Holy Spirit to convict New Agers' hearts and minds. As the Holy Spirit leads, use the FAITH gospel presentation to ask the person to make a decision for Christ.

Visitation Time

Do It
1. Be a good listener. You earn the right to share the good news by listening to the stories of the persons you visit. They may share with you some things that make you uncomfortable or may raise some questions you would rather not address—but listen. It is not necessary to be able to answer all of their questions, but it is necessary to care.
2. Are Team members becoming increasingly comfortable with making adjustments as the visit merits? Although your Team should plan in advance what is to happen and what responsibilities the various Team members will assume, the best visit is one in which visitors adjust to the needs of the situation.
3. Team Leader, as you make changes in the FAITH Visit Outline, be sure to explain why. Affirm your Team Learners as they show increasing confidence and ease in sharing their testimonies and in using the FAITH Visit Outline.
4. At the Team Leader's cue, Learners should be able to share FORGIVENESS and AVAILABLE.

Celebration Time

Share It
1. Ask a Team Learner to take the lead in sharing your Team's report.
2. Hear reports and testimonies.
3. Complete Evaluation Cards.
4. Complete Participation Cards.
5. Update visitation forms with the results of visits.

Home Study Assignments

Home Study Assignments reinforce this session by helping you apply what you have learned.

Your Discipleship Journey

Journaling activities in Your Discipleship Journey are an important part of your development as a Great Commission Christian through FAITH training.

Read the following statements of New Age beliefs and write a Christian response based on the Scriptures given.

1. People are part of God and are therefore divine.

   Deuteronomy 6:4: _____

   _____

   Mark 12:28-30: _____

   _____

   1 Timothy 2:5: _____

   _____

2. God is an impersonal energy, power, or consciousness.

   Deuteronomy 32:39: _____

   _____

   Acts 17:24-32: _____

   _____

   _____

3. New Agers do not believe that Jesus and Christ are the same person or that Jesus is the only Christ.

   Daniel 9:25-26: _____

   _____

Matthew 16:16-17: _____

_____

Matthew 22:41-45: _____

_____

John 4:25-26: _____

_____

Growing as a Life Witness

Growing as a Life Witness reminds you of your responsibility to witness and minister to others during the week.

1. Talk or meet with your accountability partner and share ways you have cultivated a lost person or have witnessed or ministered on occasions other than FAITH visits.
2. Discuss ways you can apply the session 8 content.
3. Pray for lost persons by name and for each other.

Prayer Concerns	Answers to Prayer
_____	_____
_____	_____
_____	_____
_____	_____
_____	_____

Your Weekly Sunday School Leadership Meeting

A FAITH participant is an important member of Sunday School. Encourage Team members who are elected Sunday School leaders to attend this weekly meeting. Use this section to record ways your FAITH Team influences the work of your Sunday School class or department. Use the information to report during weekly Sunday School leadership meetings. Identify actions that need to be taken through Sunday School as a result of prayer concerns, needs identified, visits made by the Team, and decisions made by the persons visited. Also identify ways you can disciple others in your Sunday School class or department and in your church.

1. Highlight FAITH needs/reports that affect your class/department or age group.

_____

_____

_____

2. In what ways does the reality that people are lost without Christ permeate your class/department? For example, is a clear explanation of the gospel periodically given in class? Is the teacher consistently ready to give an invitation during class if the session and the Holy Spirit so lead? Is the class a praying and caring body that reaches out to the lost?

_____

_____

_____

3. Participate in evaluating last week's session and discuss ways Sunday's Bible-study lesson can involve members and guests in transformational Bible study and discipleship.

_____

_____

_____

4. Pray for teacher(s) and department director(s).

_____

_____

Discipling Your Team Members

This weekly feature suggests actions the Team Leader can take to support Team members, prepare for Team Time, and improve visits. This work is part of the Team Leader's Home Study Assignments. Add any actions suggested by your church's FAITH strategy.

Support Team Members
❑ Contact Team members during the week. Remind them that you are praying for them. Discuss prayer concerns and answers to prayer.
❑ Record specific needs and concerns of Team members.

Prepare to Lead Team Time
❑ Review Team members' Home Study Assignments.
❑ Preview Leading Team Time for session 9.

Prepare to Lead Visits
❑ Review the FAITH Visit Outline.
❑ Be prepared to explain the significance of God's forgiveness being available for all but not automatic.

Link with Sunday School
❑ Participate in your weekly Sunday School leadership meeting. Share pertinent information in this meeting, using Your Weekly Sunday School Leadership Meeting (pp. 146–47) and FAITH-visit results.
❑ Encourage Sunday School teachers to periodically call on Team members to share reports from their FAITH experiences. Encourage your Team members to give periodic updates in your class.
❑ Look for ways Sunday School lessons can refute the moral relativism that is fostered by New Age teachings.

For Further Growth: The Omnipotence of Jesus Christ

For Further Growth may include additional reading or activities that will enhance your growth as a disciple and a discipler of others. These assignments are intended to be long-term projects and do not have to be completed during this semester of study.

1. Jesus is omnipotent, or all-powerful. In Matthew 28:18 what does Jesus say about His authority?
2. According to Ephesians 1:20-22, what is Jesus' position in relation to all other things?
3. True creation, making something out of nothing, is something only God can do. Read Colossians 1:16 and note Jesus' work in creation.
4. Read the following Scriptures and note the things Jesus exercised authority over: Matthew 8:1-4,16-17,26; 9:9-17; John 11:17-44; 1 John 3:8.
5. Read one or more of the following resources.
   • Millard J. Erickson, Christian Theology, part 7, "The Person of Christ," chapter 32, "The Deity of Christ" (Grand Rapids: Baker, 1985), 683–704.
   • R. C. Sproul, Essential Truths of the Christian Faith, part 4, "Jesus Christ," chapter 25, "The Deity of Christ" (Wheaton: Tyndale, 1992), 77–78.
   • Millard J. Erickson, The Word Became Flesh, chapters 17–18 (Grand Rapids: Baker, 1991), 431–80.

The New Age Movement, Part 2

BILL GORDON

In this session you will—

CHECK IT by engaging in Team Time activities;

KNOW IT by reviewing content from session 8;

HEAR IT by examining New Age beliefs and by learning ways

to witness to New Age followers;

SEE IT by viewing a video segment;

STUDY IT by overviewing Home Study Assignments;

DO IT by leading your Team in making visits;

SHARE IT by celebrating.

IN ADVANCE
- Overview content.
- Preview teaching suggestions. Prepare key points. Decide whether to use the session 9 computer presentation or the overhead cels.
- Prepare the room for teaching.
- Cue the videotape to the session 9 segment.
- Pray for participants and for Teams as they prepare to visit.
- As Teaching Time begins, direct participants to open their Journals to page 152.

If the computer presentation is used, display the agenda frame for Team Time. Add other points as needed.

CHECK IT agenda:
✔ FAITH Visit Outline
✔ Other Home Study Assignments
✔ Session 8 Debriefing
✔ Help for Strengthening a Visit

Leading Team Time

All Team members participate in Team Time. They are primarily responsible for reciting the assigned portion of the FAITH Visit Outline and for discussing other Home Study Assignments.

As you direct this important time of CHECK IT activities with your Team, keep in mind that Learners look to you as a role model, motivator, mentor, and friend. Team Time activities can continue in the car as the Team travels to and from visits.

Lead CHECK IT Activities

✔ *FAITH Visit Outline*
❏ Listen while each Learner recites the FAITH Visit Outline: all of *Preparation* and all of *Presentation*, adding *T* is for TURN to the gospel presentation, plus the key words for *Invitation*. Be aware of time limits if two Learners are sharing; someone may need to recite in the car going to and from visits.
❏ Initial each Learner's work in his or her Journal.
❏ Practice other parts of the outline as time allows.

✔ *Other Home Study Assignments*
❏ Emphasize the importance of involving the Sunday School class in FAITH, whether by prayer support, in training, or in follow-up. Explain that in this session Sunday School will be the focus of building bridges to people.
❏ Ask: Do class/department members who are not participating in FAITH still see themselves as a part of this ministry? In what ways? Are you sharing prayer needs and results of visits with fellow class members? Are they praying for you and for people you and your Team will visit? Are your class, department, and church growing spiritually and numerically?
❏ Home Study Assignments and memorization are reaching their maximum. Make a special effort during the week to personally encourage Learners, especially those who may have fallen behind in memory work or home study.

✔ *Session 8 Debriefing*
❏ Some important theological truths are communicated in this part of the gospel presentation. Are Learners at ease and confident in sharing about both God's love and His justice? About their own sinfulness?
❏ Ask Learners to recall from their personal experience—
  • their need to be saved;
  • their inability to save themselves;

- God's saving initiative in their lives (their life-changing experience). Doing so will help them continue to identify with the people they visit. All of us are sinners in need of God's grace. Some of us have been fortunate enough to receive and accept it, while others still need to know about God's forgiveness. Letting them know is a big part of what FAITH is all about.
❑ If your group needs it, overview ways to respond to a works answer to the Key Question.

✔ Help for Strengthening a Visit
❑ Have most Team members seen someone accept Christ during a home visit by this time? If so, remind Team members of how such a visit should motivate them to continue in their efforts. If not, remind Team members that God is still working, even if they have not seen specific desired results.
❑ Call on the Assistant Team Leader, if your Team has one, to encourage other Team members; he or she may have had experiences in earlier FAITH training that can motivate others.
❑ As important as practice is, it is not the same as sharing the gospel in a home visit. Acknowledge that even as you encourage your Team to practice with one another and with other believers, as the opportunity allows.

Notes

_____

_____

_____

_____

Actions I Need to Take with Team Members This Week

_____

_____

_____

_____

Transition to classrooms for instruction on the content of the session. (5 mins.)

TEACHING TIME

KNOW IT

Step 1 (5 mins.)

Direct participants to locate A Quick review on page 152 in their Journals and to complete the activities. Then give the answers, using the computer presentation or the overhead cel.

A Quick Review

HEAR IT

Step 2 (5 mins.)

Ask participants to fill in the blanks as you summarize What's New About New Age? Use the computer presentation or the overhead cel.

What's New About New Age?

A Quick Review

Last week you began a study of the New Age movement. Check the statements that represent New Age beliefs.

- ❑ 1. God is personal and separate from His creation.
- ☑ 2. All is God.
- ☑ 3. All is one.
- ❑ 4. God's creations are distinct from one another.
- ❑ 5. Humans are made in God's image.
- ❑ 6. Humans are not divine and are not basically good.
- ☑ 7. Humans are divine.
- ☑ 8. Morality is relative.
- ❑ 9. There are absolute standards of right and wrong.
- ☑ 10. Jesus was only a great teacher.
- ❑ 11. Jesus is the unique Son of God.

Check the ways you learned to witness to a New Age follower.

- ☑ 1. Point out contradictions in New Age beliefs.
- ☑ 2. Discover the person's beliefs.
- ❑ 3. Review biblical passages that support pantheism and monism.
- ❑ 4. Attend a consciousness-raising seminar with the person.
- ☑ 5. Emphasize the personal nature of God.
- ❑ 6. Explain how you gained awareness of your personal divinity.
- ☑ 7. Assert the uniqueness of Jesus Christ.
- ☑ 8. Answer objections to the gospel.
- ☑ 9. Direct the person to the New Testament.
- ☑ 10. Present the biblical plan of salvation.
- ❑ 11. Agree that each person must find his own path to truth.

What's New About New Age?

Last week you began your study of New Age beliefs by focusing on ___**pantheism**___, the idea that everything is deity; ___**monism**___, the belief that all is one; the New Age belief that humans are ___**divine**___; the contention that morality is ___**relative**___; and the teaching that Jesus was merely a great ___**teacher**___ who discovered the Christ Consciousness within. These beliefs, along with the ones you will study in this session, make it clear that New Age is not new at all but consists of a Westernized assortment of ___**Hindu**___ beliefs and ___**occult**___ practices. The term *new* does not refer to the movement's chronological age but to its dissimilarity with conventional Western ideas. New Age concepts have been held by Eastern religions for millennia.

New Age Beliefs

Although the New Age movement includes great diversity in thought and practice, most New Agers would accept the beliefs you studied last week. In this session we will examine other common New Age beliefs revealing deep spiritual needs that only Christ can satisfy.

1. Oneness with all is achieved through   <u>reincarnation</u>.
New Age followers believe in spiritual evolution through cycles of reincarnation, the theory that when people die, they are reborn and live other lives in new bodies. These cycles of birth, life, and death are necessary to lose the illusion of separateness from all and to attain oneness with all. It is believed that few people can attain this oneness in one lifetime, so they experience many deaths and births. Some proponents claim that the number of rebirths is in the millions. Oneness is attained by acquiring positive *karma*, the Hindu teaching that a person's actions determine the quality of a person's next life. Positive *karma* advances a person toward oneness, while negative *karma* prolongs the time needed to realize this unity. As far-fetched as reincarnation sounds to a Christian, the concept has been popularized in a number of books and movies. Surveys indicate that as many as one in four persons in North America believes in some form of reincarnation.

Many people find belief in reincarnation attractive for two reasons. First, it offers hope for life after death. According to reincarnation, life doesn't end at the grave, and this claim offers hope to people who do not know the true hope of eternity with Jesus Christ. Second, reincarnation offers a second chance. If you don't get life right this time, you simply keep trying. Reincarnation is the ultimate form of works salvation, claiming that people have as many lifetimes as they need to earn it. The truth is that New Agers' concept of salvation means ceasing to exist as a separate entity and being reassumed into the impersonal all. In other words, salvation means ceasing to exist. Most people do not find this an attractive prospect. Many New Agers have not thought through their beliefs in pantheism and reincarnation to this logical conclusion.

The Bible rejects a belief in reincarnation. Hebrews 9:27 teaches that people are destined to die only once: "Just as man is destined to die once, and after that to face judgment" (NIV). True salvation is found only in Christianity. Reincarnation is a form of works salvation. The Bible rejects salvation through works as impossible. Romans 11:6 says, "If by grace, then it is no longer by works; if it were, grace would no longer be grace" (NIV). Likewise, Ephesians 2:8-9 stresses that salvation from sin and its eternal consequences is a gift that God gives freely. Sin does not result in reincarnation but in death: "The wages of sin is death, but the gift of God is eternal life in Christ Jesus our Lord" (Rom. 6:23, NIV).

Step 3 (15 mins.)

Direct participants to turn to page 153 in their Journals and to fill in the blanks as you present the key points in New Age Beliefs. Use the computer presentation or the overhead cel.

New Age Beliefs

The Bible also teaches resurrection, not reincarnation. Jesus declared, " 'A time is coming when all who are in their graves will hear his voice and come out' " (John 5:28-29, NIV). The Christian hope is not to experience impersonal absorption but to spend eternity with the personal God of the Bible, who not only created us but also sent His only Son to pay the price for our salvation.

2. A __new__ __age__ of enlightenment is coming.

A central New Age belief is the idea that a new age of enlightenment is coming for humanity. It is this belief that has given the movement its name. New Agers believe that humans and history are spiritually evolving and are ready to advance to the next level of enlightenment as people move toward the goal of awareness of their divinity. Humanity is on the verge of a great personal and social transformation, when the old ways will pass away and human consciousness will shift to a higher level. Many New Agers believe that the astrological forces of the universe will inevitably bring about this new age, which is sometimes called the Age of Aquarius. August 16–17, 1987, marked the date of the harmonic convergence that began this new age.

Contrary to the beliefs of the New Age movement, the Bible teaches that the world is not awaiting the evolution of the human race but the second coming of the Lord Jesus Christ. Paul wrote that Christians look forward to "the blessed hope—the glorious appearing of our great God and Savior, Jesus Christ" (Titus 2:13, NIV). That event will bring about the consummation of history, when the world passes away and a new heaven and a new earth are created. For believers, the true new age to be anticipated is Christ's eternal reign in a world without sin and suffering, a place of joy and peace where we praise and serve the Lord and live in His presence for all eternity (see Rev. 21:1-5).

3. New Agers envision a universal __religion__.

New Age followers speak of one universal religion that draws general concepts like mysticism, love, the worth of nature, and human goodness and potential from all present religions. Individuals are allowed to hold particular beliefs with which other New Agers may vocally disagree without fear of rejection. New Agers also stress their allegiance to the planet and the human race. This allegiance is to supersede all loyalties to nation, ethnic group, and religion. Therefore, New Age concerns include ecology, peace, hunger, and global politics.

As with most Hindu-based groups, corporate worship is not an important part of the New Age movement. Several reasons may be given.
1. God is seen as an impersonal power, not a being to whom people can relate.
2. The individual is himself divine, so attention is turned inward.
3. Knowledge, not devotion, is the goal.

Christians also believe in one true world religion. It does not center on human potential, tolerance, or self-enlightenment but on the person of Jesus Christ. Only He provides salvation, meaning in life, and an eternal relationship with God. Jesus admonished: " 'Enter through the narrow gate. For wide is the gate and broad is the road that leads to destruction, and many enter through it. But small is the gate and narrow the road that leads to life, and only a few find it' " (Matt. 7:13-14, NIV). All of our worship and praise is due the one who gave His life for us (see Phil. 2:9-11; Rev. 5).

Christians can affirm a concern for and stewardship of the environment, but we must take issue with the degree of priority New Agers place on it. We are to care for the world, but we are not to worship nature or to place it above our loyalty to God and others (see Rom. 1:22-23). Jesus instructed us to give primary allegiance to His kingdom in our lives: " 'Seek first [God's] kingdom and his righteousness' " (Matt. 6:33, NIV).

4. New Age practices lead to higher ___**consciousness**___.

New Agers engage in many practices that they believe will enable them to achieve a higher state of consciousness. Such techniques as yoga, Eastern meditation, past-life regression, trance channeling, crystals, and various occult activities are employed.

Many people in North America view yoga as simply a form of physical exercise. However, in Hinduism, from which yoga is derived, the exercises are believed to be a path to enlightenment. It is doubtful that these religious presuppositions can ever be fully removed from the so-called secular form of yoga that is taught in America.

Eastern meditation differs radically from Christian prayer. In Christian prayer the believer communicates with the personal God of the Bible. In Eastern meditation no communication with a personal God is attempted. In fact, such an attempt would be considered impossible, since God is considered impersonal. Those practicing Eastern meditation try to empty the mind of all thought and to allow the divine core of their being to come to the surface.

Past-life regression is used to support belief in reincarnation. New Agers believe that discovering information about past lives and learning from their mistakes in those lives will allow them to advance toward enlightenment. However, that claim is not supported by valid evidence. Scientific studies of persons under hypnosis indicate that they often remember things that never happened. Experts believe that these false memories result from leading questions by hypnotists and the fantasies of the subjects who have been hypnotized.

Another technique used by some New Agers to advance toward enlightenment is trance channeling. Trance channelers claim that when they enter a trance, a spirit entity takes over their body. The spirit then talks through them, using their body as a speaking device. These entities

SEE IT

Step 4 (10 mins.)

Show the session 9 video segment. Briefly make the following points.

- Vernon meets two more New Age followers who are attracted to the lighthouse. Maggie is a medium who attempts to communicate with the spirits of the dead. Devin claims to detect a powerful quartz presence around the lighthouse that can release the trapped essences of human souls.
- Vernon is moved when he discovers that late in life his great-uncle accepted Jesus Christ and wanted Vernon to make the same commitment. Vernon realizes that of all the religions he has researched, only Christianity offers a relationship with the living God. He talks with Zack and prays to receive Christ.
- Vernon senses his uncle's love for his misguided friends and asks Zack to help him prepare to share with them the truth of Jesus Christ.

claim to reveal spiritual truths that help listeners advance toward enlightenment. The apostle Paul warned that "in later times some will abandon the faith and follow deceiving spirits and things taught by demons" (1 Tim. 4:1, NIV).

Many New Agers believe that crystals possess the power to manipulate the unseen energy that pulses throughout reality. Some teach that all disease is caused by energy-flow blockages. They claim that by using crystals, they can restore the energy flow to normal and therefore restore the individual's health. This concept is derived from an occult understanding of reality and has no scientific support. In fact, it represents a pre-Christian belief system. New Age medical practices can often be identified by the claim that freeing energy flows can cure illness.

The occult practices engaged in by New Agers are explicitly forbidden in Deuteronomy 18:9-14:

> When you enter the land the Lord your God is giving you, do not learn to imitate the detestable ways of the nations there. Let no one be found among you who sacrifices his son or daughter in the fire, who practices divination or sorcery, interprets omens, engages in witchcraft, or casts spells, or who is a medium or spiritualist or who consults the dead. Anyone who does these things is detestable to the Lord, and because of these detestable practices the Lord your God will drive out those nations before you. You must be blameless before the Lord your God. The nations you will dispossess listen to those who practice sorcery or divination. But as for you, the Lord your God has not permitted you to do so (NIV).

This passage strongly condemns all forms of occult practice. Divination refers to any means of foretelling the future. The biblical condemnation against divination includes all forms of this practice, including but not limited to astrology, crystal gazing, palmistry, and reading tea leaves or animal entrails. This Scripture also denounces all forms of witchcraft or neopaganism that claim to use occult powers to cast spells. Notice that the passage does not condemn only the evil witch but all witches or people who claim to cast spells. Deuteronomy 18 also censures those who attempt to contact the dead. All forms of spiritualism are strongly denounced and should not be engaged in by Christians. Rather, we are to place faith for the present and the future in God's providence and care for our well-being (see Matt. 6:25-34; 1 Pet. 5:7).

Witnessing to New Age Followers

_1. Point out _____implications_____ of reincarnation._
Gently point out some of the implications of the New Age belief system. For example, many New Agers have not considered that one implication of believing in reincarnation and _karma_ is that there are no innocent sufferers. According to reincarnation, whatever happens to a person in this life is because of something the person did in a previous life. Therefore, if a baby is murdered or a woman is raped, the law of _karma_ suggests that this person did something in a previous life to deserve this treatment. Such a belief system is morally bankrupt. Creating a crisis of belief for the New Age follower may allow you an opening to present the true way of salvation by using the FAITH gospel presentation.

_2. Explain the true nature of the coming __new__ __age__._
A look at events around us reveals that humans are no more enlightened than they have ever been. Only the elimination of sin can bring about the era of peace that New Agers long for, and that has been made possible through Jesus Christ. Use the FAITH gospel presentation to offer the New Ager the blessed hope that believers can have for eternity.

_3. Present Jesus Christ as the focus of true ___religion___._
The New Age concept of a universal religion is based on human potential and enlightenment. State that the focus of true religion is Jesus Christ, who alone provides salvation and makes eternal life possible. Use the FAITH gospel presentation to explain what Jesus has done. Use your personal testimony to reveal the centrality of Jesus in your life.

_4. Display Christian __love__ and ___kindness___._
Remember that Jesus loves followers of the New Age movement. When sharing the gospel, be filled with the Holy Spirit and allow Christ's love to show through your attitude and actions.

_5. Warn the person about involvement in the ___occult___._
Warn the New Ager about the danger of engaging in occult practices. God forbids occult activities because He is concerned about our well-being. The devil and his demons exist. Those who engage in occult activities open themselves to the activity of demonic forces (see Eph. 6:12; 1 Tim. 4:1). Explain that those who place their trust in Jesus Christ have security about the present and the future (see Phil. 1:6), as well as spiritual power to deal with life's circumstances (see Eph. 6:10-18).

HEAR IT

Step 5 (5 mins.)

Direct participants to turn to page 157 in their Journals and to fill in the blanks as you summarize Witnessing to New Age Followers. Use the computer presentation or the overhead cel.

Witnessing to New Age Followers

STUDY IT

Step 6 (5 mins.)

Overview Home Study Assignments for session 9.

Transition to assemble with FAITH Teams to prepare for home visits. (5 mins.)

Visitation Time

Do It

1. As you drive to your visit, discuss ways you are learning to reach out to persons you meet in everyday life. Suggest ways your Team's Sunday School class can begin to reach new persons for Christ.

2. In this session your Team Learners studied turning from the world to Christ. Discuss reasons people have difficulty doing this. Emphasize the need to consider the way a Christian witness is perceived by non-Christians.

3. As the Team returns to the church from its visits, the Team Leader should guide in an evaluation of what happened and what follow-through should be made by the Team and/or class/department. Discuss how the report should be presented during Celebration Time; be careful not to tell personal or sensitive details that surfaced during visits.

4. At the Team Leader's cue, Learners should be able to share IMPOSSIBLE.

Celebration Time

Share It

1. Highlight the results of ministry visits as you debrief with your Team. Indicate the different types of Sunday School ministry visits and why certain topics were discussed in the different types of visits. What would Team members suggest as actions for follow-up?

2. Hear reports and testimonies.

3. Complete Evaluation Cards.

4. Complete Participation Cards.

5. Update visitation forms with the results of visits.

Home Study Assignments

Home Study Assignments reinforce this session by helping you apply what you have learned.

Your Discipleship Journey

Journaling activities in Your Discipleship Journey are an important part of your development as a Great Commission Christian through FAITH training.

Read the following statements of New Age beliefs and write a Christian response based on the Scriptures given.

1. The New Age view of salvation is oneness with all, which is achieved through reincarnation.

   Romans 11:6: _____

   _____

   Ephesians 2:8-9: _____

   _____

   Hebrews 9:27: _____

   _____

2. A new age of enlightenment is coming, when the human race will evolve to the next step in awareness of its divinity.

   Titus 2:12-13: _____

   _____

   Revelation 21:1-5: _____

   _____

3. New Agers envision a universal religion that draws concepts like mysticism, love, the worth of nature, and human goodness and potential from present religions.

   Matthew 7:13-14: _____

Romans 1:22-23: _____

_____

Philippians 2:9-11: _____

_____

4. New Agers engage in practices like yoga, Eastern meditation, past-life regression, trance channeling, crystals, and various occult practices, all of which they believe will enable them to achieve a higher state of consciousness.

Deuteronomy 18:9-14: _____

_____

1 Timothy 4:1: _____

_____

Growing as a Life Witness

Growing as a Life Witness reminds you of your responsibility to witness and minister to others during the week.

1. Talk or meet with your accountability partner and share ways you have cultivated a lost person or have witnessed or ministered on occasions other than FAITH visits.
2. Discuss ways you can apply the session 9 content.
3. Pray for lost persons by name and for each other.

Prayer Concerns	Answers to Prayer
_____	_____
_____	_____
_____	_____
_____	_____

Your Weekly Sunday School Leadership Meeting

A FAITH participant is an important member of Sunday School. Encourage Team members who are elected Sunday School leaders to attend this weekly meeting. Use this section to record ways your FAITH Team influences the work of your Sunday School class or department. Use the information to report during weekly Sunday School leadership meetings. Identify actions that need to be taken through Sunday School as a result of prayer concerns, needs identified, visits made by the Team, and decisions made by the persons visited. Also identify ways you can disciple others in your Sunday School class or department and in your church.

1. Highlight FAITH needs/reports that affect your class/department or age group.

2. The most significant result of being saved is a restored personal relationship with God now and for all eternity. What are ways the department/class can impact persons with the truth that, for believers, heaven is HERE?

_____

That heaven is also HEREAFTER?

_____

3. How will the class begin to follow up on persons who received ministry visits?

_____

On someone who accepted Christ in an evangelistic visit?

_____

4. What areas of your Sunday School need to be started or strengthened, based on input from ministry and Opinion Poll visits?

_____

5. Pray now for your teacher(s) and department director(s).

Discipling Your Team Members

This weekly feature suggests actions the Team Leader can take to support Team members, prepare for Team Time, and improve visits. This work is part of the Team Leader's Home Study Assignments. Add any actions suggested by your church's FAITH strategy.

Support Team Members

❏ Pray for and personally follow up on any Learner who may need personal encouragement.

❑ Contact Team members during the week to remind them that you are praying for them and to discuss their participation in FAITH.

❑ Learners are memorizing the gospel presentation through *T* is for TURN. As you discuss this content with Team members, remind them that this is the heart of the gospel.

Prepare to Lead Team Time
❑ Preview Leading Team Time for session 10.
❑ Review the FAITH Visit Outline.

Prepare to Lead Visits
❑ Be prepared to explain the benefits and procedures of making Sunday School ministry visits.
❑ Be prepared to model a visit in which Team members are asked to lead in a visit up to the point of *T* is for TURN.
❑ Be prepared to lead your Team to participate during Celebration Time.

Link with Sunday School
❑ Participate in your weekly Sunday School leadership meeting. Share pertinent information in this meeting, using Your Weekly Sunday School Leadership Meeting (pp. 160–61) and FAITH-visit results.
❑ Be alert to ways Sunday School lessons can teach the true way of salvation and can highlight Jesus' second coming as the culmination of human history.

For Further Growth: The Omniscience of Jesus Christ

For Further Growth may include additional reading or activities that will enhance your growth as a disciple and a discipler of others. These assignments are intended to be long-term projects and do not have to be completed during this semester of study.

1. Even though Jesus possessed all of the attributes of God, He limited Himself and did not always exercise these attributes (see Phil. 2:5-11). Read John 2:24; 16:30. What did John and the other disciples claim about Jesus' knowledge?

2. Read Colossians 2:2-3. What treasures are hidden in Christ?

3. Note what Jesus knew in each of the following references: Matthew 12:25; Luke 5:22; John 1:48; 4:29; 6:70; 7:1,14-18,25-29.

4. Read one or more of the following resources.
   • Millard J. Erickson, *Christian Theology,* part 7, "The Person of Christ," chapter 32, "The Deity of Christ" (Grand Rapids: Baker, 1985), 683–704.
   • R. C. Sproul, *Essential Truths of the Christian Faith,* part 4, "Jesus Christ," chapter 25, "The Deity of Christ" (Wheaton: Tyndale, 1992), 77–78.
   • Millard J. Erickson, *The Word Became Flesh,* chapters 17–18 (Grand Rapids: Baker, 1991), 431–80.

SESSION 10

The Occult

JIMMY FURR

In this session you will—

CHECK IT by engaging in Team Time activities;

KNOW IT by reviewing content from session 9;

HEAR IT by examining occult beliefs and by learning ways

to witness to followers of the occult;

SEE IT by viewing a video segment;

STUDY IT by overviewing Home Study Assignments;

DO IT by leading your Team in making visits;

SHARE IT by celebrating.

IN ADVANCE

- Overview content.
- Preview teaching suggestions. Prepare key points. Decide whether to use the session 10 computer presentation or the overhead cels.
- Prepare the room for teaching.
- Cue the videotape to the session 10 segment.
- Pray for participants and for Teams as they prepare to visit.
- As Teaching Time begins, direct participants to open their Journals to page 166.

CHECK IT (15 MINS.)

If the computer presentation is used, display the agenda frame for Team Time. Add other points as needed.

CHECK IT agenda:
✔ FAITH Visit Outline
✔ Other Home Study Assignments
✔ Session 9 Debriefing
✔ Help for Strengthening a Visit

Leading Team Time

All Team members participate in Team Time. They are primarily responsible for reciting the assigned portion of the FAITH Visit Outline and for discussing other Home Study Assignments.

As you direct this important time of CHECK IT activities with your Team, keep in mind that Learners look to you as a role model, motivator, mentor, and friend. Team Time activities can continue in the car as the Team travels to and from visits.

Lead CHECK IT Activities

✔ FAITH Visit Outline
❑ Listen while each Learner recites all of the **Preparation** and **Presentation** content and key words for **Invitation**.
❑ Give opportunities for Learners to practice reciting the portions of the FAITH Visit Outline they have learned to this point.

✔ Other Home Study Assignments
❑ This may be a good time to discuss the benefits of keeping a weekly journal as part of FAITH training. Discuss some of the truths or understandings gained through the weekly Bible studies. Dialogue about how the reflective questions have influenced Learners' training experience.

✔ Session 9 Debriefing
❑ *T* is for TURN. This is the point in the gospel presentation when a person makes a significant choice—whether to receive salvation. To be forgiven, a person must turn from his sin and turn to Christ. He must trust Christ and Christ only. The imagery of turning is reinforced with the simple question, If you were driving down the road and someone asked you to turn, what would he or she be asking you to do? (Change direction) Most people can easily understand the idea of changing from one direction to another. The Bible uses the word *repent* to depict the same thing. The Bible is clear about the need for a person to repent of sin and to live for Christ (change direction) by committing to and trusting Him. Team members will need to remember the significance of the concepts behind the letter *T* to help explain and emphasize the how of the gospel.

✔ Help for Strengthening a Visit
❑ The illustration of changing directions in a car is the only dialogue that is planned as part of the actual gospel presentation. It is important to ask the person to share his or her answer to the question. The

response is predictable, but by asking the question, you call the person's attention to the gospel and increase his or her participation in the discussion. You might be talking with a child, a younger youth, or someone who obviously does not drive. If so, adapt the question to something like "If you were riding down the road and you asked the driver to turn, what would you be wanting the driver to do?" Usually, it will be significant to use the word *repent* only after the question has helped you explain what the word means. Using the turning analogy to emphasize faith in Christ also helps clarify the meaning of *repent*. For many unsaved or unchurched people, *repent* is associated with religious or churchy terms; without a relevant, contemporary explanation, this word might lose much of its significance.

❑ Remind Team members to listen during each visit for ministry opportunities, as well as for things a person might say to help you identify with his or her spiritual journey.

❑ Discuss how, as a Team Leader, you communicate follow-up information to the appropriate age group/class/department when you encounter family members of different ages in a home visit.

Notes

_____

_____

_____

_____

_____

Actions I Need to Take with Team Members This Week

_____

_____

_____

_____

_____

Transition to classrooms for instruction on the content of the session. (5 mins.)

TEACHING TIME

KNOW IT

Step 1 (5 mins.)

Direct participants to locate A Quick Review on page 166 in their Journals and to complete the activities. Then give the answers, using the computer presentation or the overhead cel.

A Quick Review

HEAR IT

Step 2 (5 mins.)

Ask participants to fill in the blanks as you summarize The Dark World of the Occult. Use the computer presentation or the overhead cel.

The Dark World of the Occult

A Quick Review

Last week you concluded your study of the New Age movement. Indicate whether the following statements express New Age (*N*) or Christian beliefs (*C*).

C 1. We die once and face God's judgment.

C 2. Salvation is by God's grace and not by works.

N 3. Oneness with all is achieved through reincarnation.

N 4. A new age of enlightenment is coming.

C 5. The new age we await is Christ's eternal reign in a new heaven and a new earth.

N 6. New Agers envision a universal religion.

C 7. The one true religion centers on Jesus Christ.

C 8. We are not to worship nature.

N 9. New Age practices lead to higher consciousness.

C 10. God condemns all forms of occult practice.

Check appropriate ways to witness to New Agers.

☑ 1. Point out implications of reincarnation.

☑ 2. Explain the true nature of the coming new age.

❑ 3. Tell New Age followers that they are very confused and cannot understand the truth.

☑ 4. Present Jesus Christ as the focus of true religion.

❑ 5. Be on the defensive when you are around New Agers.

❑ 6. Ask the person to demonstrate some occult practices.

☑ 7. Display Christian love and kindness.

☑ 8. Warn the person about involvement in the occult.

❑ 9. Assure New Agers that the devil and demons are merely fantasies.

The Dark World of the Occult

Teen Witch, a popular book on witchcraft, states that "one in every five people in the United States has dabbled in the world of the 'unknown,' whether we're talking about ESP (extrasensory perception), tarot cards, angels, creative visualization, Paganism, metaphysics, Witchcraft, New Age beliefs, et cetera."[1] Most Christians would consider this an astonishing statement. Yet when all of these activities are considered, we can understand how the statement might be true. When most of us think of the occult, perhaps only __**Satanism**__ or __**witchcraft**__ comes to mind. However, in addition to Satanism and witchcraft, many seemingly less threatening areas of the occult exist in which even many Christians participate and see no harm. ____**Divination**____, __astrology__, __spiritualism__, automatic __writings__, Atlantis __myths__, and tarot __cards__ are just a few areas of occult practice that are common in America today.

The word *occult* comes from the Latin word *occultus,* meaning __hidden__. It refers to supernatural influences, agencies, or phenomena. Many of today's superstitions are rooted in the occult. It is often said that bad luck may come from stepping on a crack or having a black cat cross your path, while good luck may come from saying, "God bless you" when someone sneezes. Although these practices may have backgrounds in the occult, most persons are not consciously practicing occult activities when they express them today. Actually, the occult encompasses a wide variety of diverse activities and beliefs, from divination to spiritualism to Satanism.

Some point to the 1960s and '70s, when the movies *Rosemary's Baby* and *The Exorcist* were popular, as the beginning of the current occult revival. By 1980 the increase in occult activity in America became more noticeable as occultists began to advertise and propagate their beliefs. Since that time the nation has witnessed a surge of interest in witchcraft, horoscopes, astrology, and occult literature.

Occult Beliefs

Christians today need to know biblical ways to respond to those who are lost in the dark world of the occult. We will examine three prominent modern occult practices and provide a Christian analysis of each.

1. Occult divination claims to predict the __future__.

Occult divination represents the most widespread practice of the occult in America today. The term *divination* refers to methods of obtaining knowledge of the unknown or the future by means of omens.[2] Probably, the most popular form of divination is astrology.

Astrology began perhaps as early as 3000 B.C. A developed belief in astrology existed as early as 2000 B.C., when the Babylonians studied the stars for clues to human destiny. In 150 B.C. the zodiac, or parade of animals, was developed. This was an imaginary belt in the sky across which the planets move. An Egyptian named Ptolemy is credited with developing astrology as it is known in the Western world in A.D. 150. Astrology became popular in this generation largely through the endeavors of Jeane Dixon, probably the most famous contemporary astrologer. In the 1950s and '60s she made a number of startling predictions about the future, some of which came true and were highly publicized. The truth is that many of Dixon's less publicized predictions failed to occur. In the 1980s many Americans were surprised when Nancy

Step 3 (15 mins.)

Direct participants to turn to page 167 in their Journals and to fill in the blanks as you present the key ideas in Occult Beliefs. Use the computer presentation or the overhead cel.

Occult Beliefs

Reagan acknowledged that she often consulted an astrologer to determine when and where President Ronald Reagan should have meetings.

The claims of astrology center on the time and place of a person's birth. Some believe that rays or vibrations from the stars and planets affect a newborn baby, endowing him or her with a certain lifelong personality. These heavenly bodies are said to continue to exert an influence as long as the person lives. The positions of planets and their relative positions to one another counteract or emphasize certain characteristics. Angles between stars and planets in the zodiac must be considered. Certain arrangements of stars and planets are good, and some are not. Different planets are said to have different characteristics.

Scientific facts do not support the practice of astrology. Astrology uses Ptolemy's Earth-centered view of the solar system. As Copernicus discovered in the 16th century, however, the sun, not Earth, is at the center of the solar system. Also, astrology claims that planets' rays or vibrations that fall on a child at birth influence his or her life. Actually, planets emit no light or cosmic rays on their own.

Most importantly, the practice of astrology is incompatible with biblical teachings. The Bible teaches that God is the Creator of everything, including the stars, moon, and planets (see Gen. 1:14-18). These bodies are created objects, not gods. Astrology violates biblical teachings in its attempt to predict details about the future (see Matt. 24:36). Jesus said that we have no reason to be anxious about tomorrow (see Matt. 6:25,34). We are to place faith in God for the future and to consult the Bible for the guidance we need for living.

The Bible condemns astrology as a pagan religious practice that God's people must reject (see Deut. 4:19; Isa. 2:6; 47:12-14). Paul wrote to the Galatians and Colossians who were involved in astrology that they had been set free from the elemental spirits of the universe (see Gal. 5; Col. 2).

In contrast to astrological predictions, the validity of biblical prophecy cannot be denied. Biblical prophecy specifically relates to God's redemptive work in history. Christians should ask two questions about all prophecy: Does the prediction always come true (see Deut. 18:22)? Do the prophet and his prediction glorify God (see Deut. 13:1-3)?

Palmistry, crystal gazing, pyramidology, and dream interpretation are also part of the world of divination. The law of Moses condemned human sacrifice, divination, witchcraft, omens, sorcery, casting spells, and spiritualism as abominations to God (see Deut. 18:9-13).

2. Spiritualism seeks to communicate with the __dead__.

Spiritism is most simply defined as the belief that spirits of the dead can and do communicate with the living. The belief is sometimes called *spiritualism*, especially by persons who have accepted the practice as a central part of their religious practice. Another term used to describe this alleged practice is *necromancy*.

Spiritualism has enjoyed widespread practice throughout American history. Swedish seer Emanuel Swendenborg (1688–1774) claimed visions and contact with persons long dead. The New Jerusalem Church, founded on his spiritualist ideas, came to America in 1792. Spiritualism was one of the many unorthodox teachings of the Shakers, founded by "Mother" Ann Lee (1733–87). Joseph Smith, the founder of the Mormon Church, was heavily involved in the occult. He claimed that Elijah, John the Baptist, Peter, James, John, Jesus, and God the Father appeared to him.

Modern spiritualism began in Hydesville, New York, in 1848. Two sisters, Margaretta Fox, age 15, and Kate Fox, age 12, claimed that they could communicate with a spirit of a deceased man who was buried beneath their house. They often publicly demonstrated this communication, which was a system of taps or knocks. Later, Margaretta admitted that the story was a hoax, explaining that they had produced the knocks by snapping their toes. However, by that time the spiritualist momentum was rolling and could not be stopped. The first spiritualist congregation in the United States began in Stirgis, Michigan, in 1858. In 1893 the National Spiritualist Association of Churches was organized in Chicago. Today Cassadega, a small town in central Florida, is the headquarters of that association and is considered the spiritualist capital of the nation.

The heart of spiritualism is the seance, through which the spirit world is allegedly contacted. A seance, which usually takes place in a dimly lighted room, may be held privately or semiprivately. A medium, who is sensitive to the "other world," makes contact with his spirit-guide, who puts the medium in contact with the spirits of the departed ones.

Spiritualists may use several methods of communication with dead spirits. The spirit may speak audibly through the medium, whose voice may change. The spirit may speak through a trumpet or may write on paper. The spirit may rap or knock, tilt or lift a table, or ring bells. The spirit may answer questions by moving an indicator on a Ouija Board. The spirit may even materialize and be photographed.

Several theories have been advanced to explain what happens during séances. Educated guesses, extrasensory perception (ESP), actual communication, or even possible demonic deception have been suggested. The theory most often given is simple fraud.

Spiritualists give the Bible a place of considerable authority in their faith, but they interpret it to reflect spiritualist teachings. They believe that the Bible is a spiritualist book, the purpose of which is to record events that may confirm a belief in communication between the living and the dead. According to spiritualists, Abraham was a powerful medium because he materialized three visitors from the spirit world at the same time (see Gen. 18:2). Moses was a medium who produced the most famous spirit writing in history when he received the tables of stone engraved by his spirit-guide named Yahweh (see Ex. 20). Daniel is also considered a master at spirit writings with the handwriting on the wall (see Dan. 5:5,24). Jesus was also a medium who materialized Moses and Elijah on the mount of transfiguration (see Matt. 17:1-8).

An objective, literal reading of Scripture does not reveal that these men practiced spiritualism. They were divinely inspired men of God who received the Word He gave them (see Heb. 1:1). Furthermore, the Bible clearly condemns spiritualism. Spiritualist practices are detestable aspects of pagan practices and inevitably defile the authentic worship of God (see Lev. 20:6; 2 Kings 23; Isa. 19:3). Believers are warned not to tolerate mediums and spiritualists in our midst. Old Testament law called for mediums and spirits to be stoned to death (see Lev. 20:27). Saul, who panicked in the face of the Philistines, consulted a witch (medium) and asked her to summon Samuel for his advice (see 1 Sam. 28:3-16). Partially because of Saul's spiritualism he died in battle with the Philistines (see 1 Chron. 10:13-14). God speaks of the foolishness of consulting mediums and spiritualists "who whisper and mutter" (Isa. 8:19, NIV). We serve a living God. "Why," as Isaiah asked, should we "consult the dead on behalf of the living?" (Isa. 8:19, NIV).

3. Satanism glorifies ___evil___.

Witchcraft and Satanism are two of the best-known expressions of the occult. Witchcraft will be the subject of session 11, so the remainder of this session will examine Satanism as practiced in North America.

Shootings in American high schools over the past few years have drawn new attention to Satanism, the darkest side of the occult. Satanists worship Satan as their lord and live their lives openly opposed to Christianity. Some Satanists insist that they do not believe in a literal Satan but consider him a symbol of evil and their lifestyle. In any case, the end result of Satanism is the destruction of the individual and/or someone else. Most Satanists utilize Satanic symbols and dark images in their practices. The grossest kinds of evil are associated with Satanism, including drug use, sexual perversion, and animal sacrifices.

The current Satanic revival began in 1966, when Anton LaVey formed the Church of Satan. His type of Satanism has spawned other Satanic churches and groups. Beginning in the 1970s, the discovery of a number of mutilated cattle in several states contributed to the belief in widespread Satanic activity. Isolated Satanic groups, primarily composed of teenagers, learned about Satanism from popular books. Drug use appears to have been widespread among these groups and may have led to Satanic involvement. Some of these groups use anti-Christian symbols to break emotional and religious ties to the Christian faith and society.

Satanism has been the theme of many movies. Rock-music groups have made Satanism attractive to teenagers with songs about sex, hell, and the devil. Participation in fantasy games, like Dungeons and Dragons, glorifies the occult world, including casting spells; evil spirits;

magicians; and a host of pagan gods, demigods, and monsters. For too many the game takes on a frightening reality as players adopt the characteristics of their gods. Some players move beyond this fantasy to deeper involvement in Satanism, drug use, or suicide.

Satanists may be divided into three types.

1. **Religious** Satanists are those who openly proclaim Satanism to be a viable religion. The most famous religious Satanist in America was Anton Szandor LaVey. In 1966 he began what we now know as the Church of Satan, headquartered in San Francisco, California. He played the part of Satan in *Rosemary's Baby*, a movie about the birth of the antichrist, and in 1969 published *The Satanic Bible*. The basic themes in LaVey's Satanism are self-assertion and self-gratification. Believing in neither God nor Satan, LaVey saw Satan as merely a symbol of humanity's carnal nature. LaVey stated: "Most Satanists do not accept Satan as an anthropomorphic being with cloven hooves, a barbed tail, and horns. He merely represents a force of nature—the powers of darkness which have been named just that because no religion has taken these forces out of the darkness."[3] LaVey rejected the supernatural, an afterlife, heaven, and hell. He also rejected the idea of sin, holding that people are superior animals who should worship their own egos and live according to their own rules. Anton LaVey died in 1997, and no leader of the Church of Satan has yet been named. Another well-known religious Satanist is Michael Aquino, who was at one time a devoted follower of LaVey and the Church of Satan and a former high-ranking member of the U.S. military. Aquino broke from LaVey's group in 1975 and formed what is known today as the Temple of Set, also headquartered in San Francisco.

2. **Lifestyle** Satanists or dabblers compose the largest category of Satanists. Most of these Satanic practitioners are white, male youth from the age of 12 or 13 to their late teens. They are usually very bright with inquisitive natures. Many have come from broken homes and have no parental supervision. Many of these youth attempt to imitate a favorite writer, actor, or rock musician by creating their own version of Satanism. Lifestyle Satanists may not believe in or worship Satan. Rather, they may see him as a symbol of the sexual abuse, drug use, or vandalism they are involved in. They are drawn by the promise of power, drugs, sex, or the desire to be included. These youth are likely to explode into violent acts like shootings and animal killings.

3. Satanic **cultists** are groups that may be involved in illegal activities, such as drugs, pornography, kidnapping, child molestation, and animal sacrifice. Rumors of human sacrifice have been leveled at Satanic cultists. Although it is possible that they have performed human sacrifices on drifters, hitchhikers, homeless people, and recently born infants whose births are unrecorded, this has not been proved. In reality, human sacrifice probably forms little or no part of

most Satanic rituals. When it does occur, it is probably performed by criminal occult groups or drug-intoxicated lifestyle Satanists.[4]

All Satanists have in common their love of evil and their opposition to Christ and His kingdom. The lord who has control of their lives is none other than Satan Himself, the archenemy of God. The Bible teaches that Satan is real and that he is dangerous. His goal is to destroy God's people. Jesus called him a murderer and the father of lies (see John 8:44). The Bible often refers to Satan as our enemy, who "prowls around like a roaring lion looking for someone to devour" (1 Pet. 5:8, NIV). Satanists yield themselves to Satan and thereby open themselves to demonic influence. Although demon possession is rare today, Satan has an opening whenever a person yields moral, spiritual, or rational control to him. Even Christians can experience demonic influence if they persistently yield to temptation and sin (see Eph. 4:27; 2 Tim. 2:26).

Yet believers must remember that Satan is not equal with God. He is a created being whom Jesus has already defeated on the cross. Christians can resist Satan by claiming Christ's victory (see 1 John 3:8; Col. 2:15), by resisting temptation (see 1 Cor. 10:13; Jas. 4:7), and by walking daily in the power of God's Holy Spirit (see 1 John 4:4). We also have spiritual weapons that God provides to fight the devil (see Eph. 6:11-18). This same spiritual power is also available to Satanists who repent of their sin and accept Christ as their Savior and Lord.

Witnessing to Followers of the Occult

1. Follow a strategy of _____prevention_____.

It is important for Christians to be alert to signs that others, especially children and youth, are attracted to the occult. Keep the lines of communication open with children. Listen to them, particularly when you do not agree with them. Let them know that they are loved and that they may always come to you for help and information. Know who children's friends are, the music they listen to, and where they spend time. Occult card games and fantasy role-playing games appeal to some young people, and the Internet has opened the door of the occult to many.

2. Prepare for spiritual _____warfare_____.

In witnessing to followers of the occult, you are engaging in spiritual warfare. Prepare yourself for battle by being filled with the Holy Spirit (see 1 John 4:4; Eph. 5:18), by employing spiritual weapons (see Eph. 6:11-17), by knowing the truth of God's Word (see John 17:17), by depending on God (see Ps. 18), and by praying (see Eph. 6:18).

HEAR IT

Step 5 (5 mins.)

Direct participants to turn to page 172 in their Journals and to fill in the blanks as you summarize Witnessing to Followers of the Occult. Use the computer presentation or the overhead cel.

Witnessing to Followers of the Occult

3. Determine the degree of occult   <u>**involvement**</u>.

Many people dabble in the occult without any real commitment. Talk with the person to determine the level of involvement, as well as to discover the needs and problems that led to this involvement. Many youth draw occult symbols and participate in practices to satisfy curiosity. Carefully listen to what is being said and do not overreact. Sometimes young people say shocking things just to elicit a reaction. If you do not react dramatically, they may feel comfortable in sharing their problems.

4. Offer Christ as the   <u>**answer**</u>.

Explain that Jesus Christ is the only answer to the occult. Occult involvement is sin, and only Christ can remove sin. He has authority and victory over the occult world, and He has power over Satan (see Mark 9:14-29; Luke 4:33-36). Spiritual victory and power are available to all who believe in Him and trust Him as Savior and Lord. Use the FAITH gospel presentation to present the way to repent of sin and find life and freedom in Jesus Christ.

Help occult followers see that Jesus is also the answer to the personal needs and problems that may have led to occult participation. Many get involved in the occult because they believe it can help them solve their difficulties, acquire spiritual power, or gain control over their circumstances or future. Meaningful solutions to problems, a purpose for living, and spiritual power come to those who have a relationship with Jesus Christ (see Rom. 8:9-13; Phil. 4:13). A believer can place problems and the future in God's hands and live according to His will instead of striving for personal power and control over others or trying to manipulate life's circumstances (see Matt. 6:25-34; Rom. 8:28-32; 1 John 5:4-5).

5. Warn of the   <u>**consequences**</u> of occult involvement.

Satanists and occult practitioners align themselves with evil. You have an obligation to point out Satan's reality and power and to warn followers that those who reject Christ will spend eternity in hell.

6. Persist in Christlike   <u>**love**</u>.

Do not give up on those who are involved in the occult. Remain accessible to them and live a life that exemplifies Christ's love. Do not be alarmed if questions arise that you cannot answer. Be honest and share that you will search for an answer and contact the person again. Keep the lines of communication open.

STUDY IT

Step 6 (5 mins.)

Overview Home Study Assignments for session 10.

Transition to assemble with FAITH Teams to prepare for home visits. (5 mins.)

Visitation Time

Do It

1. Think about being an ambassador to the persons you visit. Your goal is to share God's message of reconciliation through Jesus Christ. Your enthusiastic attitude reflects your deep conviction about the truth you share. Make sure you fulfill your responsibility as an ambassador by speaking and acting in a way that honors Christ.
2. On the drive, discuss what it means to have heaven here and now.
3. All Team members should know the FAITH presentation through *H* is for HEAVEN. While visiting, invite Team members to support you throughout the presentation. Tell them that next week they will be expected to lead the gospel presentation.

Celebration Time

Share It

1. Ask a Team member to take the lead in sharing reports.
2. Hear reports and testimonies.
3. Complete Evaluation Cards.
4. Complete Participation Cards.
5. Update visitation forms with the results of visits.

Home Study Assignments

Home Study Assignments reinforce this session by helping you apply what you have learned.

Your Discipleship Journey

Journaling activities in Your Discipleship Journey are an important part of your development as a Great Commission Christian through FAITH training.

1. Match the following Scriptures with the correct teachings about Satan.

   ___ 1. Genesis 3:1   a. Blinds minds

   ___ 2. Matthew 4:6   b. A sinner

   ___ 3. John 8:44   c. Knows the Scriptures

   ___ 4. 2 Corinthians 4:4   d. Masquerades as an angel of light

   ___ 5. 2 Corinthians 11:14   e. A murderer and the father of lies

   ___ 6. 1 Thessalonians 3:5   f. The accuser

   ___ 7. 1 John 3:8   g. Crafty

   ___ 8. Revelation 12:10   h. The tempter

2. Match the following Scriptures with the correct teachings about demons.

   ___ 1. Matthew 9:32-33   a. A spirit that does not acknowledge Jesus
                                     is a spirit of the antichrist.

   ___ 2. Matthew 17:14-20   b. Faith in God can overcome the demonic.

   ___ 3. 1 Corinthians 10:19-20   c. Jesus has power over demons.

   ___ 4. 1 Timothy 4:1   d. Pagan sacrifices are offered to demons.

   ___ 5. 1 John 4:1-3   e. People will follow deceiving spirits and
                                     demonic teachings.

3. Summarize what the following Scriptures say about occult practices.

Isaiah 47:12-15: _____

_____

Deuteronomy 4:19: _____

_____

Deuteronomy 18:9-12: _____

_____

Jeremiah 27:9-10: _____

Micah 3:7: _____

Isaiah 8:19: _____

Growing as a Life Witness

Growing as a Life Witness reminds you of your responsibility to witness and minister to others during the week.

1. Talk or meet with your accountability partner and share ways you have cultivated a lost person or have witnessed or ministered on occasions other than FAITH visits.
2. Discuss ways you can apply the session 10 content.
3. Pray for lost persons by name and for each other.

Prayer Concerns	Answers to Prayer
_____	_____
_____	_____
_____	_____
_____	_____
_____	_____

Your Weekly Sunday School Leadership Meeting

A FAITH participant is an important member of Sunday School. Encourage Team members who are elected Sunday School leaders to attend this weekly meeting. Use this section to record ways your FAITH Team influences the work of your Sunday School class or department. Use the information to report during weekly Sunday School leadership meetings. Identify actions that need to be taken through Sunday School as a result of prayer concerns, needs identified, visits made by the Team, and decisions made by the persons visited. Also identify ways you can disciple others in your Sunday School class or department and in your church.

1. Highlight FAITH needs/reports affecting your class/department or age group. Receive and provide information about future visitation assignments. Do records reflect the information that is needed for visits and for follow-up?

_____

_____

2. Periodically evaluate the growth of your class/department. Are new Christians consistently becoming part of the group? Are these new believers beginning to grow in their faith and to discover their spiritual gifts? Are mature members leaving the class to accept leadership positions? Is the class reaching out beyond itself, so much so that a new unit or more space may be needed? Is the fellowship inclusive and attractive to all people?

_____

_____

3. How should preparation for Sunday consider the needs of individuals or families visited through FAITH? Discuss ways Sunday's Bible-study lesson can involve members and guests in transformational Bible study and discipleship.

_____

_____

4. Your class/department has committed to support you throughout FAITH training. FAITH assignments are reaching their peak for many Team members, so it is appropriate to ask your leadership team to pray for you and all FAITH participants at this significant time in training.

Discipling Your Team Members

This weekly feature suggests actions the Team Leader can take to support Team members, prepare for Team Time, and improve visits. This work is part of the Team Leader's Home Study Assignments. Add any actions suggested by your church's FAITH strategy.

Support Team Members

❑ Contact Team members during the week. Remind them that you are praying for them. Discuss prayer concerns and answers to prayer.
❑ This week Learners are memorizing the FAITH presentation through the _Invitation_. As you discuss this content with Team members, remind them that this is when someone can make a life-changing decision.
❑ Learners have a significant amount of reading during home study this week. The information is important to read and understand because it interprets A _Step of Faith_. Encourage Learners to read the FAITH Tips and to be prepared to discuss the significance of this leaflet in preparation for session 11.

❑ Record specific needs and concerns shared by Team members.

Prepare to Lead Team Time
❑ Review Team members' Home Study Assignments.
❑ Preview Leading Team Time for session 11.

Prepare to Lead Visits
❑ Review the FAITH Visit Outline.

Link with Sunday School
❑ Participate in your weekly Sunday School leadership meeting. Share pertinent information in this meeting, using Your Weekly Sunday School Leadership Meeting (pp. 176–77) and FAITH-visit results.
❑ Look for opportunities in Sunday School to warn members about the danger the occult poses for society, especially for children and youth.

For Further Growth: The Omnipresence of Jesus Christ

For Further Growth may include additional reading or activities that will enhance your growth as a disciple and a discipler of others. These assignments are intended to be long-term projects and do not have to be completed during this semester of study.

1. Although Jesus continued to be God during His time on earth, He willingly limited His exercise of His attributes of deity (see Phil. 2:5-11). According to Matthew 18:20; 28:20, where did Jesus promise to be?

2. In John 14:18-20 what did Jesus promise to every believer?

3. Read Romans 8:31-39 and spend time meditating on God's promise of presence and security that is given to every believer.

4. Read one or more of the following resources.
   - Millard J. Erickson, *Christian Theology*, part 7, "The Person of Christ," chapter 32, "The Deity of Christ" (Grand Rapids: Baker, 1985), 683–704.
   - R. C. Sproul, *Essential Truths of the Christian Faith*, part 4, "Jesus Christ," chapter 25, "The Deity of Christ" (Wheaton: Tyndale, 1992), 77–78.
   - Millard J. Erickson, *The Word Became Flesh*, chapters 17–18 (Grand Rapids: Baker, 1991), 431–80.

5. Read the FAITH Tip on pages 179–80.

---

[1]Silver RavenWolf, *Teen Witch: Wicca for a New Generation* (St. Paul: Llewellyn, 1998), xiii.
[2]Lewis Spence, *An Encyclopedia of Occultism* (New York: Carol, 1996), 125.
[3]Anton Szandor LaVey, *The Satanic Bible* (New York: Avon, 1969), 62.
[4]Bob and Gretchen Passantino, *When the Devil Dares Your Kids* (Ann Arbor: Vine, 1991), 47.

Answers to matching activities on page 175:
Activity *1*: 1. g, 2. c, 3. e, 4. a, 5. d, 6. h, 7. b, 8. f
Activity *2*: 1. c, 2. b, 3. d, 4. e, 5. a

FAITH TIP

The Demonic World: Fact or Fiction?

Today many people deny the existence of a personal devil. But the Bible warns of the existence of evil spiritual entities that exercise power in this world.

Satan and the Demons Are Real

The Bible teaches that Satan and his demons are evil spiritual beings who are in rebellion against God and oppose His people (see Gen. 3:15; Job 1:6-12; Matt. 4:1; 25:41; Luke 10:18; 13:16; 1 John 3:8; 5:18; Rev. 12:9; 20:10).

Satan (the adversary; see Job 1—2) is addressed by many names in the Bible, including the devil (the accuser or slanderer; see Matt. 4:1; Luke 4:2,5; Rev. 20:2), the dragon (see Rev. 12:3), the prince of this world (see John 12:31), the serpent (see Gen. 3:4,14; 2 Cor. 11:3), Beelzebub (from a Philistine god whom Jesus identified with Satan; see Matt. 12:24; Mark 3:22; Luke 11:15), Belial (worthless one; see 2 Cor. 6:15), and Abaddon/Apollyon (the angel of the abyss; see Rev. 9:11). Jesus was tempted by the devil but successfully resisted his enticements (see Matt. 4:1-11; Mark 1:12-13; Luke 4:1-13).

The Bible also accepts the reality of demons or evil spirits who oppose God and His people. Although some people believe that demon possession in the New Testament was actually epilepsy or mental illness, Jesus distinguished between illness and demon possession (see Matt. 10:1; Mark 6:13; Luke 9:1). The cure Jesus administered for physical or emotional illness was usually a physical touch (see Luke 8:43-48). In contrast, He cast out demons by a word or a command (see Mark 9:14-29; Luke 4:33-36; 8:26-33). Jesus confronted demonic forces during His ministry (see Matt. 8:28-34; 9:32-33; 12:22; Mark 5:2-20; Luke 11:14). Other biblical characters such as Job and Jesus' disciples were also challenged by the devil and his minions.

Satan Seeks to Subvert God's Plans for His People

The goal of Satan and his demons is to render God's people useless for the Lord's kingdom. They try to do this by tempting believers to disobey God's will for their lives. Therefore, Christians must constantly be attentive to the subtle ways Satan tries to distract them from their walk with the Lord (see 1 Pet. 5:8).

Perhaps Satan's greatest aim is to prevent Christians from witnessing for Christ and seeking to lead lost people to salvation. Therefore, as a participant in FAITH, you must be alert to Satan's attacks (see 2 Cor. 2:11).

Satan Is a Defeated Enemy

Although Satan is a formidable opponent, he is not equal to God. He and the demons are created beings. Despite their rebellion, they remain under God's sovereign rule and operate only by God's permission (see Job 1:6-12).

Also remember that Satan is a defeated enemy. Jesus came into the world to destroy the works of the devil (see 1 John 3:8). His death on the cross and His resurrection sealed Satan and his minions' fate forever (see John 12:31; 16:11; Col. 2:15). We must claim that victory when Satan tempts us or seeks to distract us from God's will for our lives (see Eph. 6:11-18).

In addition, Satan can only tempt; he cannot force himself on anyone. The Holy Spirit, who dwells in our hearts, empowers us to resist Satan's attacks. John wrote that "the one who is in you is greater than the one who is in the world" (1 John 4:4, NIV). God promises that we will not be tempted beyond our power to resist (see 1 Cor. 10:13). If we submit ourselves to God and resist the devil, he will flee from us (see Jas. 4:7).

SESSION 11

Witchcraft

BILL GORDON

In this session you will—

CHECK IT by engaging in Team Time activities;

KNOW IT by reviewing content from session 10;

HEAR IT by examining beliefs of witchcraft and by learning ways

to witness to followers of witchcraft;

SAY IT by practicing the *Invitation* portion of the FAITH Visit Outline;

STUDY IT by overviewing Home Study Assignments;

DO IT by leading your Team in making visits;

SHARE IT by celebrating.

IN ADVANCE
• Overview content.
• Preview teaching suggestions. Prepare key points. Decide whether to use the session 11 computer presentation or the overhead cels.
• Prepare the room for teaching.
• Pray for participants and for Teams as they prepare to visit.
• As Teaching Time begins, direct participants to open their Journals to page 184.

If the computer presentation is used, display the agenda frame for Team Time. Add other points as needed.

CHECK IT agenda:
✔ FAITH Visit Outline
✔ Session 10 Debriefing
✔ Help for Strengthening a Visit

Leading Team Time

All Team members participate in Team Time. They are primarily responsible for reciting the assigned portion of the FAITH Visit Outline and for discussing other Home Study Assignments.

As you direct this important time of CHECK IT activities with your Team, keep in mind that Learners look to you as a role model, motivator, mentor, and friend. Team Time activities can continue in the car as the Team travels to and from visits.

Lead CHECK IT Activities

✔ FAITH Visit Outline
❑ Listen while each Learner recites the FAITH Visit Outline beginning with HOW and including all of the *Invitation*. Indicate any notes for improvement.
❑ Make sure Team members know the correct sequence in using *A Step of Faith* in making a transition from the gospel presentation to leading someone to declare commitments to Christ as Savior and Lord, to enroll in Sunday School, and to publicly acknowledge new faith in Jesus. Since several Home Study Assignments dealt with the use of *A Step of Faith*, you may not need additional review of session 10 assignments.
❑ Make certain Team members are able to lead a person to pray to receive Christ and to pray for Christian growth. Also, be certain Team members are comfortable in leading a person to record commitment(s) they have made and to provide the information the church needs.

✔ Session 10 Debriefing
❑ Heaven HERE and Heaven HEREAFTER are fundamental beliefs of the Christian. Do Learners demonstrate a sense of comfort in sharing their joy in Christ and their assurance of eternal life in God's presence?
❑ H also stands for HOW. This becomes the hinge on which a Learner is able to clarify for another person how a person can have God's forgiveness, heaven and eternal life, and Jesus as personal Savior and Lord. Make sure the person is becoming increasingly comfortable in using the picture on the cover of *A Step of Faith* to identify with the need for God's forgiveness. You received earlier training to help your Team know what to do if *A Step of Faith* is not available.

✔ Help for Strengthening a Visit

❑ Remind Team members that they are seeing the Holy Spirit at work as they make themselves available for visitation. Recall examples of ways you have seen the Holy Spirit at work when a person has heard the FAITH gospel presentation.

❑ One of the great privileges and responsibilities in FAITH training is to encounter family members of someone you are assigned to visit. Although your Team is focusing on persons from your Sunday School department or class, you quickly learn that there are many opportunities to minister to and share the gospel with persons of other age divisions. Dialogue about ways to meaningfully include preschoolers, children, youth, and adults in a visit who would not be assigned to your department or class.

❑ Indicate that next week's practice session is a good way to improve skills and increase confidence. Share schedule adjustments.

Notes

_____

_____

_____

_____

_____

Actions I Need to Take with Team Members This Week

_____

_____

_____

_____

_____

Transition to classrooms for instruction on the content of the session. (5 mins.)

KNOW IT

Direct participants to locate A Quick Review on page 184 in their Journals and to complete the activities. Then give the answers, using the computer presentation or the overhead cel.

A Quick Review

HEAR IT

Ask participants to fill in the blanks as you present the key points in A Growing Deception. Use the computer presentation or the overhead cels.

A Growing Deception

A Quick Review

Last week you studied the occult as expressed in divination, spiritualism, and Satanism. Match each Christian teaching in the left column with the occult practice it refutes.

b 1. Believers are not to tolerate mediums.
c 2. Satan is not equal with God.
a 3. Do not be anxious about the future.
c 4. Believers can resist evil and fight the devil.
b 5. Attempts to communicate with the dead defile the authentic worship of God.
b 6. We serve a living God, not a dead spirit.
a 7. The Bible condemns astrology.

a. Occult divination
b. Spiritualism
c. Satanism

Check the appropriate principles for witnessing to occult followers.
- ☑ 1. Follow a strategy of prevention.
- ❑ 2. Always wear a necklace with a cross.
- ☑ 3. Prepare for spiritual warfare.
- ☑ 4. Determine the degree of occult involvement.
- ☑ 5. Offer Christ as the answer.
- ❑ 6. Whatever you do, don't make them angry.
- ❑ 7. Begin groups at church that play Dungeons and Dragons.
- ☑ 8. Warn of the consequences of occult involvement.
- ❑ 9. Offer to read their palm, using biblical principles of divination.
- ☑ 10. Persist in Christlike love.

A Growing Deception

As you learned in session 10, witchcraft and Satanism are two of the best-known expressions of the occult today. Witchcraft, however, receives much more attention today than Satanism. While most people recognize Satanism as an evil practice, witchcraft is regarded by many as an acceptable lifestyle. TV shows like "Sabrina, the Teenage Witch" and "Charmed" have increased the acceptability of witchcraft by depicting witches as beautiful young women who combat evil.

Several reasons lie behind the increasing popularity of witchcraft in modern society. The widespread use of **occult** **themes** in movies and books since the 1960s has laid much of the groundwork for the popularity of both witchcraft and other occult beliefs. **Movie stars** who are involved in witchcraft have also given it more appeal. Witchcraft promises **empowerment** to its adherents through the practice of magic. Wicca offers a religious context for __**feminism**__, __**environmentalism**__, and __**liberalism**__. Witchcraft is probably the fastest-growing religion among __**teenage**__ __**girls**__ in North America and western Europe.

The term *witch* is derived from the old English word *wicca*, which means __**sorcerer**__. A difference of opinion exists among modern witches as to whether the term *witch* is acceptable today. Some proudly proclaim themselves as witches. Others refuse to use the word, preferring the term *wiccan*. The term *neopaganism* is often used interchangeably with the terms *witchcraft* and *wicca*. A witch or wiccan may be either male or female. A male witch is never referred to as a warlock.

Some wiccans claim that their religion is thousands of years old, the remains of a fertility or nature faith that is older than any other religion. Witchcraft is said to have begun in prehistoric times, when the worship of spirits in nature was widespread. This theory has been rejected by modern scholars. The foundation of modern wicca was built in the __**19th**__ __**century**__ with the occult practices and writings of Eliphas Levi, Aleister Crowley, and Johann Jacob Bachofen. In the 20th century wicca was popularized by the writings of __**Gerald**__ __**Gardner**__, a British amateur archaeologist and civil servant. Most researchers believe that Gardner created a new religion from his own occult studies. Gardner popularized witchcraft through his books and the initiation of others, who brought his teachings to America in the __**1960s**__.

By the 1980s the United States Air Force recognized witchcraft as a legitimate religion, granting witches the right to observe Halloween as a religious holiday. In 1994 the World Parliament of Religions acknowledged witchcraft as a legitimate religion. In addition, witchcraft as a religion has gained tax-exempt status on a national and local basis.

Beliefs of Witchcraft

Witches claim that their religion, wicca, is the fastest-growing religion in America. One of the stated goals of witchcraft is to bring about a resurgence of pagan beliefs and ideas in post-Christian America. Some wiccans claim that their religion does not have a belief system but rather is totally experiential. One wiccan pamphlet states:

> Wiccans actually believe nothing. Belief is the deceit and refuge of the credulous. Wiccans feel a closeness to the forces of nature, and recognize that there is a spiritual essence that pervades all things, places, and people. Wicca is an experiential religion, where worship is

Step 3 (15 mins.)

Direct participants to turn to page 186 in their Journals and to fill in the blanks as you summarize Beliefs of Witchcraft. Use the computer presentation or the overhead cel.

Beliefs of Witchcraft

viewed as a way of directly touching the deity that is present in all things. Wiccans view Deity as both male and female, god and goddess. These deities have been worshipped for thousands of years, under many titles, and in many forms. The God is often seen as the horned hunting and dancing God of the forest and plains. The Goddess is often characterized as the divine Mother of all life, the young maiden, and the wise grandmother. Beyond the God and Goddess, Wiccans recognize the existence of a being that is both male and female, the source of all things.[1]

This statement contradicts itself. After claiming that wiccans believe nothing, it lists a number of wiccan beliefs. This example illustrates the loose thinking and logic often found in witchcraft. Let's look at some of the teachings that characterize this deceptive form of the occult.

1. Witches worship fertility __deities__.

Wiccans worship the Lord and the Lady, terms for the impersonal male and female fertility deities who created the world. According to wiccans, these deities are the positive and negative manifestations of the divine force that fills the universe.

The Lord is the male horned deity who is worshiped from June 21 to December 21. Different branches of witchcraft use different names to refer to the horned god, who is called Cernunnas in the Gardnerian tradition, Karnayna in the Alexandrian tradition, and Kernunnos or Hern the Hunter in the Celtic tradition. Wiccans deny that their male horned deity is similar to the devil of Christianity and insist that the two are not the same.

The Lady is the earth goddess, the female deity who is worshiped from December 21 to June 21. The Lady is a fertility deity who manifests herself in three ways: as virgin, mother, and crone. These three forms are revealed in the changing seasons of the year—spring, summer, and autumn—reflecting the cycle of sowing, growth and harvest. Other deities are also acknowledged at various seasonal festivals.

Wiccans often explain that they practice a fertility religion, believing that this makes their religion legitimate and acceptable. However, fertility religions were strongly condemned by the biblical writers. The true God of the Bible requires rigorous and complete devotion: " 'If you ever forget the Lord your God and follow other gods and worship and bow down to them, I testify against you today that you will surely be destroyed' " (Deut. 8:19, NIV). The first commandment given the nation of Israel was " 'You shall have no other gods before me' " (Ex. 20:3, NIV). Exodus 23:13 forbids even mentioning a pagan god's name. The prophet Jonah summed up the futility of worshiping pagan deities:

"Those who cling to worthless idols
   forfeit the grace that could be theirs" (Jonah 2:8, NIV).

2. Witchcraft embraces __New__ __Age__ teachings.

Witchcraft shares several similarities with the New Age movement.

1. *Impersonal deity.* Like New Age followers, most witches understand deity as an impersonal force, power, or universal spirit that pervades all things and all people, not a personal, involved God. Witches "see the Lord and the Lady as aspects of this universal force."[2]

2. *Monism.* Witches accept the Hindu concept of monism, although most do not use the philosophical term. Selena Fox has written, "I also honor Divine Oneness, the Unity of All."[3] Silver RavenWolf states: "We believe that if we take something from someone else, we are really taking from ourselves. Stealing from ourselves would be stupid."[4] "One of the biggest secrets in the Craft is: We are all one. That's the Great Mystery. We all connect—people, plants, and animals. All these things, including the planet we live on, become sacred to us. Witches believe that if you hurt someone, you really hurt yourself; therefore, we don't try to harm anyone or anything."[5]

3. *Pantheism.* Most wiccans espouse pantheism, the belief that everything is divine. Selena Fox writes: "I acknowledge that the Divine is everywhere and in everything. I honor the Divine that is within the oak tree on the hill, in the herbs in the garden, in the wild birds singing in the trees, in the rock outcroppings on the hillside, in myself, and yes, even in 'things' such as my car, cameras, and computer."[6] The type of pantheism adopted by most witches also includes elements of animism and polytheism. Animism is the idea that inanimate objects have a conscious life or spirit within them. Polytheism is the belief in or worship of more than one deity.

4. *Reincarnation and karma.* Witches have adopted the New Age concepts of reincarnation and the law of *karma*. Reincarnation teaches that after death, every person is reborn and lives another life in a new body. The quality of the next life is determined by the law of *karma*, the Hindu teaching that a person's good actions earn a better life and bad actions result in a lower station in the next life. Witches believe that because we are responsible for our actions, we will pay either in this life or in the next life for bad things we do.

   You saw in a previous session that the Bible opposes all of these New Age teachings. God is not an impersonal force but a personal, loving God who relates to us as Father, Son, and Holy Spirit. Furthermore, there is only one God, the one true God of the Bible (see Deut. 4:35). The biblical account of creation refutes monism and pantheism by distinguishing between Creator and the created, as well as between the various components of God's creation (see Gen. 1).

   An incident in Jesus' life has direct implications for the wiccan belief in *karma*. When Jesus was asked why a man was born blind, Jesus said, " 'Neither this man nor his parents sinned, but this happened so that the work of God might be displayed in his life' " (John 9:3, NIV). Jesus' answer indicates that bad things do not necessarily happen because of sin in an individual's life. Therefore, it is not possible for sin in a previous life to cause bad things to happen in a present life.

Hebrews 9:27 denies the possibility of reincarnation by teaching that people are destined to die only once: "Just as man is destined to die once, and after that to face judgment" (NIV).

3. Witchcraft is ____hostile____ to Christianity.

Many witches express anger and hostility toward Christianity, often making it difficult for Christians to witness to them. Leo Martello's attack against the Bible is typical of the animosity many wiccans hold against Christianity: "Then too, if the Bible is 'the living word of God,' that God is totally unreliable, one who is constantly contradicting Himself. The Bible's wording is so vague that we now have hundreds of different and opposing churches calling themselves Christian, all claiming to base their beliefs on the 'Good Book.' "[7]

Christians know that the Bible is not contradictory when properly interpreted and understood. It is the perfect record of God's revelation to us (see 2 Tim. 3:16-17). Our response to witches' hostility must be one of love. Jesus taught us to love our enemies and to pray for those who persecute us (see Matt. 5:44). Our concern must be for the eternal souls of those who have been deceived by the false teachings of witchcraft.

4. Witchcraft denies a belief in ____Satan____.

All wiccan groups agree that they do not worship Satan. Witches reject the Christian worldview, so they believe in neither the God of the Bible nor Satan. They emphatically reject that they worship Satan, claiming that a belief in the devil is a Christian invention. According to Silver RavenWolf,

> Evil, as much as we'd like to lay blame elsewhere, does not belong to some strange entity floating around, rubbing its clawed hands in delight, salivating about what it can force us to do. It is my firm belief that we humans create the evil in the world and are too chicken to take responsibility for what our minds, hearts, and hands have wrought in negative circumstances. Humans find great joy in laying the responsibility on some mythical being rather than owning up to what we have, in error, created ourselves.[8]

In reality, Christians do not blame Satan for their evil thoughts and acts. Because of our inherited sinful nature, humans can and often do commit evil without the devil's assistance. We also know that we must take responsibility for our sins. But unlike wiccans, Christians believe the biblical teachings about the existence and work of the evil one. Unfortunately for those involved in wicca, someone does not have to believe in the devil in order to serve him. First Corinthians 10:20 indicates that "the sacrifices of pagans are offered to demons, not to God" (NIV).

5. _____**Magick**_____ *is basic to witchcraft.*

Wiccans claim to be able to cast spells and work occult magic, usually spelled *magick* to distinguish it from sleight-of-hand tricks. They define *spell* as "a thought projection used to produce a desired result."[9] Some occult magicians distinguish between two types of magic.

- _____**Black**_____ magick attempts to hurt or harm others. It involves the direct solicitation and help of evil spirits.
- _____**White**_____ magick attempts to help others and involves good spirits or forces in nature. Most witches call themselves white magicians and warn that evil wished on someone is often repaid many times.

Witches are supposed to keep a personal book of shadows. Also called a *grimoire*, this book is a collection of magical spells and rituals. Magick depends heavily on symbolism. Certain materials, such as salt and iron, as well as colors and numbers are said to have magical powers. A link between casting the spell and the intended victim is said to be important. For example, blood, hair, nail clippings, or an item of clothing from the victim is said to heighten the power of the magic. Words like the well-known *abracadabra* are believed to be powerful. Things that are backward, upside down, broken, or torn, such as an inverted or broken cross or the Lord's Prayer recited backward, are linked with magick.

The Bible shows that magick is part of pagan religion that is opposed to God (see Gen. 41:8; Ex. 9:11; Dan. 2:27-28; Acts 13:6-11; 19:19-20). The Bible also warns against any involvement in occult activity (see Ex. 22:18; Deut. 18:9-14, 2 Kings 9:22; 21:6; 2 Chron. 33:6). Christians believe that all occult magick is evil, whether black or white magick. Occult magick is the opposite of Christian love in that it attempts to force God or other powers to do the magician's will. Whereas Christ taught that a person should give of self for others (see John 3:16), magick and witchcraft feed the individual's ego and personal desires.

The existence of the devil is a reality that is attested to in Scripture (see John 8:44; 10:10; 1 Pet. 5:8). Those involved in witchcraft or other forms of the occult open themselves to the influence of the demonic.

SAY IT

Step 4 (10 mins.)

Ask accountability partners to practice sharing the *Invitation* portion of the FAITH Visit Outline with each other.

Direct participants to turn to page 190 in their Journals and to fill in the blanks as you summarize Witnessing to Wiccans. Use the computer presentation or the overhead cel.

Witnessing to Wiccans

Witnessing to Wiccans

1. Make ____spiritual____ preparation.

Although wiccans do not acknowledge Satan's existence, he is the one they serve. When you witness to wiccans, you are engaging in spiritual warfare. Prepare yourself through diligent prayer and immersion in the truths of God's Word.

2. Don't be ____afraid____.

When witnessing to those who are involved in witchcraft, you have no reason to be afraid: "God did not give us a spirit of timidity, but a spirit of power, of love and of self-discipline" (2 Tim. 1:7, NIV). "The one who is in you is greater than the one who is in the world" (1 John 4:4, NIV). Those involved in witchcraft are often afraid of the power of a genuine believer in Christ. While giving out Bibles at a neopagan meeting, I watched as a wiccan picked up a New Testament. When the woman realized that the book she was holding was a part of the Christian Bible, she began shaking, first her hands and then her whole body. She threw down the New Testament and ran away in fear.

3. Be ____gentle____ and ____loving____.

Although you must be bold in witnessing to those involved in witchcraft, you must also be gentle and loving. Your real enemy is not the wiccan but Satan, who has blinded the witch to God's truth. God loves sinners and wants their salvation (see 2 Pet. 3:9). This includes those who have committed the sin of witchcraft. "Always be prepared to give an answer to everyone who asks you to give the reason for the hope that you have. But do this with gentleness and respect" (1 Pet. 3:15, NIV).

4. Introduce the ____personal____ God of Scripture.

Wiccan's New Age concept of God and their worship of fertility deities thwart their openness to a personal God who loves them. Use biblical teachings on God's nature to dispel their misunderstandings and to show that God desires a personal relationship with them through Jesus.

5. Issue a warning of God's ____judgment____.

Warn the wiccan of God's judgment that will fall on all who do not turn in faith to the Lord Jesus. The Bible clearly teaches that those who die without Christ will spend eternity in hell (see Matt. 25:46; Luke 16:19-31; 2 Pet. 2:9; Heb. 2:2-3).

6. Proclaim Christ's power to break the hold of ___evil___.

Persons involved in witchcraft are caught in a web of fear and demonic power. Only Christ can break the stronghold of evil in a person's life (see John 8:32-36; 16:33; 1 John 4:4,18). He who overcame death and Satan has the power to cancel sin and break the power of evil in the lives of those who repent and accept Him in faith (see Col. 2:13-15). Use the FAITH gospel presentation to lead the person to salvation.

Visitation Time

Do It

1. As you visit, view the lost persons you meet with the same sense of urgency you would have for your own family members.
2. On the way to visit, ask Team members what they felt and thought when they looked at the *Step of Faith* picture.
3. Part of your discipling role is to turn over the responsibility to Learners. All Team members should know the FAITH presentation through **Invitation**. Prepare them to take the lead and present most if not all of the presentation.

Celebration Time

Share It

1. Ask a Team member to take the lead in sharing reports.
2. Hear reports and testimonies.
3. Complete Evaluation Cards.
4. Complete Participation Cards.
5. Update visitation forms with the results of visits.

STUDY IT

Step 6 (5 mins.)

Overview Home Study Assignments for session 11.

Transition to assemble with FAITH Teams to prepare for home visits. (5 mins.)

DO IT (110 MINS.)

SHARE IT (30 MINS.)

Home Study Assignments

Home Study Assignments reinforce this session by helping you apply what you have learned.

Your Discipleship Journey

Journaling activities in Your Discipleship Journey are an important part of your development as a Great Commission Christian through FAITH training.

1. One deception of witchcraft is monism, the belief that people, plants, and animals are all one. Record how the following Scriptures refute this belief.

   Genesis 1:25-26: _____

   Psalm 8:3-8: _____

   Psalm 24:1-5: _____

   Psalm 100:3: _____

   Psalm 139:13: _____

   Matthew 6:26-30: _____

   Luke 1:26-35: _____

   _____

2. Match each Scripture with the false teaching of witchcraft it refutes.
   ___ 1. Genesis 9:3-6   a. *karma*
   ___ 2. Exodus 20:1-5   b. magic
   ___ 3. Deuteronomy 18:9-12   c. monism
   ___ 4. John 9:1-3   d. reincarnation
   ___ 5. Hebrews 9:27   e. pantheism

3. Believers have no reason to fear witches. Match the following Scriptures with the correct promises of divine protection.
   ___ 1. Romans 8:31   a. God, who is in you, is greater than the one
   ___ 2. Ephesians 6:10-18   who is in the world.
   ___ 3. James 4:7   b. If God is for you, who can be against you?
   ___ 4. 1 Peter 5:8-10   c. Submit to God and resist the devil.
   ___ 5. 1 John 4:4   d. Put on the full armor of God.
                              e. Be self-controlled and alert. Resist the devil and stand firm. God will make you strong.

Growing as a Life Witness

Growing as a Life Witness reminds you of your responsibility to witness and minister to others during the week.

1. Talk or meet with your accountability partner and share ways you have cultivated a lost person or have witnessed or ministered on occasions other than FAITH visits.
2. Discuss ways you can apply the session 11 content.
3. Pray for lost persons by name and for each other.

Prayer Concerns	Answers to Prayer
_____	_____
_____	_____
_____	_____
_____	_____
_____	_____

Your Weekly Sunday School Leadership Meeting

A FAITH participant is an important member of Sunday School. Encourage Team members who are elected Sunday School leaders to attend this weekly meeting. Use this section to record ways your FAITH Team influences the work of your Sunday School class or department. Use the information to report during weekly Sunday School leadership meetings. Identify actions that need to be taken through Sunday School as a result of prayer concerns, needs identified, visits made by the Team, and decisions made by the persons visited. Also identify ways you can disciple others in your Sunday School class or department and in your church.

1. Highlight FAITH visit reports and discuss ways they affect your class/department or age group. Especially highlight results of any evangelistic visits.

_____

_____

_____

_____

2. Indicate any individuals/families who might attend on Sunday as a result of FAITH ministry visits. Will a FAITH Team member meet the guest?

How will other class members help newcomers feel at home? If any calls to class members or to prospects need to be made before Sunday, make assignments.

_____

_____

_____

3. Participate with others on your leadership team in evaluating the previous session and in discussing ways Sunday's lesson can involve members and guests in transformational Bible study and discipleship.

_____

_____

_____

4. Pray for your teacher(s), department director, and others on the leadership team. Intentionally pray for all FAITH Learners, who are at the height of their memory work and leadership in home visits.

_____

_____

_____

Discipling Your Team Members

This weekly feature suggests actions the Team Leader can take to support Team members, prepare for Team Time, and improve visits. This work is part of the Team Leader's Home Study Assignments. Add any actions suggested by your church's FAITH strategy.

Support Team Members
❑ Contact Team members during the week. Remind them that you are praying for them. Discuss prayer concerns and answers to prayer.
❑ Pray about concerns shared by Team members.

Prepare to Lead Team Time
❑ Preview Leading Team Time for session 12.

Prepare to Lead Visits

❑ Review the FAITH Visit Outline.
❑ Be prepared to explain the benefits of and procedures for making ministry visits.
❑ Be prepared to model a visit in which Team member(s) are asked to lead in a visit to the point of the letter *H* (HEAVEN).
❑ Be prepared to lead your Team to participate during Celebration Time.

Link with Sunday School

❑ Participate in your weekly Sunday School leadership meeting. Share pertinent information in this meeting, using Your Weekly Sunday School Leadership Meeting (pp. 193–94) and FAITH-visit results.
❑ Witchcraft is a self-centered system that attempts to control others through magick and to manipulate the forces of nature. In contrast, your Sunday School can teach believers to keep Christ at the center of their lives and to express their love for Him through sacrificial service to others.

For Further Growth: The Worship of Jesus Christ

For Further Growth may include additional reading or activities that will enhance your growth as a disciple and a discipler of others. These assignments are intended to be long-term projects and do not have to be completed during this semester of study.

1. A fundamental truth of the Old Testament is that only God is to be worshiped. Examine these Scriptures and note what they say about the worship of God: Exodus 34:14; Deuteronomy 6:4-5,13; Psalm 22:27.
2. Read the following passages and note from whom Jesus received worship: Matthew 2:2,11; 8:2; 14:33; 28:9; John 9:3-8; 20:28; Hebrews 1:6.
3. Read the following resource.
   - Millard J. Erickson, *The Word Became Flesh*, part 3, "The Construction of a Contemporary Incarnational Christology," chapter 18, "The New Testament Witness Regarding Jesus' Deity" (Grand Rapids: Baker, 1991), 455–80.

---

[1]"Some Questions and Answers about Wicca," pamphlet (North Hollywood: United Wiccan Church, n.d.), 1.
[2]Silver RavenWolf, *Teen Witch: Wicca for a New Generation* (St. Paul: Llewellyn, 1998), 17.
[3]Selena Fox, "I Am Pagan," (Mt. Horeb: Circle Sanctuary, 1992), 2.
[4]RavenWolf, *Teen Witch*, 14.
[5]Ibid., 21–22.
[6]Fox, "I Am Pagan," 2.
[7]Leo Louis Martello, *Witchcraft: The Old Religion* (Secaucus: Citadel, n.d.), 16.
[8]RavenWolf, *Teen Witch*, 11.
[9]Witches' League for Public Awareness, untitled brochure, 1.

Answers to matching activities on page 192:
Activity 2: 1. c, 2. e, 3. b, 4. a, 5. d
Activity 3: 1. b, 2. d, 3. c, 4. e, 5. a

FAITH AT WORK

In the midst of seeing people come to the Lord, seeing new believers baptized, and watching new Christians grow in the knowledge of Christ, a little discouragement can sneak in under the radar. One too many unanswered doorbells. Another rejection at the end of my well-rehearsed and impressively delivered FAITH presentation. "Please, God," I prayed, "let someone respond tonight."

My FAITH Team arrived at our prospect's home. We were welcomed inside and had a seat. A young child on the floor was making all kinds of noise and doing his best to steal the show. Of course, he was competing against a blaring television. I didn't see a place on the floor to play with him and distract him so that the other Team members could initiate a deeper conversation.

We visited for a while and then began our presentation. You know that the atmosphere isn't conducive for evangelism when your own foot is tapping to the music screaming from the TV. During the entire presentation the commotion continued, and it got worse. No decisions. Another rejection.

We left the family a Bible and some information about our church. I quickly wrote down a phone number and squeaked out an invitation to church and Sunday School before the door was closed. Then we all looked at one another and, as if on cue, said, "Well, that sure seemed like a waste of time!"

"O ye of little faith"—are those the Master's words? Since that evening the couple has come to our church, and both adults in the family have accepted the Lord, have been baptized, and are now involved in our Sunday school class. The visit that seemed to be going nowhere was going just where God had intended. He is faithful when we are obedient. His Word does not come back empty. FAITH, like life, isn't always about seeing an immediate result. It's often about learning to trust God with what we consider failures and successes. It's about a relationship with Him. It's hard to be discouraged about that.

Wanda Hargrave
Immanuel Baptist Church
Highland, California

Practicing FAITH

In this session you will—

CHECK IT by spending the entire time in extended Team Time/ practice activities;

STUDY IT by overviewing Home Study Assignments;

DO IT by making visits in which a Team member may take the lead;

SHARE IT by celebrating.

IN ADVANCE

• Decide whether you wish to help Teams practice by reviewing previously viewed video segments of the FAITH Visit Outline from *A Journey in FAITH*.

• Pray for Team members as they begin taking the lead in visits.

TEAM TIME

CHECK IT (60 MINS.)

CHECK IT agenda:
✔ FAITH Visit Outline

Leading Team Time

All Teams remain together during this session for an extended Team Time. All Team members participate in Team Time. They are primarily responsible for reciting the assigned portion of the FAITH Visit Outline and for discussing other Home Study Assignments.

As you direct this important time of CHECK IT activities with your Team, keep in mind that Learners look to you as a role model, motivator, mentor, and friend. Team Time activities can continue in the car as the Team travels to and from visits.

Lead CHECK IT Activities

✔ FAITH Visit Outline

Spend the entire time with your Team members, leading them to practice the entire FAITH Visit Outline. Consider rehearsing appropriate approaches to take in strengthening the skills and confidence of Learners in leading the visit. It may be helpful to suggest that the Team role-play several situations your Team or others have encountered during FAITH training.

FAITH Visit Outline

Preparation

INTRODUCTION
INTERESTS
INVOLVEMENT

Church Experience/Background
- Ask about the person's church background.
- Listen for clues about the person's spiritual involvement.

Sunday School Testimony
- Tell general benefits of Sunday School.
- Tell a current personal experience.

Evangelistic Testimony
- Tell a little of your preconversion experience.
- Say: "I had a life-changing experience."
- Tell recent benefits of your conversion.

INQUIRY

Key Question: In your personal opinion, what do you understand it takes for a person to go to heaven?

Possible Answers: Faith, works, unclear, no opinion

Transition Statement: I'd like to share with you how the Bible answers this question, if it is all right. There is a word that can be used to answer this question: FAITH (spell out on fingers).

Presentation

F is for FORGIVENESS
We cannot have eternal life and heaven without God's forgiveness.
"In Him [meaning Jesus] we have redemption through His blood, the forgiveness of sins"—Ephesians 1:7a, NKJV.

A is for AVAILABLE
Forgiveness is available. It is—

AVAILABLE FOR ALL
"For God so loved the world that He gave His only begotten Son, that whoever believes in Him should not perish but have everlasting life"—John 3:16, NKJV.

BUT NOT AUTOMATIC
"Not everyone who says to Me, 'Lord, Lord,' shall enter the kingdom of heaven"—Matthew 7:21a, NKJV.

I is for IMPOSSIBLE

It is impossible for God to allow sin into heaven.

GOD IS—
- LOVE
  John 3:16, NKJV
- JUST
  "For judgment is without mercy"—James 2:13a, NKJV.

MAN IS SINFUL

"For all have sinned and fall short of the glory of God"—Romans 3:23, NKJV.

Question: But how can a sinful person enter heaven, where God allows no sin?

T is for TURN

Question: If you were driving down the road and someone asked you to turn, what would he or she be asking you to do? (change direction)
Turn means *repent.*
TURN from something—sin and self
"But unless you repent you will all likewise perish"—Luke 13:3b, NKJV.
TURN to Someone; trust Christ only
(The Bible tells us that) *"Christ died for our sins according to the Scriptures, and that He was buried, and that He rose again the third day according to the Scriptures"—1 Corinthians 15:3b-4, NKJV.*
"If you confess with your mouth the Lord Jesus and believe in your heart that God has raised Him from the dead, you will be saved"—Romans 10:9, NKJV.

H is for HEAVEN

Heaven is eternal life.
HERE
"I have come that they may have life, and that they may have it more abundantly"—John 10:10b, NKJV.
HEREAFTER
"And if I go and prepare a place for you, I will come again and receive you to Myself; that where I am, there you may be also"—John 14:3, NKJV.
HOW
How can a person have God's forgiveness, heaven and eternal life, and Jesus as personal Savior and Lord?
Explain based on leaflet picture, FAITH (Forsaking All, I Trust Him), Romans 10:9.

Invitation

INQUIRE

Understanding what we have shared, would you like to receive this forgiveness by trusting in Christ as your personal Savior and Lord?

INVITE

- Pray to accept Christ.
- Pray for commitment/recommitment.
- Invite to join Sunday School.

INSURE

- Use A *Step of Faith* to insure decision.
- Personal Acceptance
- Sunday School Enrollment
- Public Confession

Visitation Time

Do It

1. Throughout FAITH you have been preparing your Team members to take the lead in a visit. Make sure Team members are informed that they will take the lead in specific visits.
2. As always, be prepared to assist, but do everything you can to encourage Team members to lead the entire visit. Encourage and support them when they make mistakes.

Celebration Time

Share It

1. Ask a Team member to take the lead in sharing reports.
2. Hear reports and testimonies.
3. Complete Evaluation Cards.
4. Complete Participation Cards.
5. Update visitation forms with the results of visits.

STUDY IT

Overview Home Study Assignments for session 12. (5 mins.)

Transition to prepare for home visits. (5 mins.)

DO IT (110 MINS.)

SHARE IT (30 MINS.)

Home Study Assignments

Home Study Assignments reinforce this session by helping you apply what you have learned.

Your Discipleship Journey

Journaling activities in Your Discipleship Journey are an important part of your development as a Great Commission Christian through FAITH training.

1. This week's practice session presents a good opportunity to review some habits that every growing disciple needs. Start by matching the following verses with their teachings about prayer.

     ___ 1. 1 Chronicles 16:11   a. Always pray and don't give up.
     ___ 2. Matthew 7:7   b. Watch and pray to avoid temptation.
     ___ 3. Matthew 26:41   c. Pray continually.
     ___ 4. Luke 18:1   d. Always seek the Lord.
     ___ 5. Ephesians 6:18   e. Pray in the Spirit with all kinds
     ___ 6. 1 Thessalonians 5:17   of requests.
                                         f. Ask, seek, and knock.

2. Summarize what the following verses teach that would help you grow as a Great Commission Christian.

   Psalm 119:11: _____

   _____

   2 Timothy 2:15: _____

   _____

   _____

   2 Timothy 4:1-5: _____

   _____

   _____

   1 Peter 3:15: _____

   _____

Growing as a Life Witness

Growing as a Life Witness reminds you of your responsibility to witness and minister to others during the week.

1. Talk or meet with your accountability partner and share ways you have cultivated a lost person or have witnessed or ministered on occasions other than FAITH visits.
2. Pray for lost persons by name and for each other.

Prayer Concerns	Answers to Prayer
_____	_____
_____	_____
_____	_____
_____	_____
_____	_____

Your Weekly Sunday School Leadership Meeting

A FAITH participant is an important member of Sunday School. Encourage Team members who are elected Sunday School leaders to attend this weekly meeting. Use this section to record ways your FAITH Team influences the work of your Sunday School class or department. Use the information to report during weekly Sunday School leadership meetings. Identify actions that need to be taken through Sunday School as a result of prayer concerns, needs identified, visits made by the Team, and decisions made by the persons visited. Also identify ways you can disciple others in your Sunday School class or department and in your church.

1. As a result of FAITH visits this week, have any ministry needs surfaced? Any cultivation opportunities? Any need to share information with other departments or age groups for appropriate follow-up? Record actions that need to be taken.

   _____

   _____

   _____

2. When Christians who have previously been reluctant to share their faith become confident and intentional in doing so, 2 Timothy 2:1-2 is made personal. Celebrate as a group if any Learners took the lead in a FAITH

visit and had the opportunity to share the FAITH gospel presentation. How did that Learner respond to that opportunity?

_____

_____

_____

3. With others on your leadership team, evaluate last week's session. Discuss ways Sunday's lesson can involve members and guests in transformational Bible study and discipleship.

_____

_____

_____

4. Evaluate the extent to which department/class leaders and members are following up on prospects being contacted through FAITH visits. What actions need to be started or strengthened to better assimilate newcomers into the Sunday School department or class?

_____

_____

_____

5. Pray for your teacher(s) and department director. Also pray for individuals who are considering decisions for Christ. Record names here.

_____

_____

_____

Discipling Your Team Members

This weekly feature suggests actions the Team Leader can take to support Team members, prepare for Team Time, and improve visits. This work is part of the Team Leader's Home Study Assignments. Add any actions suggested by your church's FAITH strategy.

Support Team Members

❑ Pray for and personally follow up on any Learner who may need personal encouragement.

❑ Contact Team members during the week to remind them that you are praying for them and to discuss their participation in FAITH.

❑ Learners are taking the lead in making the visits from this point on. Look for opportunities to encourage each Team member about ways he or she is successfully leading in the visit. Continue to identify ways each Learner can improve.

Prepare to Lead Time Time

❑ Preview Leading Team Time for session 13.

Prepare to Participate in Visits

❑ Review the FAITH Visit Outline.

❑ Identify the Team member who will be responsible for leading specific visits.

❑ Be prepared to lead your Team to participate during Celebration Time. Look for ways to encourage Team members to take the lead in reporting during Celebration Time.

Link with Sunday School

❑ Participate in your weekly Sunday School leadership meeting. Share pertinent information in this meeting, using Your Weekly Sunday School Leadership Meeting (pp. 203–4) and FAITH-visit results.

For Further Growth: The Offices of Jesus Christ

For Further Growth may include additional reading or activities that will enhance your growth as a disciple and a discipler of others. These assignments are intended to be long-term projects and do not have to be completed during this semester of study.

1. As a diamond is a single object with many facets, Jesus is characterized in the Bible by the three offices of prophet, priest, and king. Note the ways these offices describe Jesus in the following passages.
   • Prophet: Matthew 21:11; Luke 24:19; John 4:19
   • Priest: John 17; Hebrews 4:14-16; 8:1
   • King: John 12:14-15; 1 Timothy 6:14-15; Revelation 19:16

2. Read the following resource.
   • R. C. Sproul, *Essential Truths of the Christian Faith*, part 4, "Jesus Christ," chapter 35, "The Threefold Office of Christ" (Wheaton: Tyndale, 1992), 101–2.

Answers to matching activity on page 202: 1. d, 2. f, 3. b, 4. a, 5. e, 6. c

FAITH AT WORK

One Sunday night I introduced myself to a woman seated in the pew behind me. Dee told me that this was her first time to visit our church and introduced me to her two young children. I asked her, "Would you give me your address so that we can come to visit you on Tuesday night?" She replied that she would be glad to. Immediately after the service I rushed off to greet a friend and forgot to get Dee's address.

On the following Tuesday night when my FAITH Team and I received our assignments, the first place we visited was an apartment building. When Dee answered the door, we knew it was a divine appointment. She was elated that we were visiting her when she didn't know that anyone knew her address. After explaining that she had looked for me after the service on Sunday but couldn't find me, she exclaimed, "God must have sent you!"

While visiting, we learned that Dee was already a Christian. Recently divorced, she had moved here from another state. Her apartment was nice, but she had no furniture. I sat in a lawn chair she brought in from the garage while she and my Team members leaned against the wall. We prayed with her, and my Team members asked if we could supply her with some furniture. She quickly agreed, at the same time praising the Lord for a comfortable place to live.

Later at Celebration Time we described the way God had orchestrated our visit and reported Dee's need for furniture. Before we left, many people expressed a desire to donate items. My Team members made arrangements to pick up the donations on the following Saturday and deliver them to Dee's apartment. She was overwhelmed. Now she and her children are attending Sunday School and discipleship activities at our church. This ministry visit blessed not only Dee and her children but also those of us God so clearly led to meet this family's needs.

Lena Jackson
Immanuel Baptist Church
Highland, California

The Roman Catholic Church

BILL GORDON

In this session you will—

CHECK IT by engaging in Team Time activities;

KNOW IT by reviewing content from session 11;

HEAR IT by examining Roman Catholic beliefs and by learning ways

to witness to Roman Catholics;

STUDY IT by overviewing Home Study Assignments;

DO IT by leading your Team in making visits;

SHARE IT by celebrating.

IN ADVANCE
- Overview content.
- Preview teaching suggestions. Prepare key points. Decide whether to use the session 13 computer presentation or the overhead cels.
- Prepare the room for teaching.
- Pray for participants and for Teams as they prepare to visit.
- As Teaching Time begins, direct participants to open their Journals to page 210.

TEAM TIME

CHECK IT (15 MINS.)

If the computer presentation is used, display the agenda frame for Team Time. Add other points as needed.

CHECK IT agenda:
✔ FAITH Visit Outline
✔ Session 11 Debriefing
✔ Help for Strengthening a Visit

Leading Team Time

All Team members participate in Team Time. They are primarily responsible for reciting the assigned portion of the FAITH Visit Outline and for discussing other Home Study Assignments.

As you direct this important time of CHECK IT activities with your Team, keep in mind that Learners look to you as a role model, motivator, mentor, and friend. Team Time activities can continue in the car as the Team travels to and from visits.

Lead CHECK IT Activities

✔ FAITH *Visit Outline*
❑ Listen while each Learner recites the FAITH Visit Outline. Because there is no new memory work, it may be best to ask Learners to recite the segment they have the most difficulty sharing during a visit.

✔ *Session 11 Debriefing*
❑ Because session 12 was a practice session with no new material, debrief session 11. Session 11 focused on the important time when a person is given the opportunity to personally accept God's forgiveness and salvation, so it is important that Team members be well trained. It is even more important that they grow in their sensitivity to the Holy Spirit's prompting during visitation.
❑ Discuss ways Team members are finding A *Step of Faith* helpful in prompting discussion in a visit. If time permits, allow Team members to practice the **Invitation**, using A *Step of Faith*.

✔ *Help for Strengthening a Visit*
❑ Discuss difficulties the Team has encountered in leading someone to hear and consider the FAITH gospel presentation. Evaluate ways the Team responded to selected experiences and identify appropriate ways to improve responses. Indicate that although most visits go smoothly, next week's session will help all Team members better handle challenges in a visit. Difficulties are things that happen or are said that could keep you from sharing the gospel and leading someone who is ready to respond to make a commitment to Christ. Principles for dealing with difficulties relate primarily to building bridges of relationships with the person, dealing with questions and objections, and working through the obstacles and distractions that take place.
❑ As you talk with Team members during the week, share ways you are seeking to take advantage of your daily-life witnessing opportunities. Also talk with them about opportunities they have to share the gospel during the week with persons they encounter.

Notes

_____

_____

_____

_____

_____

_____

_____

_____

_____

Actions I Need to Take with Team Members This Week

_____

_____

_____

_____

_____

_____

_____

_____

_____

Transition to classrooms for instruction
on the content of the session. (5 mins.)

KNOW IT

Direct participants to locate A Quick Review on page 210 in their Journals and to complete the activities. Then give the answers, using the computer presentation or the overhead cel.

A Quick Review

HEAR IT

Ask participants to fill in the blanks as you present the key points in Shaped by Tradition. Use the computer presentation or the overhead cel.

Shaped by Tradition

A Quick Review

Recall the beliefs of witchcraft, which you studied in session 11, as you mark each statement *T* for true or *F* for false.

- **T** 1. Witches worship fertility deities.
- **F** 2. Witches worship the one true God.
- **F** 3. Wiccans worship the Lord and Lady as Jesus and Mary.
- **F** 4. Witchcraft rejects New Age teachings.
- **T** 5. Witchcraft embraces New Age teachings.
- **T** 6. Witchcraft is hostile to Christianity.
- **F** 7. Witchcraft joins Christian efforts because of common beliefs.
- **F** 8. Like Christians, wiccans rely on the Bible as their authority.
- **F** 9. Wiccans worship Satan.
- **T** 10. Witchcraft denies a belief in Satan.
- **T** 11. Magick is basic to witchcraft.
- **F** 12. Wiccans reject magick as a practice of early Judaism.

Check appropriate principles for witnessing to wiccans.
- ☑ 1. Make spiritual preparation.
- ❑ 2. Be careful of the spells a witch might cast on you.
- ❑ 3. Remind them of what happened in Salem.
- ☑ 4. Don't be afraid.
- ❑ 5. Avoid contact with wiccans.
- ☑ 6. Be gentle and loving.
- ☑ 7. Introduce the personal God of Scripture.
- ☑ 8. Issue a warning of God's judgment.
- ❑ 9. Seek to win their favor through white magick.
- ☑ 10. Proclaim Christ's power to break the hold of evil.

Shaped by Tradition

As a FAITH witness, you are very likely to encounter many people from a Roman Catholic background, for about __**75**__ __**million**__ of the world's __**800**__ __**million**__ Roman Catholics live in North America. It is important to be aware of Roman Catholic beliefs as you share the biblical message of salvation with the Roman Catholics God brings into your life.

The Roman Catholic Church has a long history. After the deaths of the apostles in the first century A.D., a hierarchical system slowly began to develop in the early church with the appearance of __**bishops**__. In the Latin-speaking church, situated in the western part of the Roman Empire, the bishop of Rome was considered the supreme bishop of the church. The Greek-speaking church, located in the eastern part of the

Roman Empire, never accepted the superiority of the bishop of Rome. The **Great** **Schism** of 1054 formalized the separation between the Roman Catholic Church in the west and the Eastern Orthodox Church, which will be the subject of session 14, in the east.

Most evangelical scholars place the genesis of the Roman Catholic Church with the reign of **Pope** **Gregory** **I**. In A.D. 590 Gregory I secured the supremacy of the bishop of Rome in the western church. Even after power was consolidated in the Roman bishop, it took many years for the beliefs of the contemporary Roman Catholic Church to develop. Belief in purgatory developed in the sixth century, while prayer to Mary and the saints was regularly practiced by the beginning of the seventh century. The requirement that priests could not marry began in 1079. Belief in seven sacraments was formally recognized in 1439.

Roman Catholic Beliefs

It is easier to share the gospel with Roman Catholics than with persons of other religious backgrounds because evangelical Christians share many beliefs in common with Roman Catholics that allow them to understand us when we explain the gospel. For example, Roman Catholics regard God as the all-knowing and all-powerful Creator. They also believe in the triune nature of God and affirm His attributes as revealed in Scripture. Those with a Roman Catholic background also share our beliefs about Jesus. Roman Catholics affirm Jesus' complete deity and humanity. They believe that Jesus is the second person of the Trinity and the promised Messiah of the Old Testament, who was born of the virgin Mary, lived a sinless life, died on the cross, was laid in a grave, and was resurrected from the dead through God's power. They believe that Jesus then ascended into heaven, where He sits at the right hand of God the Father.

These common beliefs do not mean that Roman Catholics and evangelical Christians do not have significant areas of disagreement. Over the centuries the Roman Catholic Church has adopted unbiblical teachings that undermine biblical authority and foster misunderstandings about the biblical way to be saved. This session will examine Roman Catholic beliefs in light of biblical truth.

1. Roman Catholics accept extrabiblical sources of **authority**.

A significant area of disagreement between Roman Catholics and evangelical Christians is their source of authority. Roman Catholics accept three sources of authority: the Bible, including the Apocrypha; Church Tradition; and the Magisterium, the teaching ministry of the Church.

1. *The Bible.* Since Vatican II in 1964 the Roman Catholic Church

Step 3 (20 mins.)

Direct participants to turn to page 211 in their Journals and to fill in the blanks as you summarize Roman Catholic Beliefs. Use the computer presentation or the overhead cels.

Roman Catholic Beliefs

has encouraged members to read the Bible. According to the official catechism of the Roman Catholic Church, "Ignorance of the Scriptures is ignorance of Christ."[1] However, while Roman Catholics and evangelical Christians affirm the same books of the New Testament, we disagree about the material that should be included in the Old Testament. In addition to the books of the Bible accepted by evangelical Christians, Roman Catholics add intertestamental writings, called **Apocrypha**, which evangelicals do not accept as inspired by God.

2. *Tradition.* The Roman Catholic Church also uses Church **Tradition** as a source of religious authority. This Tradition does not refer to customs in the Church but rather to the teachings of the apostles that they believe have been preserved apart from what has been recorded in the Scriptures. According to the catechism, "This living transmission, accomplished in the Holy Spirit, is called Tradition, since it is distinct from Sacred Scripture, though closely connected to it."[2]

3. *Magisterium.* The word *Magisterium* refers to the authority claimed by the Church to teach religious **doctrine**. Roman Catholics believe that their Church has the authority to authentically interpret the Bible. Therefore, the pope and bishops are considered divinely authoritative when speaking on faith and morals. According to the catechism, "The faithful receive with docility the teachings and directives that their pastors give them in different forms."[3]

Evangelicals regard only Scripture as the infallible Word of God (see 2 Tim. 3:15-17; 2 Pet. 1:19-21). The Bible warns about the danger of adding to or taking away from Scripture (see Deut. 4:2; Rev. 22:18-19). Jesus cautioned His disciples that tradition can distort God's revelation to humanity (see Matt. 15:2-3,6; Mark 7:8-9,13). Paul warned the Colossians of the hazard of being led off course by pursuing "the tradition of men" (Col. 2:8, NASB). Peter wrote about the "vain conversation received by tradition" (1 Pet. 1:18, KJV). Roman Catholics' Tradition and Magisterium are not equal to God's written revelation. The Bible is the only source of reliable information on spiritual issues.

2. Roman Catholics distinguish between categories of **sin**.

Roman Catholic theology distinguishes between mortal sins and venial sins. A mortal sin is a serious sin that is capable of destroying the grace of God in the Christian who commits it. A mortal sin is also done with *"full knowledge and complete consent."*[4] If a Christian dies with a mortal sin on her soul, she forfeits heaven and experiences the eternal death of hell. Once committed, a mortal sin can be removed only by a priest, who has the power to sacramentally forgive the sin.

According to Roman Catholic theology, venial sins differ from mortal sins in several significant ways. A venial sin is either a less serious sin or a sin that was committed without full consent or reflection. Unlike mortal sins, venial sins do not destroy sanctifying grace. Unfortunately for

Roman Catholics, the line between mortal and venial sins is nebulous.

Roman Catholics believe that although you have committed venial sins, you can rid yourself of them by undergoing a process of purification in purgatory, a place where Christians go after death to become worthy to enter heaven. There is no legitimate biblical basis for the doctrine of purgatory. It is derived from Church Tradition and spurious passages in the Apocrypha. Contrary to this teaching, the Bible teaches that there is "no condemnation for those who are in Christ Jesus" (Rom. 8:1, NIV).

The concepts of venial and mortal sins are not biblical. Apart from the grace of Jesus Christ, even the smallest sin would condemn a person to hell. The Bible teaches that "all have sinned and fall short of the glory of God" (Rom. 3:23, NIV) and that "the wages of sin is death" (Rom. 6:23, NIV). James 2:10 demonstrates the impossibility of venial sins by explaining that someone who keeps the entire law "and yet stumbles at just one point is guilty of breaking all of it" (NIV). The Bible also reveals that even the worst sin cannot destroy Christ's grace in a believer and that a believer cannot lose salvation (see John 10:27-29; 1 Pet. 1:4-5).

3. Salvation is imparted through _____sacraments_____.

Another difference between Roman Catholic and evangelical theology is the way Christ's grace enters the life of an individual. In Roman Catholic theology Christ's grace is imparted to an individual through the seven sacraments of the church: baptism, confirmation, Eucharist, penance, anointing of the sick, holy orders, and marriage. The Roman Catholic Church teaches that the sacraments actually "confer the grace that they signify."[5] In other words, the sacraments actually change a person inwardly through spiritual empowerment. This means that salvation is given through the sacraments. Roman Catholicism teaches that "if anyone says that the sacraments … are not necessary for salvation … and that without them … men obtain from God through faith alone the grace of justification … let him be anathema [divinely cursed]."[6]

Evangelical Christians believe that Christ's grace enters our lives when we believe in the Lord Jesus Christ. This grace is applied directly through the power of the Holy Spirit without any physical mediation (see Acts 10:43; Heb. 7:25,27). The Bible teaches that salvation is by grace through faith alone, entirely apart from works (see Eph. 2:8-9).

Of the seven Roman Catholic sacraments, baptism, confirmation, the Eucharist, and penance will be reviewed here because they are the sacraments that are most likely to arise in witnessing encounters.

4. _____Baptism_____ is necessary for salvation.

According to Roman Catholicism, a person becomes a Christian not by placing faith in the Lord Jesus Christ as personal Savior but by receiving the sacrament of baptism. According to the catechism, "Through Baptism we are freed from sin and reborn as the sons of God; we become members of Christ."[7] The sacrament of baptism is believed to remove sin and its punishment and to provide spiritual rebirth. It is seen as necessary for salvation. Roman Catholic baptism is not believer's baptism. Infant children are baptized. According to the catechism, "The Church and the parents would deny a child the priceless grace of becoming a child of God were they not to confer Baptism shortly after birth."[8]

Baptism, as practiced in the New Testament, is an outward ordinance symbolizing a person's identification with Jesus in His death and resurrection and the person's new life in Christ. Evangelical believers do not trust baptism for salvation. The apostle Paul contrasted baptism with preaching the gospel, indicating that they are not the same: "Christ did not send me to baptize, but to preach the gospel—not with words of human wisdom, lest the cross of Christ be emptied of its power" (1 Cor. 1:17, NIV). When the Philippian jailer asked Paul and Silas how he could be saved, they answered, " 'Believe in the Lord Jesus, and you will be saved' " (Acts 16:31, NIV). All that is necessary for salvation is sincere, personal faith in Jesus Christ.

5. _____Confirmation_____ *bestows the Holy Spirit.*

Roman Catholics are taught that they receive the Holy Spirit in the sacrament of confirmation. According to the catechism, "The essential rite of Confirmation is anointing the forehead of the baptized with sacred chrism ... together with the laying on of the minister's hands and the words: 'Accipe signaculum doni Spiritus Sancti' [Be sealed with the Gift of the Holy Spirit]."[9] The rite of confirmation is said to bring grace, the gifts of the Holy Spirit, spiritual power, and a sealing to the Church. Confirmation illustrates Roman Catholics' assertion that God's spiritual grace and gifts are dispensed only through their Church's sacraments.

The Bible, however, teaches that the Holy Spirit is given to those who believe in Jesus Christ as Savior and Lord (see Rom. 8:9-16). Faith in Christ is the sole criterion for receiving the Holy Spirit. The Bible does not support an intermediary role for the church in this event.

6. *Christ's body is received through the* _____Eucharist_____.

The most important sacrament in the day-to-day life of Roman Catholics is the Eucharist or Mass. Roman Catholics believe that the Eucharist communicates grace to participants by resacrificing Christ and reapplying the benefits of Calvary. Through the miracle of transubstantiation, Roman Catholics believe that they physically receive Christ in the sacrament of the Eucharist. The catechism, quoting the Council of Trent, defines *transubstantiation* in the following way.

> Because Christ our Redeemer said that it was truly his body that he was offering under the species of bread, it has always been the conviction of the Church of God, and this holy

Council now declares again, that by the consecration of the bread and the wine there takes place a change of the whole substance of the bread into the substance of the body of Christ our Lord and of the whole substance of the wine into the substance of his blood. This change the holy Catholic Church has fittingly and properly called transubstantiation.[10]

The Bible does not support Roman Catholics' literal interpretation of biblical accounts of the last supper. A literal interpretation of Matthew 26:26; Mark 14:22; and 1 Corinthians 10:16; 11:23 contradicts the context of Jesus' words. Because Jesus' physical body was present when He said, " 'This is my body' " and " 'This is my blood,' " His words must be taken figuratively. Jesus' words in Luke 22:19, " 'Do this in remembrance of me' " (NIV), convey the idea of a figurative memorial.

In addition, significant theological problems arise if Jesus' words are taken literally. For example, if Jesus' body was literally the bread in Luke 22:19, this would mean that Jesus was present in more than one place at a time. This would have violated the self-imposed limitations of Jesus' incarnation, because a human body cannot be in more than one place at a time. Another theological problem is that if transubstantiation is true, people literally consume Christ's blood in the Eucharist. This directly contradicts the prohibitions against drinking blood in both the Old and New Testaments (see Gen. 9:4; Lev. 3:17; Acts 15:29).

Evangelicals partake of the Lord's Supper as a symbolic act of obedience memorializing Christ's death and anticipating His second coming.

7. __Penance__ *removes the penalty of sins.*
Penance is a sacrament by which Roman Catholics express sorrow for their sins. This sacrament involves confessing mortal sins to a priest, who assigns Roman Catholics an act of penance through which they show the sincerity of their repentance and their desire to make amends. Roman Catholics believe that through penance, mortal sins are removed, and justification before God is restored.

The Bible indicates that believers need to confess their sins to God to maintain fellowship with Him (see 1 John 1:9). No passage in the Bible teaches Christians to confess their sins to priests.

Witnessing to Roman Catholics

1. *Determine whether the person is* __saved__ .
Roman Catholics have been taught that salvation is provided through God's grace, individual faith and works (including suffering in purgatory after death), and the seven sacraments of the Church. Evaluate the

Step 4 (10 mins.)

Direct participants to turn to page 215 in their Journals and to fill in the blanks as you summarize Witnessing to Roman Catholics. Use the computer presentation or the overhead cel.

Witnessing to Roman Catholics

person's spiritual standing by asking what he is trusting for salvation—works, the sacraments, or grace by faith in Jesus Christ alone. If the person relies on external works, sensitively explain the biblical way of salvation, using your FAITH gospel presentation.

2. Establish the Bible as the source of ___authority___.
Remember that Roman Catholics have been taught to place their faith in three sources of religious authority. Many Roman Catholic beliefs are based on Church Tradition and the Magisterium, not on the Bible. Read Acts 17:11 to show Roman Catholics that even the teachings of the apostles were compared with Scripture to verify their truthfulness. Read passages that present the truth of salvation solely by grace through faith. Trust in the Holy Spirit's ability to bring understanding, enlightenment, and conviction through an encounter with God's Word (see Heb. 4:12).

3. Use a Roman Catholic ___New___ ___Testament___.
Because evangelicals and Roman Catholics accept the same New Testament, consider giving the person a New Testament that has the Roman Catholic imprimatur (official approval). These New Testaments, available from the American Bible Society, have the same translation as non-Catholic editions. Do not use the Roman Catholic edition that contains the Old Testament, which also includes the spurious Apocryphal books.

4. Clarify ___terms___.
Roman Catholics' understanding of the sacraments may cause confusion unless you take care to clarify the terms you are using. For example, they have been taught to equate Christianity with receiving baptism. If you ask whether the person is a Christian, he hears you ask, "Have you been baptized?" Similarly, if you ask a Roman Catholic, "Have you received Christ?" the person would interpret that question to mean, "Have you received the Eucharist?" When Roman Catholics receive the elements of the Eucharist, they believe that they are receiving Christ. Explain that Christ is received not physically but spiritually through faith.

5. Give a ___Christ-centered___ testimony.
Because Roman Catholics trust in the sacraments of the church to aid them in the process of salvation, do not emphasize your church when witnessing to them. Rather, be Christ-centered when sharing the gospel. Stress your personal relationship with Jesus Christ. Share your personal testimony and the difference Jesus makes in your life. Avoid using church words that Roman Catholics may not understand. Do not get sidetracked by secondary issues that are not a part of the gospel.

6. State that salvation is through ___Christ___ alone.
Many Roman Catholics trust in their own ability to remove their venial

sins, having been taught that they need Christ's grace only for mortal sins. Therefore, although a Roman Catholic recognizes that she is a sinner, she does not necessarily realize her need for salvation. For example, if you share Romans 3:23, "All have sinned and fall short of the glory of God" (NKJV), a Roman Catholic may agree that she has sinned but may not agree that she has done anything that would make her fall short of the glory of God. In Roman Catholic theology only a mortal sin sends a person to hell.

Stress that all sins are serious and have mortal consequences. The Bible teaches that even one small sin is enough to keep us out of heaven: "Whoever keeps the whole law and yet stumbles at just one point is guilty of breaking all of it" (Jas. 2:10, NIV). When many Roman Catholics hear this truth, they sometimes ask, "If that's true, how can anyone be saved?" This is your opportunity to use Scriptures like John 3:16; Acts 10:43; Romans 11:6; Ephesians 1:7; 2:8-9; and Hebrews 7:25,27; 9:12; 10:12,14-15,17 to prove that salvation is by grace through faith in Christ, not through human works or sacraments. Explain that because salvation is by grace through faith alone, persons who have trusted Christ can know that all of their sins are forgiven—past, present, and future—and that they will spend eternity with Christ, the author and finisher of their faith (see Col. 2:13; John 5:24; 6:47; Heb. 12:2; 1 John 5:13).

Visitation Time

Do It

1. As you make visits with your Team, look for opportunities to connect lost persons with Sunday School classes that can love and minister to them.
2. This week Learners have learned how to live FAITH in daily life. Share with them how this happens in your life.
3. Learners should have memorized the entire FAITH Visit Outline. Provide opportunities to let them share in FAITH visits.

Celebration Time

Share It

1. Ask a Team member to take the lead in sharing reports.
2. Hear reports and testimonies.
3. Complete Evaluation Cards.
4. Complete Participation Cards.
5. Update visitation forms with the results of visits.

STUDY IT

Step 5 (5 mins.)

Overview Home Study Assignments for session 13.

Transition to assemble with FAITH Teams to prepare for home visits. (5 mins.)

DO IT (110 MINS.)

SHARE IT (30 MINS.)

Home Study Assignments

Home Study Assignments reinforce this session by helping you apply what you have learned.

Your Discipleship Journey

Journaling activities in Your Discipleship Journey are an important part of your development as a Great Commission Christian through FAITH training.

1. Roman Catholics ascribe authority to Tradition and the Magisterium. Match the following Scriptures with statements that give a biblical response to the Roman Catholic view of authority.

   ___ 1. Deuteronomy 4:2   a. Never add to or take away from Scripture.

   ___ 2. Matthew 15:2-3,6b   b. There is grave danger in accepting oral

   ___ 3. Mark 7:8-9,13   tradition as having scriptural authority.

   ___ 4. Acts 17:11   c. Check every Christian teacher's doctrine

   ___ 5. Colossians 2:8   against God's Word.

   ___ 6. 2 Peter 1:20-21

   ___ 7. Revelation 22:18-19

2. Roman Catholic theology has many false teachings. Read the following Roman Catholic teachings and use the verses listed to give a biblical response.

   If Christians die with mortal sins on their soul, they forfeit salvation.

   1 Peter 1:3-5: _____

   _____

   _____

   Baptism washes away sin and punishment.

   John 3:16: _____

   _____

   The Holy Spirit is given to believers through confirmation.

   Romans 8:9-16: _____

   _____

As a believer takes the Eucharist, the bread and the wine are literally transformed into Jesus' flesh and blood, thus providing grace to the believer.

Acts 15:29: _____

_____

In addition to repentance and faith, works are required for salvation.

Acts 16:31: _____

Romans 3:28: _____

Ephesians 2:8-9: _____

_____

Growing as a Life Witness

Growing as a Life Witness reminds you of your responsibility to witness and minister to others during the week.

1. Talk or meet with your accountability partner and share ways you have cultivated a lost person or have witnessed or ministered on occasions other than FAITH visits.
2. Discuss ways you can apply the session 13 content.
3. Pray for lost persons by name and for each other.

Prayer Concerns	Answers to Prayer
_____	_____
_____	_____
_____	_____
_____	_____

Your Weekly Sunday School Leadership Meeting

A FAITH participant is an important member of Sunday School. Encourage Team members who are elected Sunday School leaders to attend this weekly meeting. Use this section to record ways your FAITH Team influences the work of your Sunday School class or department. Use the information to report during weekly Sunday School leadership meetings. Identify actions that need to be taken through Sunday School as a result of prayer concerns, needs identified, visits made by the Team, and decisions made by the persons visited. Also identify ways you can disciple others in your Sunday School class or department and in your church.

1. Highlight FAITH visit results and discuss needs that affect your class/ department or age group. Are prospect-discovery activities continuing to generate good prospect information?

_____

2. Participate with others on your leadership team in evaluating last week's session and in discussing ways Sunday's lesson can involve members and guests in transformational Bible study and discipleship.

3. How should preparation for Sunday consider the needs of individuals or families visited through FAITH?

_____

4. In what ways can the truths you discovered in this session be communicated with the rest of your Sunday School leadership team? With fellow class members?

_____

5. Discuss ways to involve members in praying for and celebrating God's leadership in raising up new persons to begin FAITH training.

6. Pray for your teacher and other leadership. Request prayer for any persons contacted through Opinion Poll visits.

Discipling Your Team Members

This weekly feature suggests actions the Team Leader can take to support Team members, prepare for Team Time, and improve visits. This work is part of the Team Leader's Home Study Assignments. Add any actions suggested by your church's FAITH strategy.

Support Team Members
❑ Contact Team members during the week. Remind them that you are praying for them. Discuss prayer concerns and answers to prayer.
❑ As you talk with Learners this week, discuss opportunities they have for witnessing during the week. Encourage them as they seek to witness to persons they encounter.
❑ Pray for needs and concerns shared by Team members.

Prepare to Lead Team Time
❑ Review Team members' Home Study Assignments.
❑ Preview Leading Team Time for session 14.

Prepare to Lead Visits

❑ Review the FAITH Visit Outline.

Link with Sunday School

❑ Participate in your weekly Sunday School leadership meeting. Share pertinent information in this meeting, using Your Weekly Sunday School Leadership Meeting (pp. 219–20) and FAITH-visit results.

❑ Ask Sunday School leaders to think about others who may become involved in FAITH training.

❑ Consider ways your Sunday School lessons can foster a proper understanding of salvation by grace through faith in Christ alone.

For Further Growth: The Sacrificial Death of Jesus Christ

For Further Growth may include additional reading or activities that will enhance your growth as a disciple and a discipler of others. These assignments are intended to be long-term projects and do not have to be completed during this semester of study.

1. It is important for believers to understand the results of Christ's sacrificial death on the cross. Read what the following Scriptures say about Jesus' death and the results for believers: Romans 6:22; 1 Corinthians 1:30; Galatians 3:13; Ephesians 1:7; 1 Thessalonians 5:23; Hebrews 2:14; 9:11-14; 10:10-12; 1 John 3:8; Revelation 5:8-12.

2. Read one or more of the following resources.
   - Millard J. Erickson, *Christian Theology*, part 8, "The Work of Christ" (Grand Rapids: Baker, 1985), 761–844.
   - R. C. Sproul, *Essential Truths of the Christian Faith*, part 7, "Salvation" (Wheaton: Tyndale, 1992), 159–214.
   - John F. MacArthur, *Our Sufficiency in Christ*, chapter 11, "Sufficient Grace" (Dallas: Word, 1991), 239–57.

3. Read the FAITH Tips on pages 222–24.

[1] *Catechism of the Catholic Church* (Liguori: Liguori, 1994), no. 133.

[2] Ibid., no. 78.

[3] Ibid., no. 87.

[4] Ibid., no. 1859.

[5] Ibid., no. 1127.

[6] H. J. Shroeder, trans., *The Canons and Decrees of the Council of Trent* (Rockford: Tan, 1978), 7th Session, Canon 4, 52, as quoted by John Ankerberg and John Weldon, *The Facts on Roman Catholicism* (Eugene: Harvest House, 1993), 14.

[7] *Catechism of the Catholic Church*, no. 1213.

[8] Ibid., no. 1250.

[9] Ibid., no. 1320.

[10] Ibid., no. 1376.

Answers to matching activity on page 218: 1. a, 2. b, 3. b, 4. c, 5. b, 6. b, 7. a

FAITH TIP

The Trouble with Mary

The Bible describes Mary, the mother of Jesus, very differently from the Mary adored and worshiped by the Roman Catholic Church. The Mary of the Bible is not the Mary of Roman Catholicism.

The Female Counterpart to Jesus

In many ways the Mary of Roman Catholicism is the female counterpart to Jesus. The official catechism of the Roman Catholic Church states, "What the Catholic faith believes about Mary is based on what it believes about Christ, and what it teaches about Mary illumines in turn its faith in Christ."[1] In contrast, the Bible depicts Mary as a godly woman, not someone with Godlike qualities.

Without Sin or Impurity

Roman Catholics believe that Mary, like Jesus, was born without sin and committed no impure act while on earth. The catechism of the Roman Catholic Church teaches that Mary "was totally preserved from the stain of original sin and she remained pure from all personal sin throughout her life."[2] As part of her purity, Roman Catholics believe that Mary remained a virgin throughout her life.[3]

The Bible does not give evidence of Mary's sinlessness. In Luke 1:47 she called God her Savior, indicating that she was indeed a sinner who needed spiritual salvation. Likewise, there is no biblical evidence that Mary remained a virgin after Jesus' birth. The New Testament makes many references to Jesus' brothers and sisters. A disturbing implication of the Roman Catholic doctrine of Mary's perpetual virginity is the idea that sex in marriage is impure. The Bible does not support this view. First Corinthians 7:3 advises the husband to "fulfill his marital duty to his wife, and likewise the wife to her husband" (NIV).

Ascension into Heaven

Just as Jesus physically ascended into heaven and is exalted at the right hand of God the Father, the Roman Catholic Church teaches that Mary ascended into heaven at the end of her earthly life and has been exalted as the queen of heaven. The catechism states that Mary "was taken up body and soul into heavenly glory, and exalted by the Lord as Queen over all things."[4] There is no scriptural support for this claim. Mary will be physically resurrected along with other Christian believers when Jesus returns for His church.

A Mediator Between God and Humanity

The Roman Catholic Church believes that Mary is a co-mediator of God's grace and collaborates with the salvation of Jesus.[5] However, 1 Timothy 2:5 teaches that "there is one God and one mediator between God and men, the man Christ Jesus" (NIV). The only mediator between God and humanity is Jesus, who promised, " 'Come to me, all you who are weary and burdened, and I will give you rest' " (Matt. 11:28, NIV).

Worthy of Honor and Worship

The Roman Catholic Church teaches that "the Church's devotion to the Blessed Virgin is intrinsic to Christian worship."[6] The Bible, however, teaches that only Jesus is worthy of honor and worship (see Rev. 5:13). The Bible warns against offering worship to any being except God. Even the worship of a holy angel of God is forbidden (see Rev. 22:8-9).

Divine Titles

The Roman Catholic Church identifies Mary as "the Holy Mother of God,"[7] arguing that the title refers to the reality of the incarnation. Because Jesus was truly God and truly man while in her womb, Roman Catholics argue that the child she gave birth to was the complete Godhead. Evangelicals accept the incarnation and the full deity of Jesus, but we object to the unbiblical titles given to Mary. Although Mary is the mother of Jesus, she is not the source of His deity. The incarnation was the result of a miracle performed by the Holy Spirit.

Prayers Offered

Roman Catholics are taught that it is proper to pray to Mary.[8] But because prayer is a form of worship, it should be offered only to God. The Bible warns against any attempt to communicate with the dead (see Lev. 20:6; 2 Kings 23; Isa. 19:3). Prayers offered to Mary and other saints violate this biblical prohibition.

---

[1] *Catechism of the Catholic Church* (Liguori: Liguori, 1994), no. 487.
[2] Ibid., no. 508.
[3] Ibid., no. 499.
[4] Ibid., no. 966.
[5] Ibid., nos. 964, 969–70.
[6] Ibid., no. 971.
[7] Ibid., no. 975.
[8] Ibid., no. 971.

FAITH TIP

Evaluating the Apocrypha

"How can you expect me to take the Bible seriously when it talks about mythical creatures?" an unbeliever asked his Christian friend.

"The Bible may make references to dragons but only figuratively to refer to Satan," answered the Christian.

"Not so!" claimed the unbeliever. The unbeliever walked to his bookshelf, picked up a Bible, opened it to the Old Testament, and started reading from a book titled Bel and the Dragon.

The Christian, in shock, exclaimed, "But that's not in the Bible!"

"Sure it is," said the unbeliever, who had read from a Bible that contained what Roman Catholics refer to as the deuterocanonical books.

While Roman Catholics' New Testament is the same as the Protestant New Testament, their Old Testament contains several books that Protestants and evangelicals consider spurious. For this reason Protestants refer to these additional books as the Apocrypha. The term *Apocrypha* means *of doubtful authenticity* or *spurious*. In addition to Bel and the Dragon, the Apocrypha contains Tobit, Judith, additions to Esther and Daniel, the Wisdom of Solomon, Sirach, Baruch, the Letter of Jeremiah, and 1 and 2 Maccabees.

Evangelicals reject the Apocrypha for several reasons. Unlike the true Scriptures, the apocryphal books contain many historical errors and geographical and chronological mistakes. The Apocrypha also contains many unbiblical teachings. For example, it claims that the world was created from preexisting matter (Wisdom 11:17), while the Bible teaches that "the universe was formed at God's command, so that what is seen was not made out of what was visible" (Heb. 11:3, NIV).

The Apocrypha also indicates that giving alms and performing good works can atone for sin (Sirach 3:3,30; 35:3). Romans 3:20, however, teaches that "no one will be declared righteous in his sight by observing the law" (NIV). The Apocrypha also asserts that prayers and atonement for the dead will help the departed (2 Maccabees 12:45; Baruch 3:4). Hebrews 9:27 reveals that "man is destined to die once, and after that to face judgment" (NIV).

No Apocryphal book ever claims to be inspired by God. In fact, the author of 2 Maccabees denies that his writing is inspired, stating that his book may be "poorly done and mediocre" (2 Maccabees 15:38, RSV). The Apocrypha itself admits that there were no prophets in the land of Israel during the time when it was being written (1 Maccabees 9:27). None of the Apocryphal books contain the signs that mark true prophecy of God (see Deut. 18:21-22), nor do they record divine miracles and predictive prophecy (see Isa. 44:7; 45:21). In addition, the New Testament writers never quote from the Apocrypha. Evangelical Christians have good reasons for labeling these additional books the Apocrypha and for rejecting them as inspired Scripture.

The Eastern Orthodox Church

BILL GORDON

In this session you will—

CHECK IT by engaging in Team Time activities;

KNOW IT by reviewing content from session 13;

HEAR IT by examining Eastern Orthodox beliefs and by learning ways to witness to followers of Eastern Orthodoxy;

STUDY IT by overviewing Home Study Assignments;

DO IT by leading your Team in making visits;

SHARE IT by celebrating.

IN ADVANCE

- Overview content.
- Preview teaching suggestions. Prepare key points. Decide whether to use the session 14 computer presentation or the overhead cels.
- Prepare the room for teaching.
- Pray for participants and for Teams as they prepare to visit.
- As Teaching Time begins, direct participants to open their Journals to page 228.

CHECK IT (15 MINS.)

If the computer presentation is used, display the agenda frame for Team Time. Add other points as needed.

CHECK IT agenda:
- ✔ FAITH Visit Outline
- ✔ Session 13 Debriefing
- ✔ Help for Strengthening a Visit

Leading Team Time

All Team members participate in Team Time. They are primarily responsible for reciting the assigned portion of the FAITH Visit Outline and for discussing other Home Study Assignments.

As you direct this important time of CHECK IT activities with your Team, keep in mind that Learners look to you as a role model, motivator, mentor, and friend. Team Time activities can continue in the car as the Team travels to and from visits.

Lead CHECK IT Activities

✔ FAITH Visit Outline

❑ Listen while each Learner recites as much of the FAITH Visit Outline as time allows. Make sure each person has a turn. It may be best to ask Learners to recite the segment they have the most difficulty sharing during a visit.

❑ As time permits, allow for additional practice on any part of the visit presentation, sequence, and materials (*My Next Step of Faith— Baptism*, for example).

✔ Session 13 Debriefing

❑ Review: The FAITH Sunday School Evangelism Strategy is designed to help equip the Sunday School member and leader to share the gospel and minister to prospects and members. A strength of this evangelism training is that participants learn a simple yet direct approach to talking with people about the message of the gospel when visiting with a Team of three. Another wonderful benefit is that someone who learns to share the gospel becomes more aware of witnessing opportunities during encounters throughout the week. Remind Team members that, as they continue training, they will become more aware of opportunities to share both a verbal and a lifestyle witness with people whose lives they intersect.

✔ Help for Strengthening a Visit

❑ Discuss some of the difficulties Teams have encountered in leading someone to hear and consider the FAITH gospel presentation. Call attention to the fact that this session formally introduces Learners to ways to deal with difficulties and distractions. At the same time, Team Leaders and other participants will learn other ways to help their Teams respond appropriately.

❑ As time allows, consider sharing a copy of the Witness Awareness Quotient (from *Building Bridges Through FAITH*) for Team members to use at their convenience. Or discuss some things you learned as a result. Briefly help Team members see the impact of increasing their awareness of witnessing opportunities. It is one way to focus attention on strengthening both lifestyle and verbal opportunities to witness.

Notes

_____

_____

_____

_____

_____

_____

_____

Actions I Need to Take with Team Members This Week

_____

_____

_____

_____

_____

_____

_____

Transition to classrooms for instruction on the content of the session. (5 mins.)

Step 1 (5 mins.)

Direct participants to locate A Quick Review on page 228 in their Journals and to complete the activities. Then give the answers, using the computer presentation or the overhead cel.

A Quick Review

HEAR IT

Step 2 (5 mins.)

Ask participants to fill in the blanks as you present the ideas in Descendants of the Apostles. Use the computer presentation or the overhead cels.

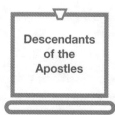

Descendants of the Apostles

A Quick Review

Last week you examined Roman Catholic beliefs. Complete the numbered statements summarizing their beliefs by selecting the correct words from the list that follows.

sacraments • confirmation • penance • Eucharist
sin • baptism • authority

1. Roman Catholics accept extrabiblical sources of _____**authority**_____.
2. Roman Catholics distinguish between categories of _____**sin**_____.
3. Salvation is imparted through _____**sacraments**_____.
4. _____**Baptism**_____ is necessary for salvation.
5. _____**Confirmation**_____ bestows the Holy Spirit.
6. Christ's body is received through the _____**Eucharist**_____.
7. _____**Penance**_____ removes the penalty of sins.

Check appropriate principles for witnessing to Roman Catholics.
- ❑ 1. State that all Roman Catholics are bound for hell.
- ☑ 2. Determine whether the person is saved.
- ☑ 3. Establish the Bible as the source of authority.
- ☑ 4. Use a Roman Catholic New Testament.
- ❑ 5. Express appreciation for the pope's authority.
- ❑ 6. Emphasize Baptist history and polity.
- ☑ 7. Clarify terms.
- ☑ 8. Give a Christ-centered testimony.
- ❑ 9. Agree that the sacraments impart saving grace.
- ☑ 10. State that salvation is through Christ alone.
- ❑ 11. Insist that the person make a decision today.
- ❑ 12. Affirm the Catholic's efforts to remove his own venial sins.

Descendants of the Apostles

A Christian was trying to share the gospel with new neighbors. When the discussion turned to spiritual matters, the neighbor announced, "We are members of the one true, holy church formed by the apostles." The witness said, "Oh, are you Roman Catholic?" "No," the neighbor emphatically stated. "We are Orthodox."

Members of Orthodox churches are very proud of their history, claiming direct descent from Christ and the apostles. For the first thousand years after Christ, the Eastern Orthodox and Roman Catholics were two branches of the same church in the _____**Roman** **Empire**_____. Inhabitants of the east spoke Greek, while those in the west spoke mostly Latin. In A.D. 330 Emperor _____**Constantine**_____, the first

Christian emperor of the Roman Empire, moved his capital from Rome to Constantinople in the Greek-speaking part of the empire. Eventually, the empire divided into two parts, east and west, which later contributed to the polarization of the eastern and western churches. The **Great Schism** of 1054 formalized the separation between the Roman Catholic Church in the west and the Eastern Orthodox Church in the east. Today the Eastern Orthodox Church claims to be the **original**, **undivided**, **universal** church of Christ.

Orthodox churches have experienced much persecution throughout their history. Like the Latin Church, they experienced sporadic persecution during the first three centuries of Christianity. Even during the Crusades, the Orthodox were persecuted by the Latin Christians who had supposedly come to aid them. In 1204 Crusaders sacked Constantinople and installed a Latin bishop in the city. This event probably contributed more to the division between the church in the east and west than did the schism of 1054. Many Orthodox Christians have not forgotten the plundering of Constantinople by those claiming to represent the western church. Although the Orthodox often enjoyed recognition by the Islamic rulers after the Muslims conquered their territories in 1453, they still experienced periods of persecution. The most severe persecution experienced by the Orthodox has occurred in the 20th century under both **Islamic** and **Communist** rulers. Many Orthodox in North America have come to North America to escape this persecution.

Unlike Roman Catholicism, Eastern Orthodoxy is divided into several groups representing various national churches, such as Greek, Russian, Syrian, Armenian, and Coptic. Although not as numerous as Roman Catholics, about **6.5** million Orthodox reside in North America. Among worldwide denominations that claim to be Christian, the Orthodox is second in size only to Roman Catholicism. It is estimated that there are as many as **250** million Orthodox worldwide.

Eastern Orthodox Beliefs

Orthodox beliefs are similar to those of Roman Catholics in several respects.

- Both emphasize liturgy and rituals.
- Both maintain a sacramental theology and practice.
- Both assign Mary the title *mother of God* and pray to Mary and the saints in heaven.
- Both offer prayers for the dead.
- Both consider faith and works necessary for salvation.

Step 3 (20 mins.)

Direct participants to turn to page 230 in their Journals and to fill in the blanks as you summarize Eastern Orthodox Beliefs. Use the computer presentation or the overhead cel.

Eastern Orthodox Beliefs

- Both believe that the bread and wine are Christ's body and blood.
- Both emphasize Church Tradition in formulating doctrine.
- Both believe in the infallibility of the Church.

In spite of these similarities, significant differences exist between the Orthodox and Roman Catholics. Some of these differences will be apparent in the overview of Orthodox beliefs that follows.

1. Church _____ **Tradition** _____ is authoritative.

The Orthodox view the Bible as the true Word of God. They believe that the miracles of the Bible really happened and that the virgin birth of Christ and His physical resurrection from the dead are historical events. However, the Bible is seen as only one strand in the cord of Church Tradition, which is the authoritative source for Orthodox doctrine. According to the Orthodox, not all of God's revelation was written down in the Bible. They claim that the Church in its oral Tradition preserved the revelation that was not written down. This Tradition is found in the statements of the early ecumenical church councils, later church councils, church liturgy, the Nicene Creed, and writings of the church fathers. While evangelicals place Scripture above Tradition, the Orthodox place Tradition above Scripture. Orthodox believers are encouraged to accept and understand Scripture in accordance with the church's interpretation.

The Eastern Orthodox Church also considers the Church to be authoritative and infallible, although these qualities do not reside in a singular leader. While Roman Catholics recognize the bishop of Rome as the infallible head of the Christian church, the Orthodox reject the supremacy and infallibility of the bishop of Rome or any other human authority. Among the Orthodox churches the ecumenical patriarch of Constantinople is considered the head bishop, but he is not equivalent to the pope in the Roman Catholic Church. The patriarch of Constantinople has only an honorary primacy. He is first among equals and is not infallible. Authority and infallibility are said to belong to the entire body of the faithful. However, bishops—individually or in ecumenical councils—are responsible for preserving and teaching truth according to Church Tradition.

Evangelicals believe that the Bible is the only reliable source of and authority for religious knowledge and practice. The Scriptures are the infallible Word of God (see 2 Tim. 3:15-17; 2 Pet. 1:19-21). The Bible warns us not to add to or take away from Scripture (see Deut. 4:2; Rev. 22:18-19). Paul warned believers not to be misled by "the tradition of men" (Col. 2:8, NKJV). Neither Orthodox Tradition nor ecclesiastic authority is equal to God's written revelation.

Although Orthodox Church Tradition may support biblical truth, we do not believe a doctrine because a church council teaches it but because the doctrine is taught in Scripture. One problem with the Orthodox position on Tradition is that Tradition is not a unified whole. The church fathers, for example, often contradicted one another, making their writings an unreliable source of authority. Only God's Word communicates God's truth in a consistent and reliable way.

2. God can be known through ____deification____.

Orthodox churches teach that God is beyond human understanding and transcends the capability of human thought or language to describe. He can be known experientially or mystically but not rationally. Therefore, the Orthodox stress a mystical approach to God, advocating the attainment of spiritual union with God. They refer to this union as deification.

Deification does not mean that a Christian becomes God or is assumed into God, as in Hindu and New Age systems of thought. The Orthodox distinguish between God's essence and His energies. In Orthodox theology God's essence is transcendent and unknowable. Created beings will never participate in God's essence. On the other hand, God's energies, such as glory, light, grace, and love, permeate the universe and can be experienced by humans. Although God's energies can be experienced in a mystical way, they cannot be intellectually comprehended.

The Bible teaches that because God created humanity in God's image (see Gen. 1:26), humans have the capacity to truly know God (see Gal. 4:9; 1 John 4:8). Because God is infinite, it is impossible for finite beings to fully comprehend Him. However, this does not mean that God cannot be truly known. Christians can truly know and experience God without fully comprehending Him. Knowledge of God comes to people when they accept the gospel of Jesus Christ (see Eph. 1:9). Paul taught that believers experience God's presence not through deification but through sanctification. The Holy Spirit experienced by every believer is not an energy of God but truly God (see 1 Cor. 3:16; 6:19).

3. The doctrine of ____original____ ____sin____ is denied.

The Orthodox do not believe in the doctrine of original sin, which is the biblical position that Adam's fall had serious spiritual implications for all his descendants. The Orthodox believe that humans are prone to sin not because of inherited sin but because of their subjection to physical needs. They also teach that this weakness was mystically removed through Christ's incarnation and is made real in our lives through the sacraments of the Church. This approach makes it difficult for Orthodox believers to understand the gravity of the fall, the seriousness of sin, and their need for Christ's substitutionary death on the cross. Rather, they believe that although human beings possess the freedom to sin, they naturally desire to be in communion with God and proceed toward fellowship with Him.

Evangelical Christians' view of our relationship with God is based on the biblical teaching of original sin—that all humanity has fallen from a state of innocence because of sin and desperately needs redemption (see Gen. 3:6; Matt. 15:19; Rom. 3:23; 5:14-21). Sin, as a violation of God's law, has not only resulted in humanity's separation from God but also merits the death of all sinners (see Rom. 6:23). Jesus Christ satisfied the demands of God's law by taking the sinner's place on the cross and paying the penalty that the law required (see Col. 2:13-14). Having fulfilled the righteous demands of the law, Jesus imparts His righteousness to everyone who places faith in Him (see 1 Cor. 1:30).

4. Salvation is gained by observing the ___sacraments___.

Deification, or union with God, is achieved through prayer, meditation, asceticism, good deeds, and the sacraments. The Orthodox Church recognizes the seven sacraments practiced by Roman Catholics but refers to them as Christian mysteries. Like Catholics, the Orthodox believe that God's grace is imparted through the sacraments and that they are vital to salvation. The sacraments are viewed not as symbols or reminders but the means by which God imparts saving and sanctifying grace to those who practice them. Baptism by threefold immersion, administered to infants, brings the remission of sins and eternal life. Like Roman Catholics, the Orthodox believe that Christ's body and blood are partaken in the elements of the Eucharist through transubstantiation.

Evangelical Christians must respond that the Bible teaches salvation by grace through faith, apart from any works (see Acts 10:43; Heb. 7:25,27). When we believe in the Lord Jesus Christ, His grace enters our lives directly through the power of the Holy Spirit without physical mediation (see Eph. 2:8-9).

As you learned in session 13, transubstantiation is not supported by Scripture. In the last supper the disciples could not have consumed Christ's body and blood, because Jesus was physically present with them. The consumption of blood also violates Old Testament law (see Lev. 3:17) and New Testament teachings by the apostles (see Acts 15:29). Evangelicals believe that the Lord's Supper is a symbolic act of obedience that memorializes Christ's death and anticipates His second coming.

5. The Orthodox pray to the ___saints___.

Orthodox believers invoke the aid and prayers of departed saints with full assurance of their help. They venerate the saints' images and relics, make pilgrimages to their shrines, and observe feasts dedicated to them. The highest of all helpers is Mary, whom the Orthodox, like Roman Catholics, regard as the mother of God and the queen of heaven. Prayers and hymns are offered to Mary, who intercedes to her Son on behalf of those who call on her.

Evangelical Christians stand on the biblical teaching that Jesus Christ is the only mediator between God and humanity (see 1 Tim. 2:5).

In addition, because prayer is a form of worship, it should be offered only to God. The Bible warns us not to attempt to communicate with the dead (see Lev. 20:6,27; 2 Kings 23:24; Isa. 19:3-4).

6. Orthodox ____worship____ brings union with God.

The goal of Orthodox worship is mystical union with God. The Orthodox liturgy, or worship practice, consists of elaborate rituals of great aesthetic detail and symbolic meaning. Candles, incense, clerical vestments, altar adornments, music, hymns, chants, prayers, processions, and the observance of the Eucharist are intended to help Orthodox worshipers praise God and receive God's presence through the Holy Spirit. Unlike Roman Catholics, the Orthodox reject the use of statues as religious objects, instead using icons, or religious images, to present the gospel message. The Orthodox claim that these images are not worshiped but are venerated as depictions of holy men and women who glorified God and now lead others into His presence. Thus, the icons are seen not merely as sacred art but as sources of revelation.

A biblical understanding of worship is based on an understanding that true union with God is spiritual, not mystical. Spiritual union with God is a personal relationship with Him, which comes only through personal faith in Jesus Christ (see John 3:16-18,36; Gal. 3:6; Phil. 3:9). The use of candles, incense, chants, processions, and elaborate rituals may appeal to human senses, but they do nothing to bring anyone closer to God. The New Testament does not advocate an endless series of rituals or external rites. Rather, it teaches that " 'God is spirit, and his worshipers must worship in spirit and in truth' " (John 4:24, NIV).

The Orthodox distinction between worship and veneration of icons is nothing more than verbal gymnastics. In day-to-day Orthodox practice there is little difference between worship and veneration. The Bible prohibits the use of two- and three-dimensional representations as aids to worship (see Deut. 4:16). God says, " 'Do not make idols or set up an image or a sacred stone for yourselves, and do not place a carved stone in your land to bow down before it' " (Lev. 26:1, NIV).

Witnessing to the Orthodox

1. Determine whether the person is ____saved____.

In Eastern Orthodoxy salvation is achieved through a mystical union with God. This union is not accomplished solely through faith but by performing good works and receiving the sacraments of the Church. Establish whether the person is trusting Christ or the sacraments for salvation. If the person is lost, use your FAITH gospel presentation

Step 4 (10 mins.)

Direct participants to turn to page 233 in their Journals and to fill in the blanks as you summarize Witnessing to the Orthodox. Use the computer presentation or the overhead cel.

Witnessing to the Orthodox

to explain that God uses our personal faith in Jesus Christ, not the sacraments, to communicate His grace to us (see Eph. 2:8-10).

2. Build a _____relationship_____.

The Orthodox history of persecution often makes followers suspicious of others. Take time to build a caring and respectful relationship, trusting the Holy Spirit to use the gospel message to reach the hearts and minds of those who are lost.

3. Affirm the authority of _____Scripture_____.

If you have an opportunity to discuss Orthodox beliefs, state that you do not disrespect Orthodox Tradition. Rather, you do not believe that it has the same authority as God's Word. Although evangelicals can agree with many teachings of the church fathers and the early ecumenical councils, our source of authority for religious belief and practice must be God's eternal Word (see 2 Tim. 3:15-17; Heb. 4:12; 2 Pet. 1:19-21).

4. Emphasize the severity and consequences of _sin_.

Because the Orthodox reject original sin, they do not share evangelicals' understanding of the serious nature of sin and our great need to accept Christ's payment for our sin on the cross. Your FAITH gospel presentation and your prior training give you tools for explaining the eternal consequences of unforgiven sin and the way to be saved by grace through faith in Jesus.

5. Share your personal _____testimony_____.

Share with your Orthodox friend your testimony of personal faith in Jesus Christ, relating the difference He makes in your life. Communicate that a personal relationship with Jesus Christ comes through faith and not through the sacraments of any church. God is concerned about sincere faith, not sacraments (see Gal. 5:6). God does not use rituals to communicate grace to His children. According to Paul, baptism is not part of the gospel (see 1 Cor. 1:17). The Lord Jesus Christ is the only mediator between God and humanity (see 1 Tim. 2:5; Heb. 9:15).

Also share your assurance of salvation (see John 14:3; Jude 24) and the freedom that comes from being saved by grace through faith rather than by works or the sacraments (see John 3:16). Keep your witness Christ-centered rather than church-centered. Avoid using evangelical terms that your Orthodox friend may not understand, like *saved, born again,* and *walk the aisle.*

STUDY IT

Step 5 (5 mins.)

Overview Home Study Assignments for session 14.

Transition to assemble with FAITH Teams to prepare for home visits. (5 mins.)

Visitation Time

Do It

1. All Team members should know the entire FAITH presentation. Are they ready to take the lead in a visit? Are they growing in their faith and in their capacity to share their faith? Are they learning to recognize when the FAITH Visit Outline needs to be adjusted in visits? Are they helping to establish bridges of relationship between the community and your Sunday School? Use your leadership role to challenge them to take the lead in visits and to offer support.

2. Share with Learners the importance of making ministry visits in order to strengthen their Sunday School and to connect members with a loving fellowship. Help them make the transition from asking, "How can I meet my needs?" to asking "How can I meet someone else's need?"

3. How far have Team members come since session 1? Have you taken the time to affirm them for their progress and to thank God for this mentoring experience?

Celebration Time

Share It

1. Ask a Team member to take the lead in sharing reports.
2. Hear reports and testimonies.
3. Complete Evaluation Cards.
4. Complete Participation Cards.
5. Update visitation forms with the results of visits.

DO IT (110 MINS.)

SHARE IT (30 MINS.)

Home Study Assignments

Home Study Assignments reinforce this session by helping you apply what you have learned.

Your Discipleship Journey

Journaling activities in Your Discipleship Journey are an important part of your development as a Great Commission Christian through FAITH training.

1. Eastern Orthodox churches teach that a believer's ultimate destiny is a mystical union with God, but this understanding is not scriptural. Record the way the following Scriptures describe our relationship with God.

Galatians 4:4-7: _____

_____

_____

_____

Ephesians 1:3-6: _____

_____

_____

_____

Colossians 1:13-14 : _____

_____

_____

_____

Revelation 22:1-5: _____

_____

_____

_____

2. The Eastern Orthodox place much importance on icons in their worship. Read John 4:21-24 and answer the following questions.

Whom are we to worship? _____

How are we to worship? _____

Growing as a Life Witness

Growing as a Life Witness reminds you of your responsibility to witness and minister to others during the week.

1. Talk or meet with your accountability partner and share ways you have cultivated a lost person or have witnessed or ministered on occasions other than FAITH visits.
2. Discuss ways you can apply the session 14 content.
3. Pray for lost persons by name and for each other.

Prayer Concerns	Answers to Prayer
_____	_____
_____	_____
_____	_____
_____	_____
_____	_____

Your Weekly Sunday School Leadership Meeting

A FAITH participant is an important member of Sunday School. Encourage Team members who are elected Sunday School leaders to attend this weekly meeting. Use this section to record ways your FAITH Team influences the work of your Sunday School class or department. Use the information to report during weekly Sunday School leadership meetings. Identify actions that need to be taken through Sunday School as a result of prayer concerns, needs identified, visits made by the Team, and decisions made by the persons visited. Also identify ways you can disciple others in your Sunday School class or department and in your church.

1. Highlight FAITH-visit results and implications for your class/department or age group. How can ministries of your class/department or Sunday School further extend bridges of relationship?

_____

_____

2. Pray for your teacher(s) and department director. Ask God to strengthen and encourage Team Leaders as they continue to train and equip new Learners. Record your requests.

_____

_____

_____

3. With others on your leadership team, evaluate last week's session and discuss ways Sunday's lesson can involve members and guests in transformational Bible study and discipleship.

_____

_____

_____

4. In what ways can the truths you discovered in this session be communicated with your Sunday School leadership team? How has FAITH changed your priorities? Those of your Team members? Those of new believers?

_____

_____

_____

Discipling Your Team Members

This weekly feature suggests actions the Team Leader can take to support Team members, prepare for Team Time, and improve visits. This work is part of the Team Leader's Home Study Assignments. Add any actions suggested by your church's FAITH strategy.

Support Team Members

❏ Contact Team members during the week. Remind them that you are praying for them. Discuss prayer concerns and answers to prayer.
❏ As you talk with Learners this week, discuss opportunities they have for witnessing during the week. Encourage them as they seek to be witnesses to persons they encounter.

❑ Record specific needs and concerns shared by Team members.

_____

_____

_____

Prepare to Lead Team Time
❑ Review Team members' Home Study Assignments.
❑ Be prepared to remind Team members to draft a "What FAITH Has Meant to Me" testimony, due in session 16.

Prepare to Lead Visits
❑ Review the FAITH Visit Outline.

Link with Sunday School
❑ Participate in your weekly Sunday School leadership meeting. Share pertinent information in this meeting, using Your Weekly Sunday School Leadership Meeting (pp. 237–38) and FAITH-visit results.
❑ Look for ways your Sunday School ministry can reinforce an understanding of the purpose of Christian worship.

For Further Growth: The Resurrection of Jesus Christ

For Further Growth may include additional reading or activities that will enhance your growth as a disciple and a discipler of others. These assignments are intended to be long-term projects and do not have to be completed during this semester of study.

1. One aspect of life that is missing in other world religions is sure hope for the future. The resurrection of Jesus Christ and the subsequent resurrection of believers bring wonderful hope to followers of Jesus. Study 1 Corinthians 15 and examine the fact of Christ's resurrection, the importance of His resurrection, the order of the resurrections, moral implications of resurrection, bodies of the resurrected dead, and bodies of the translated living.

2. Read one or more of the following resources.
   • J. I. Packer et al., _Exploring the Christian Faith_, chapter 8, "Death ... and Then" (Nashville: Thomas Nelson, 1992), 75–84.
   • Philip Yancy, _The Jesus I Never Knew_, chapter 11, "Resurrection: A Morning Beyond Belief" (Grand Rapids: Zondervan, 1995), 207–20.

FAITH AT WORK

Her name is Wendy. She's on my FAITH Team. She's a great communicator and a gifted evangelist. But that's not all. She's also glue. She has a knack for meeting people and permanently sticking them to her life. And when she's on a FAITH Team, the whole Team gets stuck too.

I can understand meeting someone, having them accept Christ before you've finished the presentation, feeling a connection with them, and keeping in touch for a few weeks after the conversion. That's natural and perhaps even expected. But what about when your message is rejected and your prospect couldn't be less interested in going to heaven? How easy is it then to stay involved and connected? Ask Wendy.

On this particular night our FAITH Team made a first-time visit to a single woman and heard the usual excuses. We left, and I tried to forget about it. But Wendy didn't forget. She began reaching out to this hurting woman. And slowly the whole Team felt their lives being stuck to hers as well. During the next several months Wendy went with her for an occasional meal, all the while sharing her relationship with Jesus. When this woman had a memorial service for her mother, we were there as part of her family and friends. And during the ongoing days of grief, Wendy was there comforting her and handling the important matters that couldn't wait. Praise God that one of those matters was leading her to the Lord. She prayed to receive Christ as her Savior and Lord, and we all rejoiced.

The woman's financial state was in ruins. The Lord directed me to hire her. As she has continued to grow in her dependence on the Lord, we've all marveled at His provision in her life. She participates in our prayer meetings at work, and we continue to meet together for special occasions such as birthdays and anniversaries. During these times we often marvel at the divine Providence that brought us together. And I stand amazed that by meeting this woman's deepest need, Wendy was able to stick another life to hers and to ours.

Sharon Lucki
Immanuel Baptist Church
Highland, California

SESSION 15

Secular Humanism

TAL DAVIS

In this session you will—

CHECK IT by engaging in Team Time activities;

KNOW IT by reviewing content from session 14;

HEAR IT by examining the beliefs of secular humanists and by learning ways

to witness to them;

SEE IT by viewing a video segment;

STUDY IT by overviewing Home Study Assignments;

DO IT by leading your Team in making visits;

SHARE IT by celebrating.

IN ADVANCE
- Overview content.
- Preview teaching suggestions. Prepare key points. Decide whether to use the session 15 computer presentation or the overhead cels.
- Be prepared to answer questions about next week's schedule.
- Prepare the room for teaching.
- Cue the videotape to the session 15 segment.
- Pray for participants and for Teams as they prepare to visit.
- As Teaching Time begins, direct participants to open their Journals to page 244.

TEAM TIME

CHECK IT (15 MINS.)

If the computer presentation is used, display the agenda frame for Team Time. Add other points as needed.

CHECK IT agenda:
- ✔ FAITH Visit Outline
- ✔ Session 14 Debriefing
- ✔ Other Home Study Assignments
- ✔ Help for Strengthening a Visit

Leading Team Time

All Team members participate in Team Time. They are primarily responsible for reciting the assigned portion of the FAITH Visit Outline and for discussing other Home Study Assignments.

As you direct this important time of CHECK IT activities with your Team, keep in mind that Learners look to you as a role model, motivator, mentor, and friend. Team Time activities can continue in the car as the Team travels to and from visits.

Lead CHECK IT Activities

✔ FAITH Visit Outline
- ❑ Listen while each Learner recites as much of the FAITH Visit Outline as time allows. It may be best to ask Learners to recite the segment they seem to have the most difficulty sharing during a visit.
- ❑ As time permits, allow for any additional practice that is needed on the visit presentation and sequence.

✔ Session 14 Debriefing
- ❑ Briefly talk about distractions Team members have encountered in earlier visits.
- ❑ While reminding Team members that most visits go smoothly, help them begin to recognize principles and actions for handling difficulties. As you model ways to handle difficult situations during visits, explain what you did and why. Deal appropriately with difficulties that could take place at any time during visits. Difficulties are things that happen or are said during the visit that could keep you from sharing the gospel and leading a person who is ready to respond to make a commitment to Christ. Principles for dealing with difficulties relate primarily to building bridges of relationship with the person, dealing with any questions and objections, and working through the obstacles and distractions that take place.

✔ Other Home Study Assignments
- ❑ Remind the group of the assignment, due next week, to write a testimony describing what FAITH has meant personally.

✔ Help for Strengthening a Visit
- ❑ Remind Team members to listen during each visit for ministry opportunities and for ways to follow up appropriately.
- ❑ If you have shared the Witness Awareness Quotient with Team members (from *Building Bridges Through FAITH*), reemphasize as follows.

- The greater the number of Unsaved identified, the greater the potential for sharing a witness. The greater the number of Yes responses, the more someone is taking advantage of witnessing opportunities.
- If No responses are higher than Yes responses, then someone can consciously strengthen awareness of opportunities to share the gospel. If Yes responses are higher, then a witness can comfortably model for others the significance of sharing FAITH during daily-life opportunities.

Notes

_____

_____

_____

_____

_____

_____

Actions I Need to Take with Team Members This Week

_____

_____

_____

_____

_____

_____

_____

Transition to classrooms for instruction on the content of the session. (5 mins.)

TEACHING TIME

KNOW IT

Step 1 (5 mins.)

Direct participants to locate A Quick Review on page 244 in their Journals and to complete the activities. Then give the answers, using the computer presentation or the overhead cel.

A Quick Review

HEAR IT

Step 2 (5 mins.)

Ask participants to turn to page 245 in their Journals and to fill in the blanks as you present the key points in The Idolatry of Self-Worship. Use the computer presentation or the overhead cels.

The Idolatry of Self-Worship

A Quick Review

The previous session examined Eastern Orthodox beliefs. Mark each statement O for *Eastern Orthodox* or C for *evangelical Christian*.

__O__ 1. Church Tradition is authoritative.
__C__ 2. Scripture is above Tradition.
__C__ 3. A teaching is true if it is taught in Scripture.
__C__ 4. We can know God personally without comprehending Him.
__O__ 5. God can be known through deification.
__O__ 6. The doctrine of original sin is denied.
__C__ 7. All humanity has fallen from innocence and needs redemption.
__C__ 8. Salvation is gained by grace through faith.
__O__ 9. Salvation is gained by observing the sacraments.
__O__ 10. The Orthodox pray to the saints.
__C__ 11. Jesus is the only mediator between God and humanity.
__C__ 12. Prayer is offered only to God.
__C__ 13. True worship is spiritual, not mystical.
__O__ 14. Orthodox worship brings union with God.
__C__ 15. God is worshiped in spirit and truth, not through rituals.

Check principles for witnessing to Eastern Orthodox followers.
❑ 1. State that mysticism really freaks you out.
❑ 2. Do not share your testimony, because it doesn't apply to Orthodoxy.
☑ 3. Determine whether the person is saved.
☑ 4. Build a relationship.
❑ 5. Tell them that icons are idols.
☑ 6. Affirm the authority of Scripture.
❑ 7. Alter the FAITH gospel presentation to downplay sin's seriousness.
☑ 8. Emphasize the severity and consequences of sin.
☑ 9. Share your personal testimony.

The Idolatry of Self-Worship

Mike excitedly awaited the beginning of his first class on his first day of college. "I want to start this class by telling all you freshmen what I tell each new class every year," Dr. Hancock began. "I am a humanist. I reject any belief in God or the supernatural. I believe that Christians and other theists are deluded. I can find no reason to believe that the earth and the universe are anything other than a gigantic accident. It and we exist completely by fixed laws of nature. There were and are no miracles or supernatural occurrences. Humans decide what is right and wrong and make our laws accordingly. There are no moral absolutes.

Furthermore, I believe that the Bible is not true but full of myths. It is on this basis that this class will proceed."

Mike was stunned. As a Christian he had always been taught that God exists, that He created the world, that the Bible is true, and that Jesus Christ is God's Son. Now without hesitancy or shame this teacher had challenged nearly everything he took for granted.

Today the skeptical philosophy of secular humanism dominates most academic fields and has come to pervade Western culture during the past several generations. Nearly every field of endeavor has adopted a naturalistic worldview—science, art, law, social science, humanities, history, philosophy, and even theology. Perhaps no other worldview has posed so great a threat to Christianity in the past century as secular humanism.

Secular humanism has been defined this way.

> The word "secularism" … means a philosophy that is completely concerned with the _____**material**_____ _____**universe**_____ that is bound by time, and thus is unconcerned with God. "Humanism" … means to be very concerned with _____**humanity**_____, with developing the abilities of humanity, and defending the dignity of individual persons. … But when the term secular is put in front of humanism, what one has is a philosophy that denies __**God**__, and which sees mankind as _____**autonomous**_____, ultimately responsible to nothing save itself.[1]

Perhaps the fuller implications of this philosophy can be revealed by the statement of a prominent humanist spokesman: "The unique message of humanism on the current world scene is its commitment to scientific _____**naturalism**_____. … Scientific naturalism enables human beings to construct a coherent worldview disentangled from metaphysics or theology and based on the sciences."[2]

The philosophical roots of secular humanism can be traced to the Greek philosophers Democritus (ca. 460 B.C.) and Epicurus (341–270 B.C.). The Chinese philosopher Confucius (551–479 B.C.) also espoused humanistic concepts. The modern formation of secular humanism dates from the European _____**Enlightenment**_____ period in the 17th and 18th centuries. Naturalistic thinkers Jacques Rousseau (1712–78) and Francois Voltaire (1694–1778) in France and Thomas Paine (1737–1809) in America challenged theistic and Christian presuppositions.

In the 19th century several prominent thinkers enhanced the influence of secularism. Karl __**Marx**__ (1818–83) and Charles __**Darwin**__ (1809–82) especially influenced intellectual thought. In the 20th century secularism and humanism reached their zenith of intellectual and political power. Totalitarian forms of naturalism gave birth to _____**Communism**_____ and __**Nazism**__, both of which culminated in tyranny and violence on a global scale. In the academic and intellectual fields secular humanists rose to prominence, including notable personalities such as Bertrand Russell (1872–1970), H. L. Mencken (1880–1956), and Sigmund Freud (1856–1939).

Beliefs of Secular Humanism

The main sources of information about humanist beliefs are two documents published by the American Humanist Association: Humanist Manifesto I (1933) and Humanist Manifesto II (1973). In 1999 a new generation of secular humanists drafted Humanist Manifesto 2000: A Call for a New Planetary Humanism. Secular humanists are a diverse group of people who differ on many specific points of belief. However, most agree on the following basic principles.

1. God is the big ___myth___.

Secular humanists, generally, are atheists, though many may describe themselves as agnostics or simply nonreligious. Some are vehemently antireligious, anti-Christian, and dogmatically naturalistic. Some humanists may describe themselves as theists, but most of those reject orthodox Christian doctrine such as Christ's deity and resurrection, preferring to focus on His moral example and teachings.

Secular humanists, therefore, regard the universe as self-existent and the material cosmos as the totality of what exists. As the late cosmologist Carl Sagan asserted, "The cosmos is all that is, or ever was, or ever will be."[3] For most humanists the idea of a God or gods is nothing more than superstition born of ignorance, fear, or psychological conditioning. Most regard a belief in God or gods as hindrances to humankind's social development and a major contributor to the world's problems.

Christians respond to the challenge of atheism by acknowledging that proving God's existence by a scientific or mathematic formula is not possible. However, we can provide cogent arguments why belief in God is reasonable. Christian philosophers Norman L. Geisler and Ronald M. Brooks argue that belief in God makes sense for four basic reasons.

1. *The argument from* ___creation___. Because the universe is limited and had a beginning, something outside it must have been its cause. Even many nonbelieving scientists now accept the evidence that the universe had a beginning point, although science cannot explain it. Christians believe that there is no reasonable explanation for the universe's existence other than a divine one (see Gen. 1:1; Col. 1:16).
2. *The argument from* ___design___. The design movement asserts that the vast complexity of the universe as a whole and the detailed complexity of molecular biology can only be explained as the plan

Step 3 (15 mins.)

Direct participants to turn to page 246 in their Journals and to fill in the blanks as you summarize Beliefs of Secular Humanism. Use the computer presentation or the overhead cels.

Beliefs of Secular Humanism

of an intelligent designer. Mere chance alone fails to explain the complex interdependence of both the macro (larger) and micro (smaller) levels of the universe. Christian scientist Hugh Ross has stated, "The estimated probability that a non-designed, Earth-sized planet will have the capacity to support life is less than one in 10^{150} (the number 1 with 150 zeroes following it)."[4] Christians argue that the most reasonable explanation for such complexity is that it was designed by the superintelligent mind of God.

3. *The argument from* __**moral**__ __**law**__. Every culture that has ever existed has acknowledged that some actions are right and some actions are wrong. This innate moral sense is evidence of a moral sense in the universe. Even most atheists (except nihilists), especially secular humanists, claim to possess high standards of ethics and morality. A moral standard requires some kind of objective basis for it. Christians hold that the only reasonable basis for absolute morality is that a personal God has established in our hearts that innate sense of right and wrong (see Rom. 1:19; 2:14-15). In addition to the innate moral sense present in all people, God has revealed His will and moral standards more fully through His Word, the Bible (see 2 Tim. 3:16-17; 2 Pet. 1:20-21), and ultimately in His Son, Jesus (see Heb. 1:1-2).

4. *The argument from* __**being**__. When God revealed his name to Moses in the burning bush, He declared, " 'I AM WHO I AM' " (Ex. 3:14, NIV). He stated, in essence, that He just was. Moses understood that God must exist by necessity because we cannot conceive of any way for Him not to exist. The argument from being says that because we can conceive of God, He must exist.[5]

2. Sources of authority are __**reason**__ *and* __**science**__.

Secular humanists generally believe that human intelligence is capable of discovering all truth. Therefore, there is no higher basis for authority in any area of knowledge or morality. Because God does not exist, any concept of divine revelation is rejected, and only human reason defines truth. In this view, science is the doorway to new discovery. As time progresses, new facts are uncovered, usually through the scientific methods of experimentation, physics, or historical research. These form the basis of a body of knowledge that can be labeled as truth. Nonetheless, new data may lead us to discard old presumptions and accept new truth. In any case we are limited from knowing ultimate truth.

Christians acknowledge the legitimacy of human discovery through valid forms of scientific research. Though some have accused Christianity of stifling scientific study, the truth is that scientific knowledge has flourished in Christian cultures. This fact may be attributable, in part, to our presumption that the world operates on reasonable laws of nature originally established by a reasonable God.

However, the Bible indicates that due to our finite and sinful natures, we are not capable of truly understanding all things, especially those of a spiritual nature. For that reason God has made Himself known to us, not only through the balance and wonder of nature (see Rom. 1:18-32) but also through special revelation. That special revelation is found in the written Word, the Bible, as given through divinely inspired writers (see 2 Tim. 3:15-17; 2 Pet. 1:19-21) and ultimately through His personal revelation of Himself in Jesus Christ (see Phil. 2:6-10; Col. 2:9; Heb. 1:1-2).

3. Moral standards are ____relative____.

If no God exists, human morality is not absolute but merely the result of subjective and changeable human opinions. The logical problem and danger in this dilemma are obvious. To say that no absolutes exist is to negate any transcendent (supernatural) basis for morality. This leads to artificial ways to determine moral standards. Responding to the humanist-pragmatist ethics of educator John Dewey, Christian philosopher John Newport has pointed out: "This method affirms that whatever works is right. The test of the validity of ethical ideas is their workability; there are no permanent principles of morality."[6] If human standards alone are the basis for morality, then whoever exercises the most power at any time or place sets the standard for law and personal behavior.

The biblical position is that God has established absolute moral standards of right and wrong. God deems human thoughts and behavior acceptable only if they conform to His moral standards (see Ps. 1). Because we are made in His image, we possess an innate, God-given sense of right and wrong (see Rom. 1:19; 2:14-15). God also reveals His moral law through His written Word (see Ps. 119:1-40) and through the Holy Spirit, who inhabits and guides every believer (see John 14:16,26).

4. Humankind is a highly evolved ____animal____.

Secular humanists assert that humanity is the highest order of life and thus the pinnacle of the evolutionary scale. As such, humans possess great potential for improving life for all people, establishing just systems of government, and perhaps even determining the future direction of their own biological evolution. Secular humanists contend that humanity's basic problem is superstition or ignorance, which can be remedied through education, science, or technology.

Thus, in one sense, secular humanism deifies humankind above all other creatures. The problem, however, is that in removing any transcendent, divine basis for humankind's existence, humanism actually devalues human life to the level of that of any other living creature. The logical conclusion of this reasoning is that we are only the sum total of our chemical components. This philosophy undercuts any objective basis for the value of human life or explanation for the human condition.

Humanists seem unwilling to admit that if humankind is a highly evolved animal, we are really nothing more than animals. Human life thus has no more intrinsic value than any other creature, living or dead. Most secular humanists, unfortunately, fail to recognize or choose to ignore this obvious implication of their perspective. Their position colors many issues of American public policy, such as abortion and euthanasia.

Christians assert that human life is the highest level of creation because we alone of all God's creatures are made in His image (see Gen. 1:27; 2:7). Our moral, spiritual, and personal natures reflect God's image. We stand as the pinnacle of creation because we are uniquely loved and valued by God (see Ps. 8:3-8). Consequently, we should love and value other people because God loves and values them (see John 3:16).

The human problem is not ignorance or superstition, as secular humanists assert. The Bible teaches that humankind, though originally created innocent and pure, has been infected by sin, which is the root cause of the world's ills (see Rom. 3:23). No amount of human reason, scientific progress, or technological advancement can solve what is essentially a spiritual problem. Only regeneration and salvation through Jesus Christ can alter humankind's evil nature (see Rom. 6:23; 12:1-2).

5. Jesus Christ was just a __man__.

Many secular humanists do not even believe that Jesus Christ existed. Those who recognize His existence acknowledge that He was, at best, a great moral teacher or a social reformer. They uniformly deny that Jesus possessed any supernatural power; that He was divine; or especially, that He rose from the dead. Most would argue that the supernatural elements of Jesus' life described in the New Testament are merely wish-fulfilling myths and legends created by the early church after His death.

Christians believe that the events described in the four Gospels about the life of Christ are historical facts (see John 21:24-25; 1 John 1:1-4). Most biblical events have been verified by archaeological research and textual study. Christ's resurrection, especially, has undergone rigorous investigation and is regarded as one the best-attested events of ancient history.

6. __Life after death__ is rejected.

Most secular humanists reject any notion of life after death. Any concept of postmortem existence, whether in heaven or hell or by reincarnation, is regarded as totally without scientific validation. To the humanist, life on earth is all there is. At its end we face nonexistence. Therefore, humanism encourages the improvement and extension of human life by scientific and medical progress. Oddly, most humanists favor legalized abortion on demand, liberal euthanasia laws, and legal assisted suicide.

For Christians, life after death is the greatest assurance we possess. This confidence is not based on mere wish fulfillment or even numerous stories of people's near-death experiences. Christians base their hope for eternal life on the historical event of Christ's resurrection (see 1 Cor. 15:13-20). The evidences for the resurrection of Christ are His empty

SEE IT

Step 4 (10 mins.)

Show the session 15 video segment. Briefly make the following points.

- This video segment highlights three areas in which secular humanism affects values in our culture: euthanasia, scientific naturalism, and abortion.

- Because Dr. Hudson is an atheist, he does not believe in prayer and does not value Bernie's life. With God's guidance and Tim and Angie's influence, Madge resists the doctor's pressure to end Bernie's life.

- Dan and Marsha's children are exposed to pantheism and evolution through children's books and TV programs. Dan and Marsha intervene with scientific and biblical truth.

- Sissy has believed humanism's lie that abortion is a viable option because it is legal and because a preborn baby is not a person. Angie's example and verbal witness influence Sissy to choose life for her unborn child.

tomb (see John 20:1-18), eyewitness reports of His physical appearances (see Acts 1:3), the founding of the church (see Acts 2:41), and the apostles' fearless preaching of the gospel at the cost of their lives (see Acts 4:1-22; 5:17-42; 7:54-60). Christians can rejoice in Jesus' promise that believers will be with Him after death for eternity (see John 14:1-4).

Witnessing to Secular Humanists

1. Develop a trustful _____relationship_____.
Build a personal, friendly, and sincere relationship with the secular humanist. Honestly show him that you are interested in his ideas and that you care about him and his family. Show him you do not reject him just because you disagree with his beliefs.

2. Discover the person's __beliefs__.
Determine exactly what the secular humanist's personal beliefs are about the supernatural, God's existence and nature, the person of Jesus Christ, life after death, and moral standards. Ask him to explain his views in his own words. You may find that he is not a committed atheist but an agnostic who does not know exactly what he believes. Patiently listen as he explains his ideas. Do not belittle his beliefs and, above all, do not argue with him about them.

3. State the __reasons__ you believe in God.
Explain to your friend why you feel that belief in God is reasonable, using the arguments presented earlier in this session. Remember that these arguments do not prove God's existence, but they demonstrate why it is reasonable and logical to believe in God.

4. Reveal the divine basis of __morality__.
Commend the secular humanist for his desire to build a moral and just world. Show him, however, that any system of morality that denies a divine basis is, at best, purely pragmatic, conditional, and arbitrary. Humanists espouse many ethical and moral principles but can provide no objective basis for them. Point out that God has designed humans with a sense of His standards of right and wrong and that these objective laws can be discerned by those who follow Him and study His Word.

5. Explain the source of human __worth__.
Commend the humanist for his high view of human life and its potential. Ask him what forms the basis for his view of human worth. He will likely say something about human intelligence or the evolutionary scale. Explain to him that, from your perspective, his view does not elevate

HEAR IT

Step 5 (5 mins.)

Ask participants to turn to page 250 in their Journals and to fill in the blanks as you summarize Witnessing to Secular Humanists. Use the computer presentation or the overhead cel.

Witnessing to Secular Humanists

people but devalues human life because its sees us as nothing more than complex animals. Show him that biblical truth elevates humanity because we are made in God's image. Explain that among all of God's creatures, human beings are uniquely valuable.

6. State your belief in ___Jesus___ ___Christ___ .
Discuss why you believe Christianity is a credible belief system. Support your views with biblical teachings about Jesus Christ. Show why you believe Christ's resurrection is a credible historical event and its implications for Jesus' identity and for our hope for life after death.

7. Present the way of ____salvation____ .
Using your FAITH gospel presentation, explain the plan of salvation and invite your friend to accept Christ as personal Savior and Lord. Patiently pray for him and trust the Holy Spirit to break down any intellectual barriers he has erected between himself and God.

Visitation Time

Do It
1. As you drive, ask Team members to recall persons who are frequently absent from Sunday School. These persons may be facing crises. Ask Learners to think about what they can do to reinvolve these persons through caring ministry and loving fellowship.
2. Remember that this is the last week to visit before the final review. By now your Learners should be accepting responsibility for the visit. You should participate as a prayer partner on the FAITH Team. Take responsibility to deal with distractions like the baby, dog, phone, and so on. Always be ready to step in if Learners need assistance.
3. As you travel, talk about whom Team members have enlisted to be on their Teams for the next semester of FAITH. If they have not enlisted their Team members, encourage them to do so this week.

Celebration Time

Share It
1. Ask a Team member to take the lead in sharing reports.
2. Hear reports and testimonies.
3. Complete Evaluation Cards.
4. Complete Participation Cards.
5. Update visitation forms with the results of visits.

STUDY IT

Step 6 (5 mins.)

Announce plans for the next semester of FAITH training in your church and encourage participants to enroll. Overview Home Study Assignments for session 15.

Transition to assemble with FAITH Teams to prepare for home visits. (5 mins.)

DO IT (110 MINS.)

SHARE IT (30 MINS.)

Home Study Assignments

Home Study Assignments reinforce this session by helping you apply what you have learned.

Your Discipleship Journey

Journaling activities in Your Discipleship Journey are an important part of your development as a Great Commission Christian through FAITH training.

1. One component of a humanist worldview is that truth is relative, not absolute. Match each Scripture with its teaching about truth.

___ 1. Psalm 31:5	a. It is impossible for God to lie.
___ 2. Psalm 96:10-13	b. God's truth will set you free.
___ 3. Isaiah 45:18-19	c. God is the God of truth.
___ 4. Matthew 22:16	d. Jesus is the truth.
___ 5. John 8:32	e. God speaks the truth.
___ 6. John 8:44	f. Jesus' teachings were based on God's truth.
___ 7. John 14:6	g. God's Word is truth.
___ 8. John 17:17	h. God will judge the world by His truth.
___ 9. Hebrews 6:18	i. Satan is a liar and the father of all lies.

2. How does each of the following Scriptures answer secular humanists' deification of humankind?

Jeremiah 17:9: _____

Mark 7:20-23: _____

_____

Romans 7:18-19: _____

_____

Romans 8:5-14: _____

_____

_____

1 John 2:15-17: _____

_____

3. Record what the following Scriptures indicate about Jesus' authority.

Matthew 9:6-8: _____

Matthew 10:1: _____

Matthew 28:18: _____

Romans 13:1-3: _____

_____

Growing as a Life Witness

Growing as a Life Witness reminds you of your responsibility to witness and minister to others during the week.

1. Talk or meet with your accountability partner and share ways you have cultivated a lost person or have witnessed or ministered on occasions other than FAITH visits.
2. Discuss ways you can apply the session 15 content.
3. Pray for lost persons by name and for each other.

Prayer Concerns	Answers to Prayer
_____	_____
_____	_____
_____	_____
_____	_____
_____	_____

Your Weekly Sunday School Leadership Meeting

A FAITH participant is an important member of Sunday School. Encourage Team members who are elected Sunday School leaders to attend this weekly meeting. Use this section to record ways your FAITH Team influences the work of your Sunday School class or department. Use the information to report during weekly Sunday School leadership meetings. Identify actions that need to be taken through Sunday School as a result of prayer concerns, needs identified, visits made by the Team, and decisions made by the persons visited. Also identify ways you can disciple others in your Sunday School class or department and in your church.

1. Discuss plans for the next semester of FAITH training. Give the dates.

2. Update the group on plans to enlist a Team of new Learners from your class/department. Who are potential Learners? Invite current Team members or new Christians to share testimonies and benefits of participating as a Team Learner. Indicate other promotional efforts that are under way.

_____

_____

3. With others on your leadership team, evaluate last week's session and discuss ways Sunday's lesson can involve members and guests in transformational Bible study and discipleship.

_____

_____

4. Discuss plans to keep evangelism and ministry contacts consistent and strong between semesters.

_____

5. Thank the Sunday School class/department leaders for their support and encouragement throughout this semester.

6. Pray for your teacher and department director. Specifically ask God to bless and multiply your church's ministry through Sunday School.

Discipling Your Team Members

This weekly feature suggests actions the Team Leader can take to support Team members, prepare for Team Time, and improve visits. This work is part of the Team Leader's Home Study Assignments. Add any actions suggested by your church's FAITH strategy.

Support Team Members

❑ Contact Team members during the week. Remind them that you are praying for them. Discuss prayer concerns and answers to prayer.
❑ Record Team members' specific needs and concerns.

_____

_____

❑ Identify specific ways you can encourage Team members as they prepare for their written and verbal reviews.

Prepare for Session 16
❑ Review Team members' Home Study Assignments.
❑ Preview instructions for session 16.
❑ Be prepared for your final verbal and written reviews.

Prepare to Lead Visits
❑ Review the FAITH Visit Outline.
❑ Make sure a Team member is ready to take the lead during visits.

Link with Sunday School
❑ Participate in your weekly Sunday School leadership meeting. Share pertinent information in this meeting, using Your Weekly Sunday School Leadership Meeting (pp. 253–54) and FAITH-visit results.
❑ Consider ways Sunday School teaching can reinforce a God-centered worldview that rejects humanistic values.

For Further Growth: The Second Coming of Jesus Christ

For Further Growth may include additional reading or activities that will enhance your growth as a disciple and a discipler of others. These assignments are intended to be long-term projects and do not have to be completed during this semester of study.

1. Just as Jesus bodily came to earth in the past, He will bodily come again to take His rightful place as King of kings and Lord of lords. Read the following Scriptures and note the assurance of His return, the circumstances of His return, and the results of His return: Daniel 7:13-14; Matthew 24:29-30; Acts 1:11; 1 Thessalonians 1:9-10; Titus 2:13; Hebrews 9:28; Revelation 19:11-16.

2. Read one or more of the following resources.
   - Herbert Lockyer, *All the Teachings of Jesus*, chapter 32, "The Second Coming" (Peabody: Hendrickson, 1991), 289–94.
   - Millard J. Erickson, *Christian Theology*, part 12, "The Last Things" (Grand Rapids: Baker, 1985), 1149–1242.
   - R. C. Sproul, *Essential Truths of the Christian Faith*, part 10, "End Times" (Wheaton: Tyndale, 1992), 273–88.

3. Read the FAITH Tip on page 256.

[1]Francis J. Beckwith and Stephen E. Parrish, *See the Gods Fall: Four Rivals to Christianity* (Joplin: College, 1997), 137.
[2]Paul Kurtz, "Humanist Manifesto 2000," 10 November 2000, <*http://www.secularhumanism.org*> (27 Feb. 2001).
[3]Carl Sagan, as quoted by Norman L. Geisler and Ronald M. Brooks, *When Skeptics Ask* (Wheaton: Victor, 1990), 16.
[4]Hugh Ross, "Planet Quest—A Recent Success," *Connections—News and Views*, 2 (2000): 2, as quoted by Hugh Ross, "Design Evidences for Life Support" (Pasadena: Reasons to Believe, 2000)
[5]Geisler and Brooks, *When Skeptics Ask*, 15–25.
[6]John P. Newport, *Life's Ultimate Questions* (Dallas: Word, 1989), 468.

Answers to matching activity on page 252: 1. c, 2. h, 3. e, 4. f, 5. b, 6. i, 7. d, 8. g, 9. a

FAITH TIP

A New Challenge: Postmodernism

In the 1990s, remarkably, the stronghold secular humanists have held on American culture has made a decided shift (and for some secular humanists, it is a troubling turn). The dogmatic naturalistic assertion that truth can be discerned by strict adherence to scientific method is now being challenged by a new intellectual paradigm called postmodernism.

Postmodernism, as its name implies, is a recent philosophical movement that rejects the naturalistic-modernist worldview. Its adherents argue that science and truth really have no objective basis whatsoever and that all academic pursuits are culturally conditioned and thus not universally relevant or applicable. This philosophical movement has swept across North America's institutions of higher learning, affecting the social sciences, humanities, and historical studies. Even the hard sciences have not gone untouched by the postmodern presupposition that no truth can be stated with any level of certainty.

Evangelical Christians survey this situation with mixed reactions. On one hand, it means that naturalism's long hold on Western culture may be waning. People who for years were rigidly opposed to any supernatural understanding of reality may now be open to the biblical concepts of God and the miraculous. On the other hand, postmodernists' radical rejection of all truth claims leaves them suspicious of any claims to absolute truth, especially those of an exclusive religious nature. Tolerance and inclusivism are elevated to the highest levels of ethical virtue, while any positions perceived as intolerance and exclusivism are regarded as the greatest vices. Thus, the Christian claim of the uniqueness of Christ as the only way of salvation is passionately rejected.

Christians' response, therefore, must be to present our case with love and assurance. We must demonstrate to postmodernists that their perspective is self-contradictory. To assert that there is no absolute truth is paradoxical and illogical, because the statement actually invalidates itself. The assertion that there is no absolute truth is itself a statement of absolute truth.

We must confidently assert that truth has an objective basis. We point to the historical facts about Christ's life, death, and resurrection, which confirm His words " 'I am the way, and the truth, and the life; no one comes to the Father but through Me' " (John 14:6, NASB).

SESSION 16

Final Review

In this session you will—

CHECK IT by engaging in Team Time activities;

KNOW IT by taking written and verbal reviews to evaluate your learning

over the past 16 weeks;

STUDY IT by overviewing Home Study Assignments;

DO IT by leading your Team in making visits;

SHARE IT by celebrating accomplishments this semester or by announcing

plans for a FAITH Festival in which the celebration will occur.

IN ADVANCE

- Be prepared to administer the written review and to explain answers.
- Preview teaching suggestions. Prepare key points. Decide whether to use the session 16 computer presentation or the overhead cel.
- Be prepared to explain the process for recognizing Learners and for certifying Team Leaders, based on information in the FAITH Administrative Guide, provided in *A Journey in FAITH Training Pack*. See your FAITH Director.
- Consult with the FAITH Director and plan to announce details for the FAITH Festival.
- Be prepared to announce dates for the next semester of training. Give Learners instructions about enlistment contacts to be made.
- Be prepared to share any special plans for Visitation Time.
- Prepare the room for teaching.
- Pray for participants and for Teams as they prepare to visit.
- As Teaching Time begins, direct participants to open their Journals to page 260.

CHECK IT (15 MINS.)

If the computer presentation is used, display the agenda frame for Team Time. Add other points as needed.

CHECK IT agenda:
- ✔ FAITH Visit Outline
- ✔ Session 15 Debriefing
- ✔ FAITH Testimony
- ✔ Help for Strengthening a Visit

Leading Team Time

All Team members participate in Team Time. They are primarily responsible for reciting the assigned portion of the FAITH Visit Outline and for discussing other Home Study Assignments.

As you direct this important time of CHECK IT activities with your Team, keep in mind that Learners look to you as a role model, motivator, mentor, and friend. Team Time activities can continue in the car as the Team travels to and from visits.

Lead CHECK IT Activities

✔ FAITH Visit Outline
❑ Listen while each Learner recites any designated portion of the FAITH Visit Outline. It may be best to ask Learners to recite the segment they seem to have the most difficulty sharing during a visit.
❑ A brief time to practice the outline can help Team members confidently approach the verbal review.

✔ Session 15 Debriefing
❑ Emphasize the importance of each Team member's being available to serve as a Team Leader during future semesters. Review the potential results of choosing not to continue participating in FAITH training.

✔ FAITH Testimony
❑ Ask participants to turn in their "What FAITH Has Meant to Me" testimonies. Present them to the FAITH Director.

✔ Help for Strengthening a Visit
❑ Discuss some of the things that have been learned by making evangelistic, ministry, and Opinion Poll visits. Make sure Team members know who will be responsible for taking the lead in making the visits after the written and verbal reviews.

Notes

_____

_____

_____

_____

_____

_____

_____

_____

Actions I Need to Take with Team Members This Week

1. Write thank-you notes to Team members. Include congratulations for their completion of this semester of training. Indicate your continued support.

_____

_____

_____

_____

_____

_____

_____

Transition to classrooms for written and verbal reviews. (5 mins.)

Jesus Christ: The Chief Cornerstone

This semester you have examined a variety of world religions, from ancient faiths like Hinduism to more recently articulated philosophies like New Age and secular humanism. As you have considered each group's beliefs, perhaps you have been struck by the overwhelming truth that all of these faiths, no matter how well-intentioned their works or sincere their devotees, are set against the one true God; His beloved Son, Jesus Christ; and His eternal truth, as revealed in Holy Scripture. The sad predicament of these followers reminds us of Paul's assessment of many first-century religionists: "Although they knew God, they neither glorified him as God nor gave thanks to him, but their thinking became futile and their foolish hearts were darkened. Although they claimed to be wise, they became fools and exchanged the glory of the immortal God for images made to look like mortal man and birds and animals and reptiles" (Rom. 1:21-23, NIV). In the end a misdirected devotion is nothing less than idolatry and a rejection of God Himself.

As a Christian, you hold in your heart the truth that is missing from the religions you have studied. That truth is Jesus Christ. As Peter explained to the Sanhedrin after Jesus' death, Jesus is

> " 'the stone you builders rejected,
>   which has become the capstone.'
> Salvation is found in no one else, for there is no other
> name under heaven given to men by which we must be
> saved" (Acts 4:11-12, NIV).

Jesus is the chief cornerstone of true religion. As a Great Commission witness, you have the obligation and privilege to share this truth with followers of false religions. We hope that this study has increased your compassion for persons of other faiths and has equipped you to share Christ's love effectively with them.

This course has also encouraged you to build an unshakable life of discipleship on the cornerstone of your Lord Jesus Christ so that you will not be "tossed back and forth by the waves, and blown here and there by every wind of teaching" (Eph. 4:14, NIV). As you have gained a deeper understanding of sound Christian doctrine, you have been equipped to share solid biblical truth with followers of other faiths.

Congratulations for completing *FAITH Discipleship: Faith Reaching Out to World Religions*. We hope that you will continue to grow as a disciple and as a witness by enrolling in another semester of FAITH training.

Written Review

Session 3: Judaism

Identify Jewish beliefs by marking each statement *T* for *true* or *F* for *false*.

F 1. A plurality of gods is worshiped in Judaism.

T 2. Scripture is inferior to tradition.

F 3. Tradition is inferior to Scripture.

T 4. Jesus' messiahship is denied.

T 5. Salvation must be earned.

T 6. There is only one God.

F 7. Jewish people acutely realize the need for a Redeemer.

F 8. Judaism teaches salvation by grace alone.

T 9. Observing the law, the Sabbath, festivals, and feasts is essential.

T 10. Humanity is basically good.

Session 4: Islam

Check effective ways to witness to Muslims.

☑ 1. Be sensitive to Muslim culture.

☑ 2. Build on respect for Jesus.

☐ 3. Repay hostility with vengeance.

☑ 4. Establish the authority of the Bible.

☑ 5. Present the good news.

☐ 6. Affirm the Muslim's good works as a valid way to get to heaven.

☑ 7. Provide follow-up.

☑ 8. Clarify biblical teachings about God.

☑ 9. Be confident and diligent in prayer.

☐ 10. Explain that it is not necessary to recognize Jesus as God's Son.

☑ 11. Cultivate relationships.

☐ 12. Concede that the Christian God is actually three different gods.

☑ 13. Demonstrate Christian love.

Session 5: The Baha'i Faith

Identify Baha'i beliefs by marking the statements *T* for *true* or *F* for *false*.

F 1. Baha'is believe that we can know God intimately.

T 2. Baha'is claim that Baha'u'llah was the last Great Manifestation of God.

T 3. Baha'is regard Baha'u'llah's writings as authoritative.

F 4. Baha'is teach the importance of maintaining distinct ethnic, linguistic, racial, and national differences.

T 5. Baha'is believe that their faith is the common foundation of all religions.

F 6. Baha'is teach salvation by grace through faith in Jesus Christ.

F 7. The Baha'i concept of heaven is a place much like the biblical picture of heaven in Revelation 21—22.

T 8. Baha'i envisions a utopian theocracy.

Step 2 (10 mins.)

Give these instructions for the written review: Take the written review, beginning on page 261 in your Journal. You will have 10 minutes. Afterward you will grade your own work as I give the answers.

Session 6: Hinduism

Write *H* beside Hindu beliefs and C beside Christian beliefs.

C 1. God is intimate and personal.

H 2. God is impersonal and unknowable.

C 3. There is only one God.

C 4. Humanity's problem is sin.

H 5. The human soul is divine.

C 6. People inherit a sinful nature.

H 7. Salvation is escaping *karma* and becoming one with God.

C 8. Salvation is being delivered from sin and receiving eternal life by God's grace through faith in Jesus Christ.

C 9. Only the Bible is the revealed Word of God.

H 10. The Veda is sacred scripture.

Session 7: Buddhism

To identify ways to witness to Buddhists, select the correct words below that complete the numbered statements.

merit • desire • future • God • suffering • testimony

1. Address Buddhists' concern with _____**suffering**_____.
2. Offer hope for the _____**future**_____.
3. Introduce the truth of the personal ____**God**____.
4. Explain the futility of trying to gain _____**merit**_____.
5. Point out contradictory teachings about _____**desire**_____.
6. Share your personal _____**testimony**_____.

Session 8: The New Age Movement, Part 1

Check the statements that represent New Age beliefs.

❑ 1. God is personal and separate from His creation.

☑ 2. All is God.

☑ 3. All is one.

❑ 4. God's creations are distinct from one another.

❑ 5. Humans are made in God's image.

❑ 6. Humans are not divine and are not basically good.

☑ 7. Humans are divine.

☑ 8. Morality is relative.

❑ 9. There are absolute standards of right and wrong.

☑ 10. Jesus was only a great teacher.

❑ 11. Jesus is the unique Son of God.

Session 9: The New Age Movement, Part 2

Check appropriate ways to witness to New Agers.

☑ 1. Point out implications of reincarnation.

☑ 2. Explain the true nature of the coming new age.

❑ 3. Tell New Age followers that they are very confused and cannot understand the truth.

☑ 4. Present Jesus Christ as the focus of true religion.
❑ 5. Be on the defensive when you are around New Agers.
❑ 6. Ask the person to demonstrate some occult practices.
☑ 7. Display Christian love and kindness.
☑ 8. Warn the person about involvement in the occult.
❑ 9. Assure New Agers that the devil and demons are merely fantasies.

Session 10: The Occult

Match each Christian teaching in the left column with the occult practice it refutes.

 b 1. Believers are not to tolerate mediums.   a. Occult divination
 c 2. Satan is not equal with God.   b. Spiritualism
 a 3. Do not be anxious about the future.   c. Satanism
 c 4. Believers can resist evil and fight the
         devil.
 b 5. Attempts to communicate with the dead
         defile the authentic worship of God.
 b 6. We serve a living God, not a dead spirit.
 a 7. The Bible condemns astrology.

Session 11: Witchcraft

Check appropriate principles for witnessing to wiccans.
☑ 1. Make spiritual preparation.
❑ 2. Be careful of the spells a witch might cast on you.
❑ 3. Remind them of what happened in Salem.
☑ 4. Don't be afraid.
❑ 5. Avoid contact with wiccans.
☑ 6. Be gentle and loving.
☑ 7. Introduce the personal God of Scripture.
☑ 8. Issue a warning of God's judgment.
❑ 9. Seek to win their favor through white magick.
☑ 10. Proclaim Christ's power to break the hold of evil.

Session 13: The Roman Catholic Church

Complete the numbered statements summarizing Roman Catholic beliefs by selecting the correct words from the list that follows.

sacraments • confirmation • penance • Eucharist
sin • baptism • authority

1. Roman Catholics accept extrabiblical sources of _____**authority**_____.
2. Roman Catholics distinguish between categories of _____**sin**_____.
3. Salvation is imparted through _____**sacraments**_____.
4. _____**Baptism**_____ is necessary for salvation.
5. _____**Confirmation**_____ bestows the Holy Spirit.
6. Christ's body is received through the _____**Eucharist**_____.
7. _____**Penance**_____ removes the penalty of sins.

Session 14: The Eastern Orthodox Church

Check principles for witnessing to Eastern Orthodox followers.

❑ 1. State that mysticism really freaks you out.
❑ 2. Do not share your testimony, because it doesn't apply to Orthodoxy.
☑ 3. Determine whether the person is saved.
☑ 4. Build a relationship.
❑ 5. Tell them that icons are idols.
☑ 6. Affirm the authority of Scripture.
❑ 7. Alter the FAITH gospel presentation to downplay sin's seriousness.
☑ 8. Emphasize the severity and consequences of sin.
☑ 9. Share your personal testimony.

Session 15: Secular Humanism

Identify humanist beliefs by underlining the correct word or words that complete each sentence.

1. God is the big (kahuna, bang, <u>myth</u>).
2. Sources of authority are (<u>reason and science</u>, the Old and New Testaments, the pope and bishops).
3. Moral standards are (overrated, important, <u>relative</u>).
4. Humankind is a highly evolved (fish, <u>animal</u>, ego).
5. Jesus Christ was just a (<u>man</u>, sociologist, fraud).
6. (Good behavior, <u>life after death</u>, self-worship) is rejected.

Grade your written review as your Facilitator gives the answers. Each item counts one point; the highest possible score is 106. Subtract the number you missed from this total to get your score.

Highest possible score: 106
Number missed: – _____
My score: = _____

Verbal Review: FAITH Visit Outline

❑ Preparation

❑ INTRODUCTION
❑ INTERESTS
❑ INVOLVEMENT
❑ Church Experience/Background
   ❑ • Ask about the person's church background.
   ❑ • Listen for clues about the person's spiritual involvement.

Step 3 (5 mins.)

Give instructions for grading and scoring the written review: As I give the correct answers, place an X beside each incorrect response. Total the number of incorrect answers and subtract from 106 to get your overall score.

Step 4 (15 mins.)

Explain the process for the verbal review: Recite the FAITH Visit Outline to your accountability partner. As you present each item, he or she will listen and mark incorrect responses in your Journal, beginning on page 264. Accountability partners will have 15 minutes to recite the outline to each other.

❑ **Sunday School Testimony**
  ❑ • Tell general benefits of Sunday School.
  ❑ • Tell a current personal experience.
❑ **Evangelistic Testimony**
  ❑ • Tell a little of your preconversion experience.
  ❑ • Say: "I had a life-changing experience."
  ❑ • Tell recent benefits of your conversion.

❑ **INQUIRY**
❑ **Key Question:** In your personal opinion, what do you understand it takes for a person to go to heaven?
❑ **Possible Answers:** Faith, works, unclear, no opinion
❑ **Transition Statement:** I'd like to share with you how the Bible answers this question, if it is all right. There is a word that can be used to answer this question: FAITH (spell out on fingers).

❑ Presentation

❑ *F is for FORGIVENESS*
❑ We cannot have eternal life and heaven without God's forgiveness.
❑ *"In Him [meaning Jesus] we have redemption through His blood, the forgiveness of sins"—Ephesians 1:7a, NKJV.*

❑ **A is for AVAILABLE**
❑ Forgiveness is available. It is—

  ❑ **AVAILABLE FOR ALL**
  ❑ *"For God so loved the world that He gave His only begotten Son, that whoever believes in Him should not perish but have everlasting life" —John 3:16, NKJV.*

  ❑ **BUT NOT AUTOMATIC**
  ❑ *"Not everyone who says to Me, 'Lord, Lord,' shall enter the kingdom of heaven"—Matthew 7:21a, NKJV.*

❑ *I is for IMPOSSIBLE*
❑ It is impossible for God to allow sin into heaven.

  ❑ **GOD IS—**
  ❑ • LOVE
     ❑ *John 3:16, NKJV*
  ❑ • JUST
     ❑ *"For judgment is without mercy"—James 2:13a, NKJV.*

❏ **MAN IS SINFUL**
  ❏ *"For all have sinned and fall short of the glory of God"*
    —*Romans 3:23, NKJV.*
  ❏ **Question:** But how can a sinful person enter heaven, where God
    allows no sin?

❏ *T* **is for TURN**
  ❏ **Question:** If you were driving down the road and someone
    asked you to turn, what would he or she be asking you to do?
    (change direction)
  ❏ *Turn* means *repent.*
  ❏ **TURN** from something—sin and self
  ❏ *"But unless you repent you will all likewise perish"*—*Luke 13:3b, NKJV.*
  ❏ **TURN** to Someone; trust Christ only
  ❏ (The Bible tells us that) *"Christ died for our sins according to the
    Scriptures, and that He was buried, and that He rose again the third
    day according to the Scriptures"*—*1 Corinthians 15:3b-4, NKJV.*
  ❏ *"If you confess with your mouth the Lord Jesus and believe in your
    heart that God has raised Him from the dead, you will be saved"*
    —*Romans 10:9, NKJV.*

❏ *H* **is for HEAVEN**
  ❏ Heaven is eternal life.
  ❏ **HERE**
  ❏ *"I have come that they may have life, and that they may have it more
    abundantly"*—*John 10:10b, NKJV.*
  ❏ **HEREAFTER**
  ❏ *"And if I go and prepare a place for you, I will come again and
    receive you to Myself; that where I am, there you may be also"*
    —*John 14:3, NKJV.*

❏ **HOW**
  ❏ How can a person have God's forgiveness, heaven and eternal life,
    and Jesus as personal Savior and Lord?
  ❏ Explain based on leaflet picture, FAITH (Forsaking All, I Trust
    Him), Romans 10:9.

❏ **Invitation**

❏ **INQUIRE**
  ❏ Understanding what we have shared, would you like to receive this
    forgiveness by trusting in Christ as your personal Savior and Lord?

❑ INVITE
- ❑ • Pray to accept Christ.
- ❑ • Pray for commitment/recommitment.
- ❑ • Invite to join Sunday School.

❑ INSURE
- ❑ • Use *A Step of Faith* to insure decision.
- ❑ • Personal Acceptance
- ❑ • Sunday School Enrollment
- ❑ • Public Confession

Grade your verbal review. Each item counts one point; the highest possible score is 67. Subtract the number you missed from this total to get your score.

Highest possible score: 67

Number missed: – _____

My score: = _____

Visitation Time

Do It

1. Your visitation schedule may be altered tonight. Allow for any schedule changes your church has agreed on.
2. Encourage Learners to make the gospel presentation by themselves.
3. Urge your Team members to continue FAITH training next semester and to continue using the FAITH Visit Outline to witness.
4. Encourage Teams to return for a special Celebration Time.

Celebration Time

Share It

1. Ask a Team member to take the lead in sharing reports.
2. Hear reports and testimonies.
3. Complete Evaluation Cards.
4. Complete Participation Cards.
5. Update visitation forms with the results of visits.
6. Allow time for testimonies about what this semester of FAITH has meant to participants and to the persons they have visited.

Step 5 (5 mins.)

Give instructions for grading and scoring the verbal review: Total the number of incorrect answers your accountability partner has marked. Subtract from 67 to get your overall score.

STUDY IT

Step 6 (5 mins.)

Overview Home Study Assignments for session 16. Close the session by praying for participants' further growth as disciples and as witnesses.

Transition to assemble with FAITH Teams to prepare for home visits. (5 mins.)

DO IT (110 MINS.)

SHARE IT (30 MINS.)

Home Study Assignments

Home Study Assignments reinforce this session by helping you apply what you have learned.

Your Discipleship Journey

Journaling activities in Your Discipleship Journey are an important part of your development as a Great Commission Christian through FAITH training.

1 When you encounter false teaching, you enter spiritual warfare. Summarize what the following verses teach about the reality of spiritual warfare.

2 Corinthians 10:3: _____

_____

Colossians 1:13: _____

_____

1 Thessalonians 5:5: _____

_____

2. Read the following verses and record what they teach about how to engage in spiritual warfare.

2 Corinthians 10:4-5: _____

_____

_____

_____

Ephesians 6:10-18: _____

_____

_____

_____

_____

1 Timothy 6:11-12: _____

_____

_____

Jude 20-25: _____

_____

_____

_____

Growing as a Life Witness

Growing as a Life Witness reminds you of your responsibility to witness and minister to others during the week.

1. Talk or meet with your accountability partner and share ways you have cultivated a lost person or have witnessed or ministered on occasions other than FAITH visits.
2. Discuss your responses to activities in Your Discipleship Journey. Share your plans for future participation in FAITH training.
3. Pray for lost persons by name and for each other.

Prayer Concerns	Answers to Prayer
_____	_____
_____	_____
_____	_____
_____	_____

Your Weekly Sunday School Leadership Meeting

A FAITH participant is an important member of Sunday School. Encourage Team members who are elected Sunday School leaders to attend this weekly meeting. Use this section to record ways your FAITH Team influences the work of your Sunday School class or department. Use the information to report during weekly Sunday School leadership meetings. Identify actions that need to be taken through Sunday School as a result of prayer concerns, needs identified, visits made by the Team, and decisions made by the persons visited. Also identify ways you can disciple others in your Sunday School class or department and in your church.

1. Highlight needs/reports affecting your class/department or age group.

_____

2. Pray for your teacher and department director.

3. What are ways the department/class can celebrate the Holy Spirit's work through members who have participated in FAITH training?

_____

_____

4. What actions can be taken to encourage members and leaders to prepare for the next semester of FAITH training?

_____

_____

5. How does preparation for Sunday need to consider persons who might attend because they received a witness by members during the week?

_____

_____

For Further Growth: The Judgment of Jesus Christ

For Further Growth may include additional reading or activities that will enhance your growth as a disciple and a discipler of others. These assignments are intended to be long-term projects and do not have to be completed during this semester of study.

1. Jesus will return to judge everyone. Read the following Scriptures and note what the Bible says about judgment: John 5:22; 2 Corinthians 5:9; Hebrews 9:27; Jude 14-15; Revelation 20:11-15.

2. Read one or more of the following resources.
   - Millard J. Erickson, *Christian Theology*, part 12, "The Last Things" (Grand Rapids: Baker, 1985), 1149–1242.
   - Millard J. Erickson, *The Word Became Flesh*, part 3, "The Construction of a Contemporary Incarnational Christology," chapter 18, "The New Testament Witness Regarding Jesus' Deity" (Grand Rapids: Baker, 1991), 455–80.
   - J. I Packer et al., *Exploring the Christian Faith*, chapter 8, "Death … and Then," and chapter 29, "Destiny" (Nashville: Thomas Nelson, 1992), 75–84, 282–89.

FAITH AT WORK

I have learned a great deal about our Lord and His Word during my 16 weeks in FAITH. I expected that. What I didn't expect were weeks of unanswered doorbells, wrong addresses, sick families, and disinterested prospects.

When I began hearing about the FAITH process, I was intrigued. For many years I had felt that something was missing in my Christian walk. This plan for visiting and sharing the gospel was exciting. I knew the first night we went out that the residents of that small home would welcome us with tears of gladness as we shared Christ's love with them. I could imagine them exclaiming: "At last you're here! We've waited our whole lives for this moment!" However, no one even answered the door.

As I returned to church that evening for Celebration Time, I didn't feel much like celebrating. *Next week,* I told myself. Next week turned to 2 weeks, then 5, then 10, and nothing changed. Disappointment began to build. I had to stop several times and take stock of the situation. I realized that I was expecting this strategy to produce results—tangible results. But it wasn't. I was doing everything right, so why wasn't it working?

As I spoke with my trainers, they began to show me the true results I had been overlooking: I was fearlessly sharing my faith in a clear, concise manner. I was praying regularly. I was memorizing Scripture. I was recognizing that God was bringing people across my path for a reason. My trainers encouraged me to keep doing my part and to trust God for the harvest.

Then it happened. It started like any other night. But this time the person we visited seemed curious. My words seemed to answer every question. I asked, "Understanding what we have shared, would you like to receive this forgiveness by trusting in Christ as your personal Savior and Lord?" I waited for what seemed like an eternity. Then the answer came: "Yes, I think I would."

My entire 16 weeks in FAITH were suddenly bathed in light and clearly focused. My job is to do the legwork, no matter how disappointing or seemingly ineffective. Jesus is the Lord of the harvest, and He will take care of the results in His own time.

Chuck Stiefken
Immanuel Baptist Church
Highland, California

A COMPARISON OF MAJOR BELIEFS

This chart does not include occult beliefs because of their diversity.

	JUDAISM	ISLAM	BAHA'I	HINDUISM	BUDDHISM	NEW AGE	WITCHCRAFT	ROMAN CATHOLIC	EASTERN ORTHODOX	SECULAR HUMANISM
GOD	Absolutely one. Not triune.	Allah is absolutely one. Not triune. Only attributes can be known.	Eternal and almighty but unknowable.	Impersonal and unknowable.	No God exists.	Impersonal energy or consciousness.	Impersonal, universal spirit. Fertility deities are worshiped.	Biblical view affirmed.	God can be known mystically, not rationally.	No God exists.
JESUS	Identity as Messiah rejected.	Prophet. Not God's Son.	A Great Manifestation of God, not His Son.	An enlightened man.	An enlightened man.	An enlightened man and a great teacher.	Only a man.	Biblical view affirmed.	Biblical view affirmed.	Only a man.
SOURCE OF AUTHORITY	The Hebrew Bible (Old Testament), which is inferior to tradition.	The Qur'an is Allah's exact words.	Writings of Baha'u'llah.	The Vedas and other writings.	Buddha's teachings.	None. Sacred writings from many traditions are valued.	None. Various occult books are studied.	The Bible, including the Apocrypha; Church Tradition; Magisterium.	Church Tradition, of which the Bible is one component.	Reason and science.
HUMANITY	Basically good.	No sinful nature. Born pure. Basically religious.	Oneness of humanity. Basically good.	Divine. Part of God. Basically good.	No soul or spirit but a flowing stream of elements.	Divine. Part of God. Basically good.	Divine. Part of God. Basically good.	Biblical view affirmed.	Humans naturally want to know God.	A highly evolved animal.
SIN	Sin and the need for atonement are denied.	Breaking Allah's law and not doing His will.	Expression of animal nature.	No sin. Ignorance of divinity is humanity's problem.	No sin. Human desire leads to suffering.	No sin. Ignorance of divinity is humanity's problem.	No sin. Ignorance of divinity is humanity's problem.	Distinction made between mortal and venial sins.	No inherited sin.	No absolute standards of right and wrong.
SALVATION	Earned through repentance, prayer, and good deeds.	Based on Allah's will. Pursued by conforming to Five Pillars.	Earned through moral lifestyle.	Escaping law of *karma* and becoming one with God.	Attaining *nirvana*— extinction— through Eightfold Path.	Achieving oneness with all through reincarnation.	Achieving oneness with all through reincarnation.	Imparted through sacraments.	Imparted through sacraments, or Christian mysteries.	Education and technology can overcome ignorance. No afterlife.